# Integrating Theory and Praxis in Education

# Integrating Theory and Praxis in Education

**Hemlata Talesra**
**M.L. Nagda**

AUTHORSPRESS

Worldwide Circulation through Authorspress Global Network
First Published 2008
by
Authorspress
E-35/103, Jawahar Park
Laxmi Nagar, Delhi-110 092
e-mail: authorspress@yahoo.com



*Integrating Theory and Praxis in Education*
ISBN 978-81-7273-420-6

Printed in India at Virgo Press, Delhi.

# Preface

In order to close the gap between theory and practice, transformational leadership is necessary. For leadership to be catalyst of change, they need to be involved or else well informed about the envisaged change. They need to be part of the designing process of the intended reform in order for them to own the results, and thus be able to communicate it to their subordinates and monitor its proper implementation. By doing so the contextual realities will be addressed in order to try to reach the ideal situation. The gap that exists between theory and practice, or policy and praxis, is due to the absence of participation in designing and the knowledge of the reforms and most likely the rationale behind the design of such reforms. The contextual realism overlooked in favour of idealism in the passing and implementing of these policies.

Several educational reforms were made as an effort to redress the imbalances of the past, to make education accessible and equitable to all its citizens and to promote democracy in educational institutions. It is, therefore, imperative to recreate linkage between theory and practice in order for the transformation to be successful on the basis of different surveys and studies, that most of the reforms had a negative impact on educational leadership, compared to these which had a positive impact. The most cited reforms that they perceived as impacting negatively on leadership are the curriculum changes, the abolition of corporal punishment, inclusive education policy and the language policy. Reviewed literature confirmed some revelations made by respondents that some theories impacted negatively on leadership. Literature also revealed that there was a gap between theory and practice, and also between policy and praxis.

Keeping in view the crucial importance of integrating theory and praxis in education we propose to publish this book on the papers presented in the CCEAM International Conference on the above theme which is very relevant for shaping the future of educational endeavours. The integration between theory and practice, and between policy and praxis, has to be maintained and carried into the new millennium.

It is indeed high time that the incorporation between the theory and praxis found the deserved priority in the national policy goals in a global perspective. It is earnestly hoped that the papers published in the book will throw light on the integration of theory and praxis, and take proper strategies. The present book is a compendium of fourteen important papers presented and written by eminent experts.

*Editors*

# Contents

# 1

# Praxis-oriented Framework for Educational Leadership

—*Carolyn M. Shields* and *Steven Lynn Oberg*

Leadership and leadership theory are, in some ways, as old as society itself. From early days of social organisation, and especially with the emergence of political or military institutions, one can find discussion of what makes for good leadership. Sun Tsu, writing in sixth century China, for example, provides aphorisms of advice about leadership in times of war that still inform theories and business practices today. Other well-known writers, such as Plato or Machiavelli, are still commonly referenced in discussions of leadership. From Samuel Smiles in the Victorian era to Steven Covey's modern catalogue of a leader's prerequisite "Seven Habits", everyone seems to have a working hypothesis about the how, why, who, and when of leadership. However, despite the myriad of pages written and seemingly endless number of volumes published on the subject, there is an ongoing interest in almost every field—with new theories, models, or approaches to the topic appear annually.

In education, the field of leadership studies, first known as administrative science, is relatively new, having its origins in a group known as the Vienna Circle in the early 1920s. In North America, it developed most fully in the 1950s, with the discussions of the Chicago Cooperative Program in Educational Administration (CPEA). Culbertson (1988) writes that "CPEA leaders agreed they should make greater use of the social sciences in training and inquiry" (p. 15a). One of the early seminal works in the field was Simon's (1945) *Administrative Behaviour* in which he focused on decisionmaking, a task he considered to be central to administrative work.

Since those early days, when educational leadership was developing into both a science and a discipline, educators have been bombarded by theories related to decisionmaking, planning organisational change, personnel administration, teacher supervision and other tasks of leadership.

There have been studies of leadership traits and behaviours (Caldwell & Wellman, 1926; Stogdill, 1974), leadership styles and approaches (Fiedler, 1967; McGregor, 1960) that extend from scientific to organic and from transactional to transformational. In recent years, the barrage continues unabated with work on feminist leadership, critical race theories and leadership, distributed or distributive leadership, servant leadership, spiritual leadership, emotional leadership and so on. It seems there would remain little to be said about the topic.

At the same time, of course, researchers in many countries have begun to demonstrate that leadership is important, that it does make a difference to such things as the quality of the workplace, the organisational culture, or its goal attainment (Morgan, 1997). Some (Hill, 1998; Silins & Mulford, 2002) have found that leadership also has a direct impact on student learning.

With the common press for accountability found in the United States, Britain, and other developed countries, the question as to leader efficacy has taken on new importance. As legislators, politicians, and the general public demand to know whether or not educational leaders and the schools which they lead are actually making a difference to student learning, the subject has become crucial. With the increasing diversity in many schools, there is also indication of increasing disparities in student learning between groups of children who have traditionally comprised the dominant group and those who are in some ways minoritised or marginalised due to factors such as race, ethnicity, family socioeconomic background, or home language—factors that are largely beyond their control. Accomplishing what is often referred to as "gap reduction"—enhancing the academic performance of traditionally lower performing sub-groups—has become the gold standard for success.

To address these latter demands for equity in terms of demonstrable improvement, studies of educational reforms and restructuring have also proliferated. Yet, some children still fail in today's schools. Poor children and children of colour are less likely to succeed in North America than white middle class children. Educational leaders are expected to cope with inadequate buildings, uncertified teachers, insufficient resources, and an uncertain and shifting political climate. They are expected to address and overcome many wider societal issues such as lack of early childhood education, poverty, lack of medical care, or substandard housing—all of which impinge on children's ability to learn.

## Purpose

This paper is based on insights acquired by the authors over years of engaging in educational leadership and of conducting educational leadership research. Here we present a framework for educational leadership that we posit has the ability to move us beyond models and prescriptions to focus on the (many and still contested) purposes and goals of the endeavour. We agree with many others who have found a lack of clear-cut differentiation related to various leadership traits, styles, or approaches. We are convinced that there are highly successful hierarchical leaders as well as equally successful collaborative leaders; we have found as many highly regarded extroverted leaders as highly respected introverts. Some educational leaders seem to lead from the heart and shoot from the hip, while others appear to plan every move as if it were an elaborate military campaign.

In spite of this, we have found some common threads or themes, often in ways and places that were totally unexpected. We have found there to be a significant difference in the ability of educators to exercise leadership based on the clarity of their moral purpose, their willingness and ability to exercise agency, and the presence or lack thereof of something we are calling savvy. The purpose of this paper is to explore and develop this framework, drawing on examples from research sites we have studied over the past 15 years. This is, therefore, not an empirical piece *per se*, but draws from both theory and practice to develop a praxis-oriented framework for educational leadership.

## Theories and Definitions: Some Clarification

We have used several terms in the previous section that warrant clarification (at least in how we are using them) before we proceed; they are *leadership, moral purpose, agency,* and *savvy.* In this section, we do not provide short, dictionary-type definitions, but instead, describe some of the current theories that embody these terms and explain the ways in which we are thinking about them.

At the outset we also want to be clear that we are not creating yet another list of leadership traits, nor are we thinking of these as topics to be taught during a preparation programme. We are also not very comfortable with words like attributes, components, or facets as they all seem to imply something relatively fixed that can be clearly defined and bounded. We do not suggest that the elements of our framework are innate—you either have them or you don't, nor that they are immutable—once you have acquired, learned, or demonstrated. certain characteristics, you cannot change. These are essentialising ways of thinking about something we see as dynamic and interactive, aspects of leadership for which we seek an appropriate term.

Instead, we will be talking about *moral purpose, agency,* and *savvy* as aspects or elements of a praxis-oriented leadership framework in order to acknowledge their fluidity and imprecision. At most, we consider them to be dispositions, not in a fixed sense of one's usual mood or temperament, but more as a combination of qualities, inclinations, or tendencies that help to shape and define an approach to leadership. Taken together they represent manifestations of beliefs, values, attitudes, and practices learned over time through interaction with our social groups and the "discursive culture that these people inhabit" (Burr, 1995, p. 50). Tendencies toward one or another of these dispositions may even be inborn—a little like the tendency for extroversion or introversion. They are ways of thinking and acting that may be both inherited and learned, but are undoubtedly shaped by the dominant discourses (words and practices) of the societies in which we have lived (Foucault, 1980).

### Leadership

We do not attempt to define leadership, but take as a starting point, Bogotch's (2000) suggestion that it is "deliberate intervention that requires the moral use of power." Implicit in this statement are a number of ideas we tease out as we talk about a framework that includes moral purpose, agency, and savvy. For example, the notion of deliberate intervention implies action. Here the statement does not suggest the kind of intervention: it might be top down and mandated; it might come from the grassroots; it might be instigated by a large pressure group or by a single individual. We are making explicit the notion that there are many ways to exercise leadership. Bogotch suggests that a leader (or leaders) need to deliberately intervene—in other words, they need to act in order to exercise leadership. Action, too, is fundamental to our concept of agency. Bogotch then introduces the concept of morality related to a leader's use of power. As we will elaborate later, moral purpose is an intrinsic component of the framework we develop in this paper, and power is inherent in one's ability to act, either for good or ill. As we will demonstrate later, our findings clearly demonstrate that a component missing in much of the literature is that of savvy; yet, we posit that without what we are calling savvy, moral purpose and willingness to intervene are less likely to succeed.

However defined, there is considerable evidence emerging about the importance of educational leaders. Silins and Mulford (2002) state that "the contributions of school leadership to past and current ... school reform efforts have been found to be undeniably significant, even if these contributions are indirect" (p. 564). Some have suggested that one of the most promising approaches to leadership that makes a difference to student outcomes is transformational leadership. Sleegers, Geijsel, and van den Berg (2002) indicate that "transformational leadership has emerged as one alternative model with potential for enriching our understanding of innovation in schooling" (p. 84). Drawing on the work of Leithwood and colleagues, they identify six dimensions of transformational leadership (vision building, individualised consideration, intellectual stimulation, fostering the acceptance of group goals, creating high performance expectations, and modelling important values and practices) (p. 86). In addition to these organisational dimensions to which leaders attend, some approaches to leadership are more broadly focused. Astin and Astin (2000) describe transformative leadership in the following terms:

> We believe that the value ends of leadership should be to enhance equity, social justice, and the quality of life; to expand access and opportunity; to encourage respect for difference and diversity; to strengthen democracy, civic life, and civic responsibility; and to promote cultural enrichment, creative expression, intellectual honesty, the advancement of knowledge, and personal freedom coupled with responsibility. (p. 6)

This emphasis on leadership that enhances equity and social justice, that is interested in enhancing the quality of life for students and their families and in increasing access and opportunity, is closely related to our understanding of moral purpose.

**Moral Purpose**

While the ways in which moral purpose is exhibited may vary according to context, here we adopt Fullan's (2003) framework. Fullan identifies four levels of what he calls the moral imperative—the individual, school, regional, and societal (p. 30). In talking about what connotes a moral purpose for schools, he states:

> The criteria of moral purpose are the following: that all students and teachers benefit in term of identified desirable goals, that the gap between high and low performers becomes less as the bar for all is raised, that ever-deeper educational goals are pursued, and that the culture of the school becomes so transformed that continuous improvement relative to the previous three components becomes built in (p.31).

Fullan sums up what this means by saying, "Moral purpose of the highest order is having a system where all students learn, the gap between high and low performance becomes greatly reduced, and what people learn enables them to be successful citizens and workers in a morally based knowledge society" (p. 29).

Purpose itself suggests a clear relationship between the goals of educational leadership and the ways in which it is practised. In our conception of moral purpose related to *educational* leadership, the goal is closely tied to what some would describe as social justice: instituting equitable and inclusive learning environments in which all children reach their highest potential.

Brown (2005) declares that "at times there has been little relationship between the expressed goals of education and actual educational practices" (p. 110). Leading with moral purpose would require a groundedness in which there is congruence between expressed purpose and practice. Some (for example Evans, 1996; Terry, 1993) call this authentic leadership. Terry says that authentic leadership is not just action but ethical action—being "true to ourselves and true to the world, real in ourselves and real in the world" (p. 139). Dantley (2005) summarises many of these themes when he says that:

> Moral leadership, therefore, is broader than traditional school management. It demands a deep investment of the genuine or authentic self of the educational leader. Moral leaders have the courage to locate their work in a broader as well as deeper space as they work to (ring about societal transformation. Moral leadership is problematic because it interrogates what school systems and communities have essentialised. It is problematic because it dares to demystify those structures and rituals that have become almost reified after so many years of acceptance. (p. 45).

It is important to recognise, however, as Fairholm (2000) does, that moral leadership is not new. He explains: "the problem is we have not thought of our leadership in values terms. So the idea of values leadership is 'new', while the *practice* is much more common" (p. xxi).

We note here that when we suggest a leader is lacking moral purpose, we are not implying that leader is immoral or amoral. For the purposes of this paper, we are saying that educational moral purpose necessarily focuses on providing the optimal environment to enhance student learning. Naturally, there are other moral purposes. We recognise that all too frequently disparate moral purposes compete with each other for an educational leader's attention. Our argument for moral purpose sides with that of enhanced student learning, whether it be intellectual, emotional, social, or spiritual.

## Agency

Agency, as we are using it, implies both the willingness and the ability to act in order to achieve one's mission, goals, and objectives in a proactive way Ogawa (2005) suggests that agency is held in balance by forces outside of individual control but also acknowledges the individual responsibility to exercise agency. He adopts the concept of human agency

> as a heuristic for examining theory and research on educational leadership. Agency involves the control that people exert over their destiny, which is matched against deterministic forces assumed to lie largely beyond their control. (p. 90)

Ogawa further states that much current theory treats organisations as a constraint on leadership, but argues for the alternative approach of Katz and Kahn (1966) who think of leadership as "outside the bounds of organisation's routine directives, or structures" (2005, p. 93). He goes on to quote Schein (1992) who defines leadership as "the ability to step outside the [organisation's] culture" (p. 93). Rather than think about leadership as constrained by the norms of the institution in some way, an agentic perspective on leadership takes the leader outside the bounds of the organisation's culture in such a way as to take deliberate action that may make a difference.

We have not chosen to add power as a separate component in our framework, because it permeates both moral purpose and agency. For the most part, power has become perceived as a negative element of human interaction. Senge and colleagues (2000) believe that today too much of the

> discussion around school reform takes place in a power-coercive framework. State legislatures announce that, in effect, "These children *will* achieve." Regardless of whether they have been fed well, live in safe neighbourhoods, have parents at home, have good medical care, or live in a peaceful and tranquil environment, they will be judged against children who have those things. Teachers, similarly, are told, "You will have high test scores or we will close you down." ... The results they want are laudable but they show no awareness of the process that must occur naturally to produce those results. (p. 393-394).

Obviously, this is not the use of power that generates successful educational reform. But it is the type of power, too often seen in educational reform processes, and the one that gives the term power itself negative connotations and implications.

One of Foucault's contributions to our understanding of power was the notion that "the effective exercise of power [may] be disguised" (in Seidman & Alexander, 2001, p. 72). He asserts that power is exercised, not just through sovereignty, but also through techniques and discourses. Power, as Foucault conceptualised it, is neither inherently negative nor positive. His argument is that its discourses must be interrogated to determine who is served and who is oppressed. To understand power, one must examine its social and historical contexts, the regimes of "truth" of any given society (Rainbow, 1984, p. 73).

There is little doubt that power, whether personal, positional, or discursive may perpetuate inequities or may be used to overcome them. Hence it is closely tied to our concepts of moral purpose and agency.

**Savvy**

Savvy is defined by the American Heritage Dictionary as "practical understanding or shrewdness." It is widely used to describe knowledge about such mundane things as shoes, sunscreen, or technology. Terry (2006), with no definition or explanation, uses the term 'administrative savvy'. Barton (2005) says that nurses "must become savvy in the use of informatics" and students must become savvy in evidence-based practice" again without any further comment or explanation of the term. Rivero (2005) talks about "web savvy K-12 students" and the need to "develop a new generation of tech-savvy leaders" (p. 33). Johnson (2005) asks, "What does a tech-savvy administrator look like" and concludes he is one who incorporates the six Technology Standards for School Administrators (TSSA) adopted in 2002 by the International Society for Technology in Education (¶, 2). This person therefore understands leadership and vision, learning and teaching, productivity and professional practice, support, management and operations; assessment and evaluation; and social, legal and ethical issues—a vague list of terms, with no direction about how to get there. In these and most other references one can find to savvy, the authors simply assume that people know what it is—some sort of practical knowledge related to a topic.

There are a few references to savvy in which there are implicit if not explicit explanations. Gregory (2005) argues that because liberal education is in a battle for survival, it "needs fewer friends who are merely well meaning and more friends who train themselves to flight for liberal education's distinctive goals—not to mention its very survival—the way they train themselves to be smart, savvy, and successful in their disciplines" (p. 56). He further says that because "no one within universities receives any particular training in how to think critically, comprehensively, or philosophically about it," they do not know how to talk about liberal education. Moreover, few would know "where to begin to bring themselves up to speed" to adequately and intelligently discuss the topic. The implication is that to be savvy, one needs to be more than well intentioned. One needs to know how to think critically, comprehensively, and philosophically about a given topic. One needs to be "up to speed" so to speak.

In *The Survival of the Savvy* (Seldman & Thomas-Williams, 2004), an "organisational savvy model" is introduced in which a savvy leader is described as one who is receptive to feedback and challenge, admits mistakes, changes the risks and rewards equation for candour, detects deception, and exposes and eliminates closed shops—those situations in which "an overly political leader gets into power or a pocket of power in an organisation and established control over information" (Seldman & Thomas-Williams, 2005, p. 61). We could find no comparable discussions in educational leadership literature, although we find mention of "professional savvy" regarding the processes and politics of change (see Fullan, 2003; Leithwood & Steinbach, 1995). For our purposes, the ideas outlined by Selman and Thomas-Williams are constructive in helping us to begin to clarify our use of the term. We combine these ideas with the notion of being shrewd and having practical insight as a starting point for what we mean by savvy.

**The Framework**

In the next section, we want to illustrate the tendencies, dispositions, and inclinations that together seem to provide a sound framework for effective educational leadership. Based on our observations of leaders over time, and the date from the sample for this paper (see Table 1), we have found that despite other differences, where leaders consistently demonstrate all three inclinations, they are prone to success, whereas if any one of the three is missing, success is elusive. We reiterate that among the principals with whom we have worked and whom we have studied, some were introverts, some extroverts; some were male, some female; some white, some black; some straight, some gay. Some were implementing reforms that they had conceived or developed; others were implementing reforms mandated from an outside jurisdiction. None of these differences could consistently be associated with success or failure. In this section, we will illustrate, the importance of our framework for a praxis-oriented approach to educational leadership using data from only five respondents.

## Learning from Practice

As one examines Table 1, it is readily apparent that each principal was able to make some changes in his or her school, most exercised considerable agency related to the changes they wanted, but that only two demonstrated clear and consistent connections among the goal of adequate student achievement, the action they took, and their ability to achieve success. In this section, using pseudonyms to preserve confidentiality, we will give a flavour of the leadership of each in turn, before turning, in the last section, to a discussion of some of the implications for leadership praxis.

### Alisha: A Voracious Innovator

Alisha has been a dedicated educator: classroom teacher, guidance counsellor, and principal, for over 25 years. As principal of a small (200 students in grades 7-12) Navajo School in the United States, she has instituted numerous positive changes. Among other things, she has overseen multiple facility renovations to provide a bigger library, excellent computer and technology labs, and a well-equipped art room. She has been instrumental in changing the look of her school from a "school just like any other," to one that reflects the dominant Navajo culture at every turn. Pillars and walls display Navajo art and images,

*Table 1. Overview of Participants*

| *Person* | *Demographics & Context* | *Reform Particulars* | *Moral Purpose* | *Agency* | *Savvy* |
|---|---|---|---|---|---|
| Alisha female, white principal | Small Navajo HS, low performing | Multiple annual reforms, many physical changes, cultural programs, football lights, unrealistic low expectations<br>Both top down & bottom-up reforms, NCLB | Mixed<br>All students do not learn - disconnect between explicit goal & activities | Active interaction with community, fund raising, failure to address poor teaching, football lights | Mixed<br>Knows how to get things done, understands culture<br>No risks, ignores feedback, does not explicitly admit mistakes |
| Luke male, white failing principal | Inner city urban school, diverse, low income bottom-up | Extra personnel, parents, culture change, low adult-student ratio. achievement | XX<br>Did not focus on student surface changes but a culture of safety & security | Mixed<br>Worked within BCTF structure | XX<br>Desire to be liked, safe, burnt-out, did not challenge BCTF, personal interest in students & families XX |
| Naomi female, white principal | Large JHS, diverse, low income | MY-YRS, flexible groups, learning leaders, multiple reforms | Instituted to make a difference for students | Able to get resources, permission to innovate, overcame structures, new policies | Too much going on, too much flexibility, freedom, risks, lack of attention to feedback |

*(Contd....)*

| *Person* | *Demographics & Context* | *Reform Particulars* | *Moral Purpose* | *Agency* | *Savvy* |
|---|---|---|---|---|---|
| Sandy female, white, principal | 40% poverty, diverse, award for achievement | Rejection of deficit thinking, fun, collaboration, staff study, use of data Bottom-up, but NCLB, | Clear focus on achievement, inclusion, empowerment | Active leadership, parent & community involvement, advocacy with board | Risks, feedback, proactive, rewards candour, effort, no closed shop |
| Esther female, black, principal | Large school, high minority, low income | MT-YRS, parent programmes, intersession, class size, teacher training, focus on learning, high expectations, Both top down & bottom-up, NCLB | Dramatic improvement, disbelief in state capital | Active interaction with community, Willing to take a stand, move teachers on | Risks, feedback, admits mistakes |

posters in the building display pictures of successful Navajo people and their guiding Beauty Way; and outside, there is a traditional Hogan, a shade house, a Churro sheep project, and an ethno-botany garden.

Indicative of Alisha's agency is the story of how she worked to install lights in her football stadium. As one can imagine with such a small school, the football team is generally small (sometimes only 8-10 students) and rarely very successful—in one recent season it lost every game.

Yet, Alisha was convinced that, like other schools, hers should be able to host evening games and thus needed stadium lights. In part, she believed this could send a positive message of valuing the community. For over five years, she worked to raise enough money and finally the lights had arrived. When she contacted the district to arrange installation, she was told there would be an additional charge of several thousand dollars. After bargaining with the district and arranging some cost sharing, she was still short. Undaunted, she wrote a letter to Tony Hillerman, the famous southwestern fiction writer, who had often set his novels in her area, asking if he might be interested in donating enough money to install the lights. To her surprise, Hillerman soon contacted her and arranged for the donation. The lights were installed and inaugurated in a celebratory evening that concluded with many students and community members dancing and singing spontaneously on the field.

Alisha is extensively involved in her community in many ways. Parents and students knock on her door at all hours seeking assistance, and her home is a designated emergency care home. She cares deeply about her community and exhibits strong and positive relationships with them. She can muster the resources to make significant physical changes in her building. However, despite multiple changes in the organisation of classes and the grouping of students over 13 years of her principalship academic achievement has barely changed. Less than 50 per cent of students still meet or exceed statewide expectations in language arts, less than 40 per cent in math, and less than 33 per cent in science. One of Alisha's difficulties is that although she talks about wanting all students to achieve, she expends considerable energy on making changes in areas in which she feels competent and in which change is more visible and concrete.

When asked about what she wanted to accomplish before she retired, for example, she stated that she wanted to enlarge the parking lot and fix the tennis courts. There was no sense that she wanted to improve overall student achievement. Herein lies Alisha's difficulty. She has, over the years, hired several teachers with inadequate skills or experience to promote academic success among students. After an intensive year-long staff development programme in which an outside consultative team provided intensive training, classroom support and mentoring, and regular feedback to teachers and to Alisha, both she and the team sat down to discuss the next steps to be taken. Despite every indication that one probationary teacher was incompetent, had not responded to feedback, and had been unsuccessful in helping students to achieve academically, Alisha renewed the teacher's contract. She needed a teacher to oversee the yearbook; the teacher had voluntarily taken on some staff responsibilities; and the teacher's mother sat in the state legislature.

The foregoing is one illustration of many of Alisha's lack of savvy. She seems unaware of the disconnect between her advocacy and support of the community ire tangible ways and her lack of ability to focus on what is best to promote student learning in her school. She tends to discount external feedback if it requires risk-taking on her part or if it demands that she institute deep and difficult changes in teacher position, pedagogy, and practice. On the other hand, Alisha demonstrated a remarkable degree of savvy regarding the installation on lights on the school football field. She negotiated with the district to get the extra prohibitive costs down, and then turned to an outside source to get financial assistance on the balance.

In this instance, Alisha does not demonstrate a clear focus on what we have identified (with Fullan, 2003) as the central moral purposes of schooling. Where she has a clear and definable goal, she is purposeful and successful in achieving it. Where there is less clarity and where the goal seems more remote, she does not seem to have the ability—the savvy—to take the risks.

### Luke: A Well-intentioned Care-giver

We first met Luke when his school was selected to participate in a longitudinal study about student engagement in learning and school life. He was a friendly, dedicated educator, who, like Alisha, had developed positive relationships with his students and who cared deeply about their welfare. According to census data, the students (67% of whom speak English as a second language), live in one of the poorest areas of British Columbia. Like Alisha, Luke had worked hard to change the appearance and culture of the school from "one of violence to one of community." He created an inviting space with a carpet, couches, and toys in which elders (40% of the students are indigenous) and parents could come and sit and talk to one another. He developed a strong volunteer program in which adults came and read to students and in which community members volunteered to teach crafts or tell stories in classrooms. The school had a food bank, a clothing depot, and a community and family worker to assist parents with shopping, nutrition, and other needs. A local artist involved parents and students in the creation and painting of a large multicultural mural for the foyer. Another group instituted Native Indian drumming in the foyer each morning intended to "drum the children to school" in a culturally appropriate manner.

Luke was so successful in creating an inviting climate that during the first year of our study, the school hid an adult-student ratio of one to four (50 staff members plus some volunteers for a student population of under 250). But, students still failed to achieve academically. Students were pulled out of so many classes that teachers sought to institute a mentor programme in which each child might have a positive interaction with the same caring adult on a daily basis. Luke responded to each teacher request sympathetically, but failed to exercise the leadership required to stabilise instruction and to institute high expectations and standards. On one occasion, when a particularly ineffective and somewhat obstreperous teacher whose position was funded from a special district fund targeted for inner city schools, Luke indicated that as much as he might want to reassign other classroom teachers in the light of the availability of a new staff member, his hands were tied by the Teachers' Union and the contract. He was unwilling and apparently unable to seek permission to try something different to promote success among his students.

At the time of Luke's leadership, a commonly heard phrase in the school was, "These students have so many problems." In fact, most teachers expressed a deficit perspective (see Valencia, 1997; Shields, Bishop, & Mazawi, 2005) in which they stated that with the poverty and crime in the area all they could do was provide a safe place for students; academic goals were unrealistic. On one occasion, during "a professional development workshop held for teachers in April, one teacher stated, "I finally began teaching the 5th grade curriculum this week." When asked what she had been doing until then, she replied that she had "been helping the students to feel safe."

Several other comments provide a sense of the deficit thinking and lack of expectations at the school. On one occasion, when a child refused a teacher's request that she "get a book," the teacher backed down saying, "It's okay then, if you want to lie down, lie down. I'm glad you came." The teacher explained to the researcher that she chose to give the girl the power rather than engage in an inappropriate power struggle. On another occasion, a teacher commented:

> There's nothing to do about those kids; there's no back-up for you anymore; the Youth Worker can't manage them, Social Services can't manage them, they can't be in the classroom, they can't be in the hallway, and the administrators are not managing them so you're basically having kids that are just running around and you can't really make that progress any more; and that happens a lot in this kind of school ....Their homes are always in a disaster, ... they won't work, they won't work for anybody; you can't send them home because there's nobody at home; and if you send them home, they come back.

There is clear indication here of a general lack of moral purpose. Nowhere did we find a sense that these students could achieve academic success if teachers actually taught them and expected them to do well. There was no attempt on the part of the administrator to make changes that might have turned the school around, except to make it a safe and welcoming place. Perhaps most importantly, Luke seemed to be unaware that this could or should occur.

It is worthy of note that several administrators later, and with a similar student demographic, the students are achieving above provincial levels in every subject area tested. For example, at the 7th grade level, 85 per cent meet or exceed expectations in reading, 100 per cent in writing, and 100 per cent in math, compared to previous provincial achievement levels of 77 per cent, 90 per cent, and 83 per cent respectively (under Luke's administration).

This narrative demonstrates clearly that Luke's focus on safety, although a necessary precondition for learning, is insufficient in and of itself and is not consistent with the way we are defining moral purpose. He demonstrated agency in terms of developer closer relations with the community and in bringing parents into the school. Where it was a question of acting with respect to school organisation, class assignments, and ensuring appropriate instruction and pedagogy, he failed to act. Moreover, he seemed to believe that he had little agency apart from fulfilling the regulations of his district or of the teacher's federation. Moreover, he did not believe in the capacity of his students to succeed. His inability to make the requisite changes, when seen in the light of the subsequent success of similar populations of students in the school, is strong indication of lack of savvy.

### Naomi St. John: A Go-getter

When we first met Naomi, she had just opened a new school in a rapidly growing area of a mid-size western city. Having been appointed a year prior to the opening, she had worked with both builders and board members to achieve the kind of school she wanted: one that operated on a rotating, year-round schedule; specially constructed with pods or learning communities; and flexible spaces for various kinds of pedagogical interactions and student learning. She had convinced the district to permit her not to hire the traditional vice-principal, but to identify a learning leader for each of the five "tracks" she would be operating in this multi-track year-round junior high school. Everyone was excited. The school had opened with no rules, no processes, and the opportunity for extensive participation on the part of all students, teachers, and parents. For example, at first washrooms were not designated male or female; there were no processes for reporting student achievement; and there were no rules—could the children wear hats? There were no elected members of the student council—it was open to all students (with the result that few attended meetings).

The school had been built to fill a perceived need in this rapidly growing, diverse, working class community and Naomi was convinced that giving everyone a voice and instituting a cutting edge middle school approach to teaching and learning would result in high levels of student achievement. She recognised that not all children learn in the same way and that not all activities needed the same 30 to 1 student-teacher ratio with which most schools and classes in the district operated. So she introduced a system in which each learning team developed its curriculum, its schedule, and grouped and regrouped its students and teachers according to their perceived needs. In theory, the cutting edge approach was strong. Naomi had already proven she had a clear sense of moral purpose and singular focus on students by her inclusive and responsive approach. She had demonstrated clearly agentic behaviour in her persuasive interactions with the builders and school board members. But somehow, things went wrong.

The collaborative approach began to polarise the community—staff, students, and parents. One original learning leader stated that

> it was exciting. The teams were working together. The administration was working together. There were all the things that when you open a brand new school. There were no traditions. So expectations had to be set. Our principal was a strong advocate of stewardship and collaborative decision making. Then that process tends to take a little bit of time . ... We didn't have any infighting on the admin team. We're still close friends .... I still believe in it. I believe in the learning community approach. I believe in year-round schooling.

Many found it overwhelming, however, and expressed less positive impressions recalled that

> "The philosophy of the school looks so good on paper, total integration, total inclusion, total integration of subjects. We tried to do everything all at once ... one of the philosophies

> of the school was 'student voice, student choice'... There was such destruction the first year. The walls, everything. Six months and the school looked like it had been lived in for thirty years.

In fact, at the end of the second year, we found that only 13 of the original 40+ teachers would return for the third year; one learning community had lost all of its teachers. At the same time, Naomi announced she would leave the school to take a position as CEO of a non-profit organisation. There is no way to know if the original plan would have succeeded had she stayed, but many indications that the writing was already on the wall. By year five, when the school opened with its third principal, little was left of the original plan: walls had been erected, the multi-age, multi-grade flexible learning communities had returned to fixed classes; a vice-principal had replaced the learning leaders; and the school calendar had moved from multi-track year-round to a single-track schedule.

It is our perception that Naomi's lack of success may be explained, at least in part, by a lack of savvy. There were signs of difficulty early in the first year, with many teachers expressing a high degree of stress and a sense of constantly being overwhelmed. Student involvement had not translated into students' taking responsibility for the school building; students and parents had expressed concern that the multi-age approach would not prepare them for High School. But Naomi persisted, claiming everything was going well, citing some positive feed back she had received but neglecting the negative. She was willing to take risks in terms of implementing an innovative program, but failed to attend to the details necessary to make it work. Further evidence of her lack of savvy is contained in this summation by a former teacher in the school: "The administration can really set the tone of the school. Not to say that Naomi didn't have the best interest of the students in mind, but I think she was too idealistic."

### Sandy: A Community Success Story

Sandy's story has a happier ending. In contrast to Naomi, she did not come into a new school with exciting programmes and permit them to slip away. She was appointed to a newly merged school in an older building, one in which the wealthier children were now forced to attend school with "white trash", African-Americans, and a rapidly growing Hispanic population. She set about to help teachers identify what kind of school they wanted to work in, constantly asking questions, and setting a tone of inquiry (Palmer, 1998). In fact, she was so successful that between her first and second years, student achievement as reported by the state under the NCLB mandate changed from 59 per cent of students meeting or exceeding expectations to 76 per cent at those levels.

Teachers report that she turned previously boring staff meetings into times of discussion, data-examination, and fun. Sandy kept her staff off-guard by introducing activities that she said were reminiscent of outdoor experiential education, as well as cartoons and unanticipated competitions with silly prizes. She engaged her teachers in processes of reflection, taught them the importance of using data to make decisions about children, and empowered them to make appropriate changes.

After carefully examining student achievement data, teachers noted that the children who were not achieving well in math at the end of the year were the same children who had begun the year with deficiencies in math. To overcome this, teachers decided to group and regroup children, testing them every eight weeks, and assigning them to flexible groups based on their prior knowledge and achievement level of the specific task at hand. For example, a child might have some advanced understanding of graphs but struggle with long division. It made no sense to them to place that child either in an advanced or a remedial class for the whole year, when the tasks and students' prior knowledge changed frequently. As part of this empowering, inquiry approach to change, she gave teachers a choice of group depending on what they felt most comfortable teaching, but expected that the levels they taught would also change frequently. Through additional probing, they came to the place where they all agreed that the teacher with the lowest performing group at a given time would have the smallest number of students and first call on volunteers and school resources. When they instituted similar groups in reading, everyone participated enthusiastically—Sandy, the district personnel manager, and the district curriculum specialist all taught a group.

When we visited the school, we had occasion to participate in one of the now weekly assemblies. It was a vibrant celebration of school life in which everyone sang the school song (a rap written by a teacher), the teachers taught the children a dance, first grade students performed a readers' theater, and awards of every description were distributed. Pride in the school was evident both in the enthusiastic response of teachers and students and, when appropriate, in their quiet and respectful behaviour. What was interesting was that both principal and teachers told us that when the assemblies were first instituted, teachers had complained, worrying that the time away from instruction would negatively affect test scores. They had found however, that when the school came together as a community, the sense of belonging and pride in achievement was so enhanced that it become simply another vehicle for student learning.

Sandy is not a typical principal. She is outgoing, creative, and willing to take immense risks to achieve her goal of creating a warm and caring school community in which every child successfully acquires a deep understanding and mastery of the academic material. She knows when to push her teachers and when to back off. In her first year, although some sympathetic board members warned her she risked being fired; she challenged the closed shop of the principal meetings and superintendent's decisions. She received the lowest salary increases in the district but persisted because she constantly asked herself, "What am I really here for" and then "just did it." Here is a principal who showed evidence of all three interactive dispositions of our framework: a clear sense of moral purpose, agency, and savvy to accomplish what needed to be done.

### Esther: A Principal with a Mission

Newly-appointed principal Esther Harwood found a sprawling, overcrowded school with two new wings and 28 portable classrooms. In response to a district mandate that if a school exceeded its designated capacity by at least 20 per cent, the principal was to introduce multi-track year-round schooling. Although the mandate had not been enforced in more affluent areas, it was enforced for Jericho Elementary School, a low performing school in a low SES area. The school's population included 50 per cent Hispanic students and a large group (33%) of children whose parents who were migrant workers. Jericho Elementary School was included on Florida's list of "critically low performing schools."

Esther threw herself into the change, believing it might be a way of shaking up the staff and helping the teachers think about new approaches to instruction and to involving the community in the programmes of the school. She asked her teachers "Do you think kids can learn? Do you believe we can teach?" Upon receiving affirmative responses, she replied, "Well then let's do it." Despite the fact that the school had what she described as "real challenges, with some of the migrant kids coming in and out five times a year as they follow the apples and the tomatoes," her bottom line was that she would accept "no excuses."

Esther made numerous changes such as GED tutoring Parents, Drive-Through Fridays when parents could drop off their children and pick up a cold breakfast with an accompanying sheet of parenting tips, Wonderful Wednesdays when breakfast was served to both parents and children, Make-and-Take for Parents—a room in which parents could make educational materials to use with their children. Esther and her staff worked to make the school the centre of the community, but her focus was always primarily targeted on improving student academic achievement.

Recognising the need for a great deal of support to meet her goal of success for all students, Esther made numerous changes. Among others, she used part of her school's Title 1 money to reduce class size, particularly in the problem area of maths. Teachers decided to introduce extra tutoring programmes to meet individual needs even when it meant finding a room in an adjacent apartment complex or church basement because there were no spare facilities on the school premises. Esther then assigned some special education teachers to a four-day week, and then asked them to teach classes to small groups of students who needed remediation. This instruction was supplemented by a three hour Saturday school held on Saturday mornings and staffed by teachers she hired front around the district (Esther's husband, a teacher in another district school, taught for free).

After one year, Esther submitted her school's test results as required to the State Office of Education. Although not every principal whose scores increased considerably was asked to do so, she was "called to Tallahassee" to defend her school's results. She explained that she thought part of the reason was that the others were white and there is still a lot of racism in the state and district. She recounted the dramatic tale:

> I took a van to tallahassee with some teachers, our test scores, enrollment lists, and videos of the school, and I responded to their concerns by saying, 'You told us to do it, you told us we could do it, and we did it and now you don't believe us!' I told them to come to see for themselves and not waste my time driving all that way. Only two of them ever came.

The state did, however, send a team to her school because her math scores had gone "over the top," even higher than most of the other schools' maths scores and they wouldn't accept them. She continued,

> They came in one day and told me to take a day off and go to Orlando and shop. While I was in Orlando, unsuspecting, they took 12 of my fourth graders and re-tested them. They thought I had cheated but they tested just as well as they had before!

Esther's story is dramatic in that not only did she achieve success; she had to prove several times over that she had done so ethically and honestly. She turned around a school in which deficit thinking and failure had been the norm. Her clear sense of moral purpose, her ability to act proactively, and having enough savvy to withstand the scepticism of the state legislators and implicit personal attacks, won the day.

## Implications and Discussion

We began this paper conscious that many people talk about a divide between theory and practice or between scholars and practitioners in ways that are unproductive and that unnecessarily polarise the discourse about education. In most developed countries, public education is being played out in a political climate of high stakes testing, intense demands for accountability, and increased concern over sub-groups of children who continuously seem to be underachieving. We acknowledge that much prior research has resulted in useful models, strategies, and approaches to educational leadership. At the same time, we are concerned about the ongoing proliferation of studies and the concomitant inability of educational reform efforts and educational leaders to achieve sustained and positive change. For that reason, we revisited all of our data, gathered over 15 years of research in educational leadership, coded interviews and observations of dozens of school-based and district leaders, and identified what we believe to be three underlying essential and inseparable dispositions: agency, savvy, and moral purpose.

We have selected five exemplars from our data to emphasize that our discussion is both generalisable and context dependent. Although it is possible to state that educational moral purpose must focus on student achievement, it is not possible to provide a prescription for what the focus must look like in a specific setting. Alisha, in her Navajo setting, will have to find a different approach than Luke, in an urban inner city elementary school, or than Naomi, in a newly constructed middle school, for example. Although we can posit, with considerable assurance, the need for agency, the specific actions related to goal attainment will vary considerably, as Esther and Sandy clearly illustrate. Thus, it is savvy—the ability to identify, understand, and work with both the constraining and the supporting factors of one's specific context that enables one to be successful in a given situation.

We defined moral purpose in education relatively narrowly, taking seriously Fullan's (2003) assertion that "Moral purpose of the highest order is having a system where all students learn" one in which the "gap between high and low performance becomes greatly reduced" and which prepares students for full participation and citizenship in a "morally based knowledge society" (p. 29). Once again, we acknowledge that there are other purposes one might describe as moral. Moreover, saying that someone lacks this particular moral purpose does not imply a general lack of morality. We do, however, believe that in today's explosive political climate, educators must take seriously the requirement that schools help all children—no matter what their class, economic circumstances, ethnicity, or home language—to learn. Note here that learning is not narrowly defined only in terms of scores on standardised tests, but also in terms of citizenship and participation in a morally-based knowledge society. Esther demonstrated that this is possible despite the disbelief of legislators and policy makers. Sandy showed that when the community engages in dialogue about what is right, about what kind of learning students require, they achieve to high levels. Moreover, we have seen in the exemplars of Alisha, Luke, and Naomi that unless a leader focuses explicitly on developing high standards and rejecting deficit thinking (Wagstaff & Fusarelli, 1995), it does not happen.

At the same time, explicit goals are not enough, no matter how often they are said. Having a stated desire to improve student learning but demonstrating implicitly that other goals take priority is a misuse and misunderstanding of agency. We have chosen five educators who demonstrated different kinds of agency. In some instances they were highly successful in some activities (as in Alisha and Naomi) but less successful in bringing about the conditions that promote student learning. Expending the majority of one's time and energy as a leader on tasks that are unrelated to student learning may change the physical plant, or even the culture of the school, but it does not enhance learning. A safe school, as Luke showed us, does not necessarily produce good students. Agency must, as Bogotch (2000) stated, and as Sandy and Esther demonstrated, must be "deliberate" if it is to work towards the fulfilment of moral purpose.

Finally, we discuss the notion of savvy. Although the term is widely used in both technical and colloquial settings, it is rarely defined. We believe savvy to be so important that it needs more investigation and clarification. At the very least, it underlies the notion of praxis—moral action that is theoretically grounded. Savvy requires, as we have seen, a combination of practical insight and shrewdness, a willingness to take risks, to step outside the bounds of tradition, to attend carefully to feedback that points to needed change, to discriminate what is important, or truthful, or desirable from what is not. It is the ability to think critically, comprehensively, and philosophically about what one is doing, to navigate the social, cultural, and political minefields that surround public education.

The savvy we have identified here is savvy that permits one to negotiate the social, cultural, and political environment in ways that permit consistent progress towards the goal of emulsive and equitable student achievement. As we saw with Sandy and Esther, savvy involves being willing to take flak, to stand firm even in the face of threats to one's job security. It is unfortunate that sometimes, as in the case of Naomi (and perhaps to a lesser extent both Alisha and Luke), idealism, charisma, and even achievement can masquerade as savvy.

Heilbrun (1996) traced the quest for a "scientific formula of leadership" (p. 3). It is our contention that there is no such thing. He concluded that to grow as a discipline, leadership studies needed to "cast a wider net" (p. 11), and that in doing so, one might "discover that the most important qualities about leadership lie far beyond the capabilities of science to analyse" (p. 11). Here, we posit what we have called a praxisoriented framework for leadership. It is not "scientific" although its success may be empirically demonstrated. Moreover, we argue that unless these tendencies, qualities, dispositions are probed, explored, studied, and practised in formal programmes of leadership preparation, educational leaders will be ill-equipped to implement them in practice.

We recognise the obvious. There is a considerable overlap among the concepts of moral purpose, agency, and savvy-especially as we are using them. None of them really fully exists without the other two. Moral purpose cannot be said to be authentic if one is not willing to be agentic (to actually do something about one's beliefs), and must be informed by savvy to keep from lapsing into a kind of ineffectual idealism. Agency needs to be undergirded by both moral purpose and savvy about both the content and context of a proposed change. Otherwise it can become—what we sometimes sadly see in education—change for the sake of change. And, of course, savvy itself, is nothing without both the will and ability to act and a good moral compass to point the way. Bottled wisdom lacking in moral foundation is no good to anyone. We, therefore, argue that whether one takes a hierarchical or distributed approach, whether one leads authoritatively or collaboratively, whether one is charismatic and outgoing or quiet and unassuming, to be successful, it is critically important to ensure the presence of moral purpose, agency, and savvy in educational leadership.

## References

Astin, A.W., & Astin, H. S. (2000). *Leadership Reconsidered: Engaging higher education in social change*. Kellogg Foundation. Available: http://www.wkkf.orq/documents/youthed/leadershipreconsidered/ accessed Dec. 2003.

Barton, A. J. (2005). Cultivating competencies in a community of practice. *Nursing Administration Quarterly*, 28(4), 323-328.

Bogotch, I. E. (2000). Educational leadership and social justice: Theory into practice. Revised version of a paper presented at the annual conference of the University Council for Educational Administration. Albuquerque, NM. ED 452 585.

Brown, K. M. (2005). Pivotal points: History, development, and promise of the principalship. In F, W, English (ed.), *The Sage Handbook of Educational Leadership: Advances in Theory, Research, and Practice.* Thousand Oaks, CA: SAGE, 109-141.

Burr, V. (1995) *An introduction to Social Constructionism.* London. Routledge.

Caldwell, O. W., & Wellman, B. (1926). Characteristics of school leaders. *Journal of Educational Research*, 14, 1-15.

Culbertson, J. A. (1988). A century's quest for a knowledge base. In N. J. Boyan (ed.), *Handbook of Research on Rducational Administration.* New York: Longman.

Dantley, M. E., (2005). Moral leadership: Shifting the management paradigm. In F, W, English (ed.), op.cit., 34-46.

Evans, R. (1996). *The Human Side of Change*. San Francisco: Jossey-Bass.

Fairholm, G. W. 12000). *Perspectives on Leadership: From the Science of Management to its Spiritual Heart*. Westport, CT: Praeger.

Fiedler, F. E. (1967). *A Theory of Leadership Effectiveness.* New York: McGrawHill.

Foucault. M. (1980). *Power/Knowledge: Selected Interviews and Other Writings.* (ed. Colin Gordon). New York. Pantheon.

Fullan M. (2003) *The Moral Imperative of School Leadership.* Thousand Oaks, CA: Corwin.

Gregory, M. (2005). Why are liberal education's friends of so little help? My view. Education, 91(2), 56-59.

Heilbrun, J. (1996). Can leadership be studied? In P. S. Temes (ed.), *Teaching Leadership*, New York: Peter Lang.

Hill, P. (1998). Shaking the foundations: Research driven school reform. *School Effectiveness and School Improvement*, 9(4), 419-436.

Johnson, D. (2005). What does a tech-savvy administrator look like ? *School Administrator*, 62(5), p8. May 2005

Leithwood, K., & Steinbach, R. (1995). *Expert Problem Solving.* Albany, NY: SUNY Press.

McGregor, D. (1960). *The Human Side of Enterprise.* New York: McGraw-Hill.

Morgan, G. (1997). *Images of Organisation,* Newbury Park, CA: SAGE.

Ogawa, R. T. (2005). Leadership as a social construct: The expression of human agency within organisational constraint. In F, W, English (ed.),

Palmer, P. J. (1998). *The Courage to Teach: Exploring the inner Landscape of a Teacher's Life.* San Francisco, Jossey-Bass.

Rainbow, P. (1984, ed.), *The Foucault Reader.* New York: Pantheon.

Rivero, V. (2005). Moving it forward. *American School Board Journal,* 192(9), 3234.

Seidman, S., & Alexander, J. C. (Eds.), (2001). *The New Social Theory Reader: Contemporary Debates.* New York: Routledge.

Seldman, M., & Thomas-Williams, J. (2004). *Survival of the savvy.* Free Press.

_______________ , (2005). *Savvy Training.* J&T, 59(5), 60-62.

Senge, P., Cambron-McCabe, N., Lucas, T., Smith, B., Dutton, J., & Kleiner, A. (2000). *Schools that learn: A fifth discipline field book for educators, parents, and everyone who cares about education.* New York: Doubleday.

Shields, C. M., Bishop, R., & Mazawi, A. E. (2005). *Pathologising Practices: Deficit thinking in Education.* New York: Peter Lang.

Silins H., & Mulf-rd, B. (2002). Leadership and school results. In K. Leithwood & P. Hallinger (Eds.), *Second International Handbook of Educational Leadership and Administration* (pp. 561-612). Boston: Kluwer.

Simon, H. A. (1945). Administrative Behaviour— *A Study of Decision-making Processes in Administrative Organisations.* New York: Macmillan.

Sleegers, P., Geijsel, F., and van den Berg, R. (2002). Conditions fostering educational change. In K. Leithwood & P. Hallinger (Eds.), *Second International Handbook of Educational Leadership and Administration.* Boston, MA: Kluwer. p. 75-102.

Stogdill, R. M. (1974). *Handbook of Leadership* (1st ed.), New York: Free Press.

Terry, R. W. (1993). *Authentic Leadership: Courage in Action.* San Francisco: Jossey-Bass.

Terry. M. (2006). Who's in charge here? The administrative challenges of being a volunteer board member for a community-based adult literacy program. Online submission. ED 491595.

The American Heritage@ Dictionary of the English Language, Fourth Edition Copyright © 2000 by Houghton Mifflin Company.

Valencia, R. R. (Ed.). (1997). *The Evolution of Deficit Thinking*. London: Falmer.

Wagstaff, L., & Fusarelli, L. (1995). Establishing, collaborative governance and leadership. In P. Reyes., J. Scribner, & A. Scribner. (Eds). (1999). *Lessons from Highperforming Hispanic Schools: Creating Learning Communities,* New York: Teachers College Press.

# 2

# Integrating Theory and Praxis in Teacher Education

*—Hemlata Talesra*

Teacher education in India today is burdened with heavy assignments for qualitative improvement of teaching, and the role of teacher educators has been to a great extent geared to teacher preparation *vis-à-vis* practice teaching and teacher orientation to motivate and create patterns of teaching. The traditional, stereotyped, lifeless and dull pattern of "Chalk, Talk and Teach" by a teacher is replaced by a creative and critical approach to teaching for manifestation of pupils' innovative personality.

A teacher now is no longer considered as a disseminator or transmitter of knowledge; rather he is considered as a catalyst and facilitator of knowledge. Therefore, the teacher education should be an effort to translate theory into practice.

With the rapid expansion of education the duties and responsibilities of the teacher today take him far beyond the boundaries of the classroom. This presents new challenges to him. Teacher. Hence, the teacher in preparation should be helped to realise his role not only theoretically, not only in the classroom, but also in the total school programme.

A theory of teaching answers three questions:

1. How do teachers behave?
2. Why do they behave as they do?
3. What are the effects?

In this direction three perspectives appear relevant:

1. Instructional theories, teacher education practices and expectations;
2. Education technology process; and
3. Information technology and emergence of cyberspace.

The paper discusses in detailed the theoretical and practical aspects of teacher education programme and their integration.

## Need for Integrated Teacher Education Programme

In recent years the teacher education curriculum in India has been revised as per the recommendations of the NCTE and elaborated in the documented titled "Teacher Education Curriculum: A Framework". The structure of the curriculum for the secondary teacher education as visualised by the NCTE consists of three major areas of work:

1. Pedagogical theory
2. Working with community
3. Context-cum-methodology and practice including related practical works.

The first part of the course dealing with the pedagogical theory covers three main areas, viz., teacher and education in the emerging Indian society; educational psychology, educational management and school organisation; computer education and special courses according to the need and facilities available.

The second part deals with participation and link learning with the local conditions, problems and issues.

The third part of the course deals with content-cum-methodology and practice teaching. This is the core of the training package which is designed to help teacher trainees to acquire the basic skills of teaching.

The core of all improvements and experiments in teacher education curriculum points out the need for an integration of theory and practice. Three major models are described in the encyclopedia of teacher education with regard to the integration of theory and practice in teacher training programmes.

The first one is the apprenticeship model, which focuses on teaching as a practical activity that claims the best way to learn it, is on the job, taught by successful practitioners. Critics of this model argue that this model encourages imitations rather than understanding, and fosters maintenance of existing standards and practice.

The relationalist model rectifies the defects involved in the first model, and provides ample footing and foundation by skewing the relationship between educational theory and practice. Teacher education practised on this view, therefore, has included a ground in the so-called foundation disciplines, viz., philosophy of education, psychology of education, society of education and history of education. This ground will supply new entrants in training with a whole set of theoretical frameworks, from which general principles and empirical considerations and relevant successful practices can be derived.

In the third-reflective model of teacher training, when the practitioners engage in effective teaching, they demonstrate a capacity to analyse the process of what they are doing, and to reconstruct their professional and personal knowledge schemes, while simultaneously making judgement to adopt their practice so that it best matches the needs of students. Theoretically, it connotes conceptually complex, ethical, caring and flexible persons who consider alternative viewpoints.

These three models lay emphasis on instructions which involve both theory and practice. The act of teaching must be directly related to the act of learning. Teacher reflectivity should be considered as a means of integrating practice teaching experience with relevant knowledge base. Reflectivity may be considered as a milestone skill for professional practice. A person's conceptual complexity determines how deeply that person can perceive practical experience.

## Quality of Teachers and Practice Teaching

The quality of teachers depends upon the soundness of teacher education programmes. Practice teaching is providing the best opportunity to the trainees to have a high level of competence. It is not only giving and observing certain number of lessons but truly integrating the theory and practice with the educational administrator, curriculum framers, teacher educators, school teachers, teaching aids and teaching material. The practicum component of teacher education provides an insight among the future teachers as to how to translate theory into practice. The practice teaching programme exposes student teachers to the actual situations.

## Pedagogical Knowledge

Knowing how to teach is another critical domain for successful teaching. Future teachers need to develop an array of knowledge and skill related to the act of teaching. Many of these tend to be independent from the subject matter and level being taught. Pedagogical knowledge includes such areas as theories, strategies for assessing student learning, classroom management, use of technology in teaching as multicultural issues in education, etc.

## Development of Competencies through Methods of Teaching

The curriculum integrates subject matter for the development of competencies through methods of teaching. An example of such integration is provided by the teacher education programme of the independence movement in India. In the methods of teaching history this movement can teach in historical perspective in civics the political perspective in Hindi in the form of a poem or prose, in social studies in the form of cultural perspective. In these programmes the subject domains are taught in the teachers training institute with concurrent emphasis on educational and intellectual issues. These programmes may be more appropriate for the preparation of teachers because they tend to focus on pedagogical content knowledge and not solely on the substantive knowledge of a discipline. Such programmes reflect an orientation towards specific, rather than generic aspects of learning. To teach treatment of subject matter in a way that relates it to pedagogic issues may yield more valued and useful knowledge for the prospective teacher.

## Assessment Dilemmas

Assessment dilemmas encourage the faculty to test the strategic for elevating programme quality while exposing them to the responsibility for students' learning. This localised accountability may prove beneficial in promoting innovation as a continuing dynamic in teacher education.

New business of teacher educator's agenda joins issues left over from the past. Racial and cultural diversity, equity, inclusion and inadequate funding head the list of programme and policy concerns urgently demanding effective responses. We need teachers who advance student learning in elementary and secondary schools. But teachers who meet high performance expectations require preparation infused with compelling ideals, challenging curricula and tough-indent inquiry on the changing conditions of teaching and learning.

## Student-oriented Teaching

According to Bloom in the cognitive domain the synthesis is at the higher place. At this stage the student is able to form his own concept and judgement, whether it is beneficial to him or not. As we consider integration is the ability to synthesise, teacher education must be able to develop these abilities in his students. He should be aware of the identification of learner's ability. The following diagram shows the integration between theory and practice in teacher and student-oriented teaching.

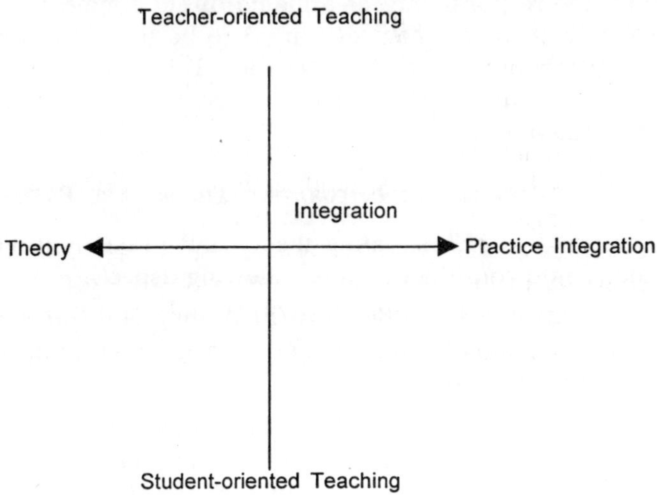


The above diagram shows that when teacher education travels from teacher-oriented teaching to student-oriented teaching the teacher integrates theory into practice. But from teacher-oriented teaching to student-oriented teaching he has to master many things. He has to understand his students, he has to understand; the science of teaching; and he has to develop the insight.

There are two dimensions of teaching: one is selection of content (need of the student), and the other is the presentation of content. The first dimension is related with students' need, and the second is related with content which is reaching to him. Those who understand these two dimensions of teaching would no doubt be able to integrate different theories into practice.

These two dimensions require scholarship, pedagogical knowledge, technology, interdisciplinary approach, devotion, knowledge of organisational behaviour, knowledge of task analysis, etc. Ultimately, no doubt that each teacher educator, with his own area of knowledge, may become a theorist and then he would be successful in integrating theory and practice in teacher education.

## Environmental Education as an Innovative Approach

Environmental education has its own content and methodological characteristics. If teachers are to be entrusted with the responsibility of bringing in environmental education focus in their teaching, they need to be trained to understand and internalise these characteristics. This brings into focus the need for building capabilities and environmental education in their classroom teaching.

## Problems of Integrating Theory and Praxis

The problem of integrating theory and praxis is to be viewed taking into consideration the following aspects:

a. Three 'R's : (i) Reading (ii) Writing and (iii) Arithmetic
b. Recently we have added three H's : (i) Head (ii) Heart and (iii) Hand
c. Five 'F's are also added : (i) Focus Oriented (ii) Fast moving (iii) Friendly approach (iv) Friendly Environment (v) Fun Approach.

The objective of imparting integrated education on the above 3 R's, 3 H's and 5 F's is to:

1) Convert the reservoir of manpower of this country into talented and skill persons.
2) The reservoir is to be skilled and to be raised to the international standards.
3) The country will get competitive advantage over others.
4) We can match our productivity level against global giants.
5) The high standard of human resources can make a market difference as compared to others in respect of:
   i) Innovation of super technology
   ii) Technological development
   iii) Adaptability to changing knowhow
   iv) Adaptability for diversification, if needed
   v) Conquering new frontiers so as to lead the country into the era of plenty and peace.
   vi) Provision of brighter career options to the young men and women
   vii) Breaking the barriers of static society and turning the society into dynamic one.
   viii) By integration the young men and women can understand the different types of Indians and different periods of India, as a large country, i.e., ancient India. Advocacy people, nomadic people, agricultural workers, medieval India, developing India, silicon valleys developing in India, which are embracing the computerised education, internet and the latest information technology in education in places like Bangalore, Hyderabad, Pune.
      i) The children of technocrats, highly skilled persons.
      ii) The children of industrialists and businessmen who desire to train their children in high technology.
      iii) Children of bureaucrats and the citizens belonging to economically high echelon definitely prefer to get their children educated in such institutions which provide high-tech learning.

The third aspect which we have to consider while integrating theory and practice in teacher education is:

i) The environment in which the teaching and learning is carried out at present in our country.

a) The condition of primary schools:

   i) Schools run by government local self-bodies and private agencies.

   ii) Medium of teaching—regional languages.

   iii) English medium schools.

   iv) Primary schools in remote places having not sufficient children to learn. Not sufficient teachers to teach and paucity of number of students in schools.

b) Secondary school, higher secondary schools, junior colleges, senior colleges:

   i) Run by government and semi-government bodies.

   ii) Private institutions — NGO's

   iii) Medium of instruction — Regional languages — English medium.

The conditions in respect of the following differ from place to place and the agencies through which the education is imparted:

a. Funding of education

b. Equipment — resources — teaching materials

c. Qualities of teachers — trained — untrained.

d. Qualities of learners.

e. Atmosphere in which teaching and learning is conducted viz.:

   i) The dynamics of classroom.

   ii) Teacher and student behaviour.

   iii) Intellectual excitement of teachers and learners.

   iv) Inter-personal rapport envisaged by Lowma's two-dimensional models.

f. The existing scenario of our education is shocking:

   i) More than 90 per cent of primary school run by government bodies are nonperforming institutions.

ii) The students completing four to five years of education do not acquire the literacy and numerical skills.

iii) One-third of the students cannot correctly write the letters of the alphabet of regional language.

iv) They cannot correctly distinguished between living and non-living things.

v) Most of the students who failed in our schools and colleges are predominately are from the poor strata of society. Their parents have limited educational background.

g. The fourth aspect is the theories which are taught in the colleges of education to the teacher trainees.

The time has come when we have to screen out the theories which are taught at present to our teacher education in respect of the following aspects:

1. a. Whether the theories taught are relevant to the Indian conditions prevailing as described above?

   b. Whether the theories advocated by the foreign theoreticians based on the conditions prevailing in their respective countries and validated them on the basis of their experience suit the conditions prevailing in India with regard to the social background from which the learners and teachers come.

The growth of software industry all over the world witnesses the Indian brain and Indian mind.

Those persons can be appealed and got involved in the preparation of software suited for this purpose.

It is true that effective knowledge management requires a combination of many organisational elements— technology, human resources, practices, organisation, structure and culture — in order to ensure that right knowledge is brought out to bear at the right time.

For new technology teachers will have to provide with the professional training and on-site training to learn how to effectively incorporate information technology into the curriculum.

## Strategy for Future

We have enough opportunities in the twenty-first century to incorporate effectively theory into practice. The following points will help in this regards:

1. Shifting from traditional to advance.
2. Global thinking.
3. Inculcation of values.
4. Utilisation of resources.
5. Rising efficiency.
6. Accountability.
7. Performance-oriented management.
8. Rising competencies.
9. Commitment of teachers to the new systems and their training.
10. Inspiring the teachers to exhibit their excellence.

# 3

# Leadership Capacity Building in School Environment

*—Zandile Kunene*

## Introduction

The Matthew Goniwe School of Leadership and Governance (MGSLG) is a semi-autonomous organisation set up by the Gauteng Provincial Department of Education in South Africa. As one of its core functions, MSGLG focuses on building the capacity of school leaders in Gauteng. Underpinning MGSLG's work is a fundamental conviction that capacity-building should lead to improved organisational performance, and that the most relevant and appropriate measure of such improved organisational performance is through on-site monitoring, integrated with formative and summative assessment of change. MGSLG has adopted and customised the practice-based methodology used in the training of head teachers (principals) by the Scottish Executive Department (*The Scottish Qualification for Headship*) and has also taken stock of successful programmes developed and run during the past ten years within South Africa. Through examining best practice locally and internationally, MGSLG believes that it is able to offer cutting-edge programmes that address the real needs of South African school leaders.

With that in mind, this paper will provide an overview of leadership constructs that have influenced the design of leadership programmes, and will explore *instructional leadership, transformational leadership and integrated leadership* as major constructs in the leadership debate. It will also discuss the emerging concept of Ubuntu as a leadership construct. In doing so, it will briefly engage with and appraise educational leadership issues in the post-modern era.

## Synthesising Perspectives on Leadership Training

### *Instructional Leadership*

Instructional leadership as a model for educational leadership rose to prominence in America and the Western world in the 1980s. Bush and Glover (2002) define instructional leadership as focusing

> ...on teaching and learning and on the behaviour of teachers working with students. Leaders' influence is targeted at student learning via teachers. The emphasis is on the direction and impact of influence rather than the influence itself.

In South Africa, instructional leadership has taken a centre-stage position and school principals are urged to concentrate on producing better exam results and better-educated children through becoming more involved in the rollout of the curriculum.

Within Gauteng, training programmes for principals and others have focused on Instructional Leadership but not without problems. Often this approach has been to the detriment of creating a better-organised school structure and system — ignoring the macro picture to concentrate on the micro picture, important though both may be. It has in some cases unwittingly diverted attention away from issues such as school welfare, school life and the creation of learner self-esteem — often forgotten because they are labelled psychological skills, deemed not to be so essential in a system that favours managerialism and the measurement of outcomes above all others.

Below is a summary of the last two learner evaluations:

National Report — Systemic Evaluation of Grade 3 Learners: 2003.

Findings on learner performance (National average scores):

a) Life Skills - 54%

b) Literacy - 54%

i) 68% - Listening and comprehension

ii) 39% - Reading

iii) 39% - Writing

c) Numeracy - 30%

Despite many good policies of the National Department of Education to encourage access, many learners have been denied quality education.

**Western Cape Systemic Evaluation of Grade 6 Learners: 2003**

Of 35 000 Grade 6 learners tested around the country, only 0.1 per cent of schools with a majority of Black learners (or one in a thousand) could meet the standards for literacy and numeracy set by the National Department of Education. However, children in predominantly Coloured schools at the same level faired better with 3 per cent meeting the standard, while learners from former White schools scored 65 per cent.

**Transformational Leadership**

Transformational Leadership is a form of leadership that assumes

> ...the central focus of leadership ought to be the commitment and capacities of organisational members. Higher levels of personal commitment to organisational goals and greater capacities for accomplishing those goals are assumed to result in extra effort and greater productivity. (Leithwood, Jantzi and Steinbach, 1999, p.9)

Leithwood (1994), quoted in Bush (2003), conceptualises transformational leadership along eight dimensions:

— Building school vision;

— Establishing school goals;

— Providing intellectual stimulation;

— Offering individualised support;

— Modelling best practices and important organisational values;

— Demonstrating high performance expectations;

— Creating a productive school culture; and

— Developing structures to foster participation in school decisions.

From this one can conclude that Transformational Leadership presents a normative approach to school leadership whereby leaders seek to influence school outcomes, rather than the nature or directions of those outcomes.

The proposition is that schools in transition need to be led democratically and not told what to do. (This offers an interesting reflection point for Gauteng schools: Where are the schools in the process of transition and transformation? What type or styles of leadership are found in the schools?) Leithwood's (1992) work sees leadership as focused on the organisation as a whole being the main purpose of leadership.

The weaknesses of the Transformational Leadership model according to Leithwood (1994, p489-518) are:

— It maybe used as a vehicle for the manipulation or control of teachers who are required to support the 'vision' and aims of the leader.

— In other countries, the governments use the language of transformation but this is about the implementation, of centrally determined policies not the identification of, and commitment to, school-level vision and goals.

In Gauteng, during the early 90s, models of training concentrated on developing Transformational Leaders. The emphasis was on getting school systems and structures in place, and this was seen as the role of the principal. The principal used the School Development Plan as the pivotal tool to guide transformation.

**Integrated Leadership**

Marks & Printy (2003) conducted a study on twenty-four schools that recently experienced restructuring. The focus of the study was to find out what kind of leadership prevailed in the schools that were showing improvement. Their hypothesis was: "transformational leadership is a necessary but not sufficient condition for improved teaching and learning".

The research confirmed the hypothesis as posed by the researchers that there are two different, innovative styles of leadership that correlate with School Improvement. These are:

— Shared instructional leadership

— Transformational leadership

Previously, Instructional Leadership was defined as the sole responsibility of the principal who gives directives and support to teachers. Marks and Printy introduce the notion of Shared Instructional Leadership, which means that the principal functions collaboratively with teachers or groups of teachers to define and set curriculum and assessment standards and practice. They further argue that it is a mixture of Shared Instructional Leadership with Transformational Leadership, defined as Integrated Leadership, that is needed in our twenty-first century schools.

**Leadership and the Post-modern Era**

Starrat (2001) examines the significance and usefulness of democratic leadership in the post-modern era. He looks at the constraints of democratic leadership with regard to racism, sexism, and class, and in doing so examines at length the following underlying themes:

— Representative democracy in the American context;

— American pragmatism with reference to the writings of John Dewey; and

— The constructivist approach to knowledge.

Starrat proposes that each of these perspectives can be considered in the practice of democratic school leadership. He says from the three themes above it can be acknowledged that in the twenty-first century:

— Schools exist in a partially compromised democracy;

— Children will learn that which is useful and practical to them and this should be informed by civic responsibility;

— There are no solid and undisputed answers to key issues and problems in education and we are constantly learning, unlearning and relearning new knowledge.

It is assumed that democracy underpins how schools operate but a reflection on the weaknesses of the two discussed models of school leadership show that democratic principles, in fact, are forgotten/usurped by a leader neglecting to consult properly.

Such a leader withdraws from debates and does not support classroom interventions positively,; he manipulates teachers to follow the vision of the school; he who is only concerned with results (the what) and not how these have been achieved.

Gronn and Ribbins (1996) argue that the leadership debate has not been discussed fully within the opposing perspectives of the positivist era. They further argue that in analysing the roles leaders play in School Improvement this has happened without acknowledging the importance of institutional context in defining the impact of leadership. They propose ethnography and biography as alternative perspectives to understanding leadership. The school leadership literature has emphasised agency and voluntarism in a naive and simplistic manner as a means of defining leadership. Gronn and Ribbins argue that we need more research studies that link leadership to "structure" "structurisation". They argue that we can only understand leadership through understanding context, and that some of the studies that have given some reference to context have been done badly and in a hazy manner.

What is acknowledged is that institutional context "predates" and "postdates" the lives of particular individuals who inhabit them. The contexts include *interalia* social class, caste, status, political affiliations, gender, ethnicity and religion. In South Africa, it is important to pay particular attention to the range of different contexts, so the concept of 'one-sock-fits-all' as an approach to training school leadership is not meaningful. Differences should be acknowledged accordingly in interventions and training programmes. In summary, the post-modern era challenges us to think about leadership within the frameworks of our contextual reality, which is not just broadly democratic but is also about "who we are and where we come from". It implies adding another layer of thinking to the integrated leadership model.

This is where I submit that Ubuntu has a role to play.

The Ubuntu discussion will have three components:

— Definition of Ubuntu

— The life of Albert Luthuli as a leader guided by the Ubuntu principle

— Lessons for school leaders in the twenty-first century

**What is Ubuntu?**

Ubuntu simply defined means "Umuntu ngumuntu ngabantu" loosely translated as "I am a person through other people." (Broodryk, 2005)

Mbiji (2004) defines Ubuntu in a similar way: We are who we are through others. He argues that the concept of Ubuntu is deeply rooted in African culture and its central values are diametrically opposed to the Western culture. He says this antithesis can be explained in terms of the African "I am because we exist" versus the Western "I think therefore I am."

Steve Biko (Biko, 1970) a human rights activist who was assassinated by the apartheid regime, said the following: "We believe that in the long run the special contribution to the world by Africa will be in the field of human relationships. The great countries of the world may have done wonders in giving the world an industrial and military look, but the great gift still has to come from Africa, giving the world a more humane face." Biko was talking about Africa giving the world the spirit of Ubuntu or Umoja, the spirit of togetherness.

There may be a perception that the notion of Ubuntu is being romanticised and being refuted left, right and centre by what Africa has become notorious for in the twentieth and, twenty-first century: the despots that rule Africa with the most appalling human atrocities: the armed militias that maim women, children and the elderly; and various forms of corruption that sell food aid intended for the starving. The easy conclusion may be that Africa is the last continent to speak on Ubuntu or humanity (the quality of being humane or human).

By elucidating the life of Inkosi Albert Luthuli as an educationist and great achiever, I want to demonstrate how Africa nurtures the spirit of Ubuntu and how this legacy can be continued by embracing Ubuntu.

**Who was Inkosi Albert Luthuli?**

Inkosi Albert Luthuli won the Nobel Peace Prize in 1961, the first African to do so. He was the president of the African

National Congress between 1952 and 1967. He was elected president of the African Teachers Association and appointed Rector of Glasgow University. He was indeed a great man.

**His Background**

He was born in Groutville in KwaZulu-Natal and studied there and at Ohlange; trained at Edendale as a teacher; he taught as a teacher at Adams College and was appointed principal in Blaaubach. He married a teacher Mama Nokulunga. When asked about his life as a teacher, he said "Adams College is a pleasant place and I like teaching." In 1935 he was elected as Chief of the Amakholwa people. He had to leave teaching where he was earning 30 pounds sterling a month in order to be a chief, in those days not a reputable position as chiefdom was associated with barbaric practices. When asked about his choice, he responded: "If people want me to come home and be chief who am I to say no?" In our organisations how many leaders are servant leaders like Chief Luthuli?

## Lessons for School Leadership

The definition of Ubuntu that I chose highlights two principles, humility and fairness. I want to extract from the life of Albert Luthuli the following useful lessons for school leadership:

- One of the key issues about Albert Luthuli is his humble beginnings and how these grounded him throughout the rest of his life in matters concerning equality.
- As early as the 1930s, as a teacher and principal he raised issues concerning the crucial role that education plays in improving people's chances in life.
- As early as the 1930s, he also raised issues about "quality education".

As people in leadership positions in education, to what extent do matters concerning the poor, the nature and quality of education inform our discussions, or is it something we have chosen to leave to the policy makers?

- In one of the writings by Inkosi Luthuli, on urbanisation, he raised his concerns about eroding good cultural practices as the unintended consequence of urbanisation.

To what extent do we as school leaders in meaningful and profound ways uphold our culture and promote understanding of other cultures?

— In the early 1920s, Inkosi Albert Luthuli in his writing and public speeches denounced all forms of exclusion, be it race, colour, gender or tribal exclusions, etc.

— As school leaders or people with an interest in education, in what profound and sustained ways do we commit (in both speech and practice) our schools to eradicating these forms of exclusion?

In the life and achievements of Inkosi Albert Luthuli I see a great African that lived by the notions of Ubuntu. A few leaders have emerged that came through the notion of Ubuntu as well; for example, Nelson Mandela, Julius Nyerere, Archbishop Desmond Tutu and President Thabo Mbeki.

At MGSLG we have started a desktop research project that identifies prominent leaders in sub-Saharan Africa and their views on leadership so that we can infuse in our programmes concept of Ubuntu alongside concepts of instructional and transformational leadership.

## Conclusion

To conclude I quote the writings of Lovemore Mbigi, who is an exciting and creative thinker specialising in the area of managing transformation in South Africa. He is probably the most influential proponent of an African philosophy of management. When he turns to the theme of Ubuntu, Mbigi is using terminology that is central to African philosophy. He is the author of *UBUNTU: The Spirit of African Transformation in Management* (co-authored with Jenny Maree), 1995.

The rapid pace of change makes the conventional management approach inadequate, and calls for other management paradigms. African traditional practices and wisdom need to become the basis for management and institutional innovation. Visionary management is the most appropriate in meeting African management challenges. It is capable of synthesising all the polarities.

It can integrate ancient wisdom of the past with the modern science of the present, as well as reality and vision. It turns them into the dynamic energy, which is essential for undertaking the task of transformation required, if Africa is to catch up with the rest of the world. The metaphysical manager is an inspirational preacher, a man who lives in the grip of a vision and shares his experience with the organisation he leads and is seeking to transform.

I invite you to join us on this journey trying to unravel this rich concept of Ubuntu.

## References


Brookdryk, J. (2005) *Ubuntu Management Philosophy,* Republic of South Africa: Knowledge Resources Publishing (Pvt) Ltd.

Bush, T. (2003) *Theories of Educational Leadership and Management,* Sage: UK

__________, & Glover, D. (2002) *School Leadership: Concepts & Evidence,* Nottingham: National College for School Leadership p.10

Gronn, P., and Ribbins, P. (1996), Leaders in Context: Post Positivist Approaches to Understanding Educational Leadership, *Educational Administration Quarterly,* 32 (3), 452-473.

Leithwood, K., and Montgomery, D. (1982), The role of the elementary principal in program improvement. *Review of Educational Research,* 52, 309-339.

__________, Jantzi, D. And Steinbach, R. (1999), *Changing Leadership for Changing Times,* Buckingham: Open University Press

Leithwood, K. A. (1992), Transformational Leadership: Where does it stand? *Educational Digest* 58 (3), 17-21.

Leithwood, K. (1994) *Leadership for School Restructuring,* Educational Administration Quarterly, 30 (4): 498-518

Marks, H., and Printy, S. (2003), Principal Leadership and School Performance: An Integration of Transformational and Instructional Leadership, *Educational Administration Quarterly,* 39 (3), 370 - 397.

Mbigi, L. (1993) The spirit of African management, in Christie, P Eds et al (1993) African Management. Knowledge Resources. Pretoria.

Starrat, R. (2001), Democratic Leadership Theory in Late Modernity: An Oxymoron or Ironic Possibility? *International Journal of Leadership in Education,* 4 (4), 333 - 352.

Weber,G. (1971), *Inner-City Children Can Be Taught to Read: Four Successful Schools,* Washington, DC Council for Basic Education

## APPENDIX : PRESIDENT THABO MIBEKI'S SPEECH—I AM AN AFRICAN

Chairperson, Esteemed President of the democratic public, Honourable Members of the Constitutional Assembly, Our distinguished domestic and foreign guests, friends,

On an occasion such as this, we should, perhaps, start from the beginning. So, let me begin.

I am an African.

I owe my being to the hills and the valleys, the mountains and the glades, the rivers, the deserts, the trees, the flowers, the seas and the ever-changing seasons that define the face of our native land.

My body has frozen in our frosts and in our latter-day snows. It has thawed in the warmth of our sunshine and melted in the heat of the midday sun. The crack and the rumble of the summer thunders, lashed by startling lightning, have been a cause both of trembling and of hope.

The fragrances of nature have been as pleasant to us as the sight of the wild blooms of the citizens of the veld.

The dramatic shapes of the Drakensberg, the soil-coloured waters of the Lekoa, iGgili noThukela, and the sands of the Kgalagadi, have all been panels of the set on the natural stage on which we act out the foolish deeds of the theatre of our day.

At times, and in fear, I have wondered whether I should concede equal citizenship of our country to the leopard and the lion, the elephant and the springbok, the hyena, the black mamba and the pestilential mosquito.

A human presence among all these, a feature on the face of our native land thus defined, I know that none dare challenge me when I say — I am an African!

I owe my being to the Khoi and the San whose desolate souls haunt the great expanses of the beautiful Cape—they who fell victim to the most merciless genocide our native land has ever seen, they who were the first to lose their lives in the struggle to defend our freedom and dependence and they who, as a people, perished in the result.

Today, as a country, we keep an audible silence about these ancestors of the generations that live, fearful to admit the horror of a former deed, seeking to obliterate from our memories a cruel occurrence which, in its remembering, should teach us not and never to be inhuman again.

I am formed of the migrants who left Europe to find a new home on our native land. Whatever their own actions, they remain still, part of me.

In my veins courses the blood of the Malay slaves who came from the East. Their proud dignity informs my bearing, their culture a part of my essence. The stripes they bore on their bodies from the lash of the slave master are a reminder embossed orb my consciousness of what should not be done.

I am the grandchild of the warrior men and women that Hintsa and Sekhukhune led, the patriots that Cetshwayo and Mphephu took to battle, the soldiers Moshoeshoe and Ngungunyane taught never to dishonour the cause of freedom.

My mind and my knowledge of myself is formed by the victories that are the jewels in our African crown, the victories we earned from Isandhlwana to Khartoum, as Ethiopians and as the Ashanti of Ghana, as the Berbers of the desert.

I am the grandchild who lays fresh flowers on the Boer graves at St. Helena and the Bahamas, who sees in the minds eye and suffers the suffering of a simple peasant folk, death, concentration camps, destroyed homesteads, a dream in ruins.

I am the child of Nongqause. I am he who made it possible to trade in the world markets in diamonds, in gold, in the same food for which my stomach yearns.

I come of those who were transported from India and China, whose being resided in the fact, solely, that they were able to provide physical labour, who taught me that we could both be at home and be foreign, who taught me that human existence itself demanded that freedom was a necessary condition for that human existence.

Being part of all these people, and in the knowledge that none dare contest that assertion, I shall claim that — I am an African.

I have seen our country torn asunder as these, all of whom are my people, engaged one another in a titanic battle, the one redress a wrong that had been caused by one to another and the other, to defend the indefensible.

I have seen what happens when one person has superiority of force over another, when the stronger appropriate to themselves the prerogative even to annul the injunction that God created all men and women in His image.

I know what if signifies when race and colour are used to determine who is human and who subhuman.

I have seen the destruction of all sense of self-esteem, the consequent striving to be what one is not, simply to acquire some of the benefits which those who had improved themselves as masters had ensured that they enjoy.

I have experience of the situation in which race and colour is used to enrich some and impoverish the rest.

I have seen the corruption of minds and souls in the pursuit of an ignoble effort to perpetrate a veritable crime against humanity.

I have seen concrete expression of the denial of the dignity of a human being emanating from the conscious, systemic and systematic oppressive and repressive activities of other human beings.

There the victims parade with no mask to hide the brutish reality—the beggars, the prostitutes, the street children, those who seek solace in substance abuse, those who have to steal to assuage, hunger, those who have to lose their sanity because to be sane is to invite pain.

Perhaps the worst among these, who are my people, are those who have learnt to kill for a wage. To these the extent of death is directly proportional to their personal welfare.

And so, like pawns in the service of demented souls, they kill in furtherance of the political violence in KwaZulu-Natal. They murder the innocent in the taxi wars.

They kill slowly or quickly in order to make profits from the illegal trade in narcotics. They are available for hire when husband wants to murder wife and wife, husband.

Among us prowl the products of our immoral and amoral past — killers who have no sense of the worth of human life, rapists who have absolute disdain for the women of our country, animals who would seek to benefit from the vulnerability of the children, the disabled and the old, the rapacious who brook no obstacle in their quest for self enrichment.

All this I know and know to be true because I am an African!

Because of that, I am also able to state this fundamental truth that I am born of a people who are heroes and heroines.

I am born of a people who would not tolerate oppression.

I am of a nation that would not allow that fear of death, torture, imprisonment, exile or persecution should result in the perpetuation of injustice.

The great masses who are our mother and father will not permit that the behaviour of the few results in the description of our country and people as barbaric.

Patient because history is on their side, these masses do not despair because today the weather is bad. Nor do they turn triumphalist when, tomorrow, the sun shines.

Whatever the circumstances they have lived through and because of that experience, they are determined to define for themselves who they are and who they should be.

We are assembled here today to mark their victory in acquiring and exercising their right to formulate their own definition of what it means to be African.

The constitution whose adoption we celebrate constitutes and unequivocal statement that we refuse to accept that our Africanness shall be defined by our race, colour, gender of historical origins.

It is a firm assertion made by ourselves that South Africa belongs to all who live in it, black and white.

It gives concrete expression to the sentiment we share as Africans, and will defend to the death, that the people shall govern.

It recognises the fact that the dignity of the individual is both an objective which society must pursue, and is a goal which cannot be separated from the material well-being of that individual.

It seeks to create the situation in which all our people shall be free from fear, including the fear of the oppression of one national group by another, the fear of the disempowerment of one social echelon by another, the fear of the use of state power to deny anybody their fundamental human rights and the fear of tyranny.

It aims to open the doors so that those who were disadvantaged can assume their place in society as equals with their fellow human beings without regard to colour, race, gender, age or geographic dispersal.

It provides the opportunity to enable each one and all to scare their views, promote them, strive for their implementation in the process of governance without fear that a contrary view will be met with repression.

It creates a law-governed society which shall be inimical to arbitrary rule.

It enables the resolution of conflicts by peaceful means rather than resort to force.

It rejoices in the diversity of our people and creates the space for all of us voluntarily to define ourselves as one people.

As an African, this is an achievement of which I am proud, proud without reservation and proud without any feeling of conceit.

Our sense of elevation at this moment also derives from the fact that this magnificent product is the unique creation of African hands and African minds.

But it is also constitutes a tribute to our loss of vanity that we could, despite the temptation to treat ourselves as an exceptional fragment of humanity, draw on the accumulated experience and wisdom of all humankind, to define for ourselves what we want to be.

Together with the best in the world, we too are prone to pettiness, petulance, selfishness and short-sightedness.

But it seems to have happened that we looked at ourselves and said the time had come that we make a super-human effort to be other than human, to respond to the call to create for ourselves a glorious future, to remind ourselves of the Latin saying: Gloria est consequenda — Glory must be sought after!

Today it feels good to be an African.

It feels good that I can stand here as a south African and as a foot soldier of a titanic African army, the African National Congress, to say to all the parties represented here, to the millions who made an input into the processes we are concluding, to our outstanding compatriots who have presided over the birch of our founding document, to the negotiators who pitted their wits one against the other, to the unseen stars who shone unseen as the management and administration of the Constitutional Assembly, the advisers, experts and publicists, to the mass communication media, to our friends across the globe — congratulations and well done!

I am an African.

I am born of the peoples of the continent of Africa.

The pain of the violent conflict that the peoples of Liberia, Somalia, the Sudan, Burundi and Algeria is a pain I also bear.

The dismal shame of poverty, suffering and human degradation of my continent is a blight that we share.

The blight on our happiness that derives from this and from our drift to the periphery of the ordering of human affairs leaves us in a persistent shadow of despair.

This is a savage road to which nobody should be condemned.

This thing that we have done today, in this small corner of a great continent that has contributed so decisively to the evolution of humanity says that Africa reaffirms that she is continuing her rise from the ashes.

Whatever the setbacks of the moment, nothing can stop us now!

Whatever the difficulties, Africa shall be at peace!

However improbable it may sound to the sceptics, Africa will prosper!

Whoever we may be, whatever our immediate interest, however much we carry baggage from our past, however much we have been caught by the fashion of cynicism and loss of faith in the capacity of the people, let us err today and say : nothing can stop us now!

# 4

# A CEO's Five-year Journey: Translating Theory into Practice

—*Bruce Sheppar* and *Jean Brown*

## Introduction

School district leadership is essential to systemic improvement of our school systems. While there are many examples of successful schools that are professional learning communities, these are isolated cases, and unfortunately, we have evidence that many of these professional learning schools are not sustained when key leaders move from the school (Giles & Hargreaves, 2006). As a result of our work over the last decade or so that has been focused on developing schools as learning organisations, we have been convinced that schools, for the most part, continue to operate as traditional bureaucratic organisations that are highly resistant to organisational learning. Often intervention and sustained external pressure and support are required to bring about change (Sheppard, 2003; Sheppard 8: Brown, 2000c). In fact, our research suggests that

> We cannot assume that all educators endorse team leadership or organisational learning as a means to successful change .... Furthermore, we learned that one cannot assume that those who are willing to accept the potential of team leadership and organisational learning will be able to make the shifts in leadership approach without effort or difficulty. (Sheppard, 2003a)

Our analysis of one school district CEO's practice led us to conclude that neither shared leadership, organisational learning, or changes in other school and classroom practices is likely to happen Without the strong leadership of the CEO. Similarly, Louis, Toole, and Hargreaves (1999) conclude that "the most recent literature suggests that we need to reassert that [while] the school is a critical focus, ... Without stable policy environments and resources outside of the school, the chances of enduring change are limited" (p. 269). This position has been reiterated more recently, as well (Fullan, 2005; Giles & Hargreaves, 2006). For example, Fullan (2005) laments the fact that many jurisdictions have set in play "deliberate strategies from the state level [that] have played down or bypassed the district" (p. 65). It is his contention that such actions are ill founded and that, "If you have your systems hat on, you know right away that this is a mistake. You cannot omit any part of the system without paying the price" (p.65). He emphasizes the importance of the district role in the provision of leadership, noting that schools differ in their capacity to engage in continuous improvement; therefore, if the system is to be changed, districts must foster across school and across district sharing and capacity development.

Even though the critical nature of district CEO leadership to sustaining school and school district improvement is well documented (Fullan, 2005; Maguire, 2004; Teitel, 2006), there exists a scarcity of evidence related to the role of CEOs in bringing, about these improvements (Leithwood, 1995; Leithwood, Louis, Anderson, & Wahlstrom 2004). In particular, our evidence is very thin in respect to our understanding of the challenges faced by a district CEO who ascribes to emergent leadership principles such as inclusiveness, collaboration, team learning and shared decisionmaking as a means of fostering organisational learning in a district where the accepted model of leadership and administration is a top-down hierarchical bureaucracy. Leavitt (2003) recounts problems encountered by Mike, a rookie manager, who did not fully comprehend the hierarchy reality. As a result of his naïve understanding of emergent leadership concepts of shared leadership, teamwork, and empowerment, he implemented these ideas fully without consideration of the hierarchical context. As a result, he did not remain fully informed of the details of activities that were happening in his area of responsibility. When he met with his executive committee, they expected him to know the details and the result was disastrous.

In the context of the pervasiveness of hierarchy in our school boards, the purpose of the research presented in this paper is to contribute to the empirical evidence related specifically to the following question: how might a district CEO foster organisational learning in a district that is a traditional bureaucratic hierarchy? While exploring answers to that question, we will particularly focus on the limitations imposed by the hierarchical bureaucratic leadership paradigm operating within the school district and the ideas, methods, and structures employed by the CEO to implement emergent leadership and to foster organisational learning in the district.

## The Conceptual Framework

This paper is set in the context of a focused research agenda on educational leadership and organisational learning that the authors have pursued over the last decade (Brown, Dibbon, & Sheppard, 200 3; Brown & Sheppard, 1999; Sheppard & Brown, 1996, 1997, 1998, 1999, 2000a, 2000b, 2000c; Sheppard, Brown, Genge, & Waiters 1996, Sheppard, 2003). In this particular paper, our focus is on district-level leadership. The theoretical framework for our research and reflective practice is what we will identify as emergent leadership. It draws extensively upon our own work as well as the work of others, with specific reference to the following: (1) Non-educational sources: Kouzes & Posner (2003), O'Toole (1996); Senae (1990) and (2) Education Specific sources: Fullan (2005); Hall & Hord (006); Leithwood, Louis, Anderson, & Wahlstrom (2004). The basic tenets of the emergent leadership approach as described in this paper are based on concepts of leadership that are transformational, inclusive, value-based, and focused on organisational learning and the achievement of purposes that transcend the surface constituent noises of pettiness and self interest. Guided by an emergent leadership approach, a leader would be expected to establish and maintain credibility, understand the theoretical frameworks related to organisations, administration and change, and be able to apply theory to practice within the differing contexts. Such a leader would attend effectively to the technical core as an instructional leader, and would attend, as well, to the administrative, managerial, and institutional systems that include the financial, legal, political, human resource, and symbolic roles (Barth, 1990; Bolman & Deal, 1992; Cuban, 1988; Hoy & Miskel 2005).

The emergent leader recognises that leadership success is contingent upon the perceptions of the Constituents, those that are to be led (Angus, 1989; Blase, 199 3; Blase & Blase, 1998; Foster, 1989; Gardner, 1990; Hallinger, 3005; Kouzes & Posner, 200 3; Lord R. Maher, 1990; Marks & Printy, 2004; Sergiovanni, 1995). Kouzes and Posner (2003) contend that "leadership is personal. ...If people don't believe in the messenger, they won't believe the message" (p. xv). Similarly, Sheppard (1996) found that instructional leadership behaviours that were accepted as appropriate by teachers were more likely to gain their support gild, and therefore, have a transformational effect on them. Kouzes and Posner (2003) refer to this as the leader's credibility. O'Toole (1996) recognises it as "enlisting the hearts and minds of followers" (p. 11).

These emergent concepts of leadership have remained theoretically robust, but have not found their way in mainstream practice of chief executive officers in our corporations, government, or education (Leavitt, 2003). Kouzes gild Posner (2004) contend that "the dominant metaphor of our time is still the hierarchy, organised by rank and authority" (p. 3). The most popular acceptable leadership models focus on one person (usually charismatic) who engages in top-down management using one of three generic approaches to leadership: command, manipulate, and paternalise (O'Toole, 1996). O'Toole asks, "How can... a CEO... overcome resistance to change [to a differing model of leadership] when the CEO's power is constrained by diverse and conflicting interests of investors, board members, union chiefs, environmentalists, government regulators, and careerist fellow managers, all intent on marching to the beat of their own drummers?"(p.7).

## Methodology

In writing this paper, the thinking and reflections of the CEO are intertwined with the interpretations of the University researcher; therefore we have written the paper using the third person, even though the CEO is one of the co-authors (Sheppard). This is important as we are emphasizing the role rather than the personality of the CEO. Prior to Sheppard's assuming the role of CEO, both authors had been involved in Driftwood School District as critical friends and action researchers focused on the development of schools as learning organisations. Becoming the CEO presented an opportunity for "real" participatory action research in a district that would be led by a CEO who understood theoretical frameworks related to emergent leadership and organisational learning and was committed to applying them to practice. The other researcher (Brown) continued to be a participant observer as the university partner acting as a critical friend and researcher. As used in this paper, a critical friend is

> A trusted person who asks provocative questions, provides data to be examined through another lens, and offers critique of a person's work is a friend. A critical friend takes the time to fully understand the content of the work presented and the outcomes that the person or group is working toward. The friend is an advocate for the success of that work. (Costa & Kallick, 1996, p. 50)

The CEO kept a journal throughout his five-year term as CEO, particularly of his involvement in attempting to foster organisational learning in the district. His journal that included links to district documents and personal reflections, together with indepth interviews and aggressive interrogations of his actions and thought processes conducted by the university researcher, compose our primary data sources. As well, the university researcher collected qualitative data through interviews with board trustees and detailed notes taken during her involvement in various retreats, workshops, and meetings that she facilitated with teachers, principals, district office staff, and board trustees. She was an observer as both a participant-as-observer (observers engage with the participants, but the participants are aware that they are being observed) and as an observer-as-participant (participants are aware that they are being observed and the observers remain separate from the participants) (Martella, Nelson, & Marchand-Martella, 1999).

Interview protocols, analysis of documents, field notes, and the CEO's journal were grounded in the emergent leadership literature. Survey data on leadership and organisational learning were collected in 1999 and 2004 from all teachers throughout the district. While analysis of these data was not employed specifically for this paper, descriptive data from these surveys provide contextual knowledge that informed analysts of other data.

## Hierarchical Bureaucratic Leadership Context

Within days of assuming the position, the CEO recognised that the mental model of leadership that was the most pervasive in Driftwood School District was one that placed the leader as the "person in charge". Initial separate meetings with the three assistant directors confirmed for the CEO the existence of the traditional bureaucratic model. Each assistant director was unequivocal that the district had been run as a traditional hierarchical bureaucracy. It was apparent that hierarchy was a reality that, for the most part, they accepted as an organisational reality. Two of the assistant directors stressed that the CEO's office (CEO and executive assistant) was set apart from the remainder of the organisation, being clearly placed at the apex of the organisation as demonstrated through power-over relationships and the symbols of the office. When the CEO or his executive assistant requested something, everyone understood that it took precedent over all other priorities. As for symbols of power, during special occasions, such as Christmas or Easter, special recognitions or decorations were distributed in a hierarchical fashion with the most flamboyant going to the CEO's office. Similarly, designated parking areas were arranged preferentially according to the hierarchy.

One assistant director was anxious to move forward with a shared decision-making model for the district with a focus on students. A second assistant director indicated that he preferred to continue to work alone within his zone of authority and essentially viewed collaboration as a waste of time. He believed organisational learning and collaboration to be theoretical constructs without merit in practice. He indicated that he had worked at the district level for more than 15 years and that, in his view, the only model that worked was the bureaucratic hierarchical model. He had worked with CEOs that tried to operate using a more collaborative model and they were unsuccessful.

A third assistant director confirmed that throughout his entire career of more than 20 years at the district level, and having worked with four previous CEOs, the only model that he knew was hierarchical. While he was willing to go along with a more participative model of leadership; he was sceptical that it would work. In his view, other assistant directors, program specialists, and principals did not have the skills or the will to participate in financial decisionmaking. Each group appeared to be self-centred in respect of budgets, wanting more for their specific field or school while using a zero-summed approach. In his view, strong decisive, directive leadership was required.

Informal interviews with school principals and other staff, and casual observation revealed that staff morale was poor and trust levels were very low between management and staff throughout the district. There were dozens of outstanding grievances and the relationship between management and staff was one of "two solitudes". In a preliminary meeting with union officials for support staff, this was confirmed. Union officials stated that they and their members perceived district administrators to be arrogant and inflexible and they claimed that the board followed unfair labour practices. It is interesting, however, that while support staff and union officials were discontented, they did not associate their discontent with the hierarchical structure. In fact, they were relying upon that structure to "fix" their problems as they called upon the new CEO to use his power to change the labour climate. The assistant director responsible for labour relations recalled the details of the first meeting between the union president and the new CEO in which the union president described the poor labour relations in the district. The president demanded that the CEO remove current district labour relations personnel from their role, claiming that they were the cause of all labour problems in the district. He was quite disappointed when the CEO indicated that he (the CEO) was willing to work with the union and current district staff to resolve the outstanding grievances, but he was not willing to act unilaterally to deal with outstanding labour issues (personal communications, assistant director, February 20, 2006).

Emergent leadership was not consistent with board norms of practice either. Board meetings were conducted following *Robert's Rules of Order*. As a result, decisions were made in a win/lose model following the debate of possible solutions put forth as motions that were either approved or rejected. Such a model is contrary to all principles of dialogue and collaboration that are essential to emergent leadership (Doyle & Straus, 1982; Newton & Tunison, 2001). *The Schools Act 1997* (2005) required that the CEO attend all meetings. His role was to provide advice as requested and to respond to questions of board trustees. While the CEO was successful in having all assistant directors join him at board meetings, the board was quite clear in their expectations. Assistant directors were welcomed at meetings, but they would be resource persons for the CEO who was the only person directly answerable to the Board. They expected that the CEO would respond directly to all their questions and that he "must" be well informed on all issues. In their interpretations of *The Schools Act 1997* (2005), the CEO was their only employee. He was directly accountable to the board while all other employees were accountable to the board, through him.

The CEO observed that the media held a very traditional hierarchical view of leadership, as well. They appeared to hold an underlying assumption that the CEO and the board make all decisions, and they were quick to publish any story that might negatively reflect on the board or the CEO. Often, the media appeared to sensationalise issues and to be supportive of calls to have either the Minister of Education or the Premier overrule board decisions with no deference to the *Schools Act 1997* (2005), thereby perpetuating in the public forum an acceptance of the dominate model of hierarchy. For example, several editorials written by parents and the editor of a local newspaper contained derogatory comments about both the board and CEO gild called upon the Provincial Government to intervene.

Other external groups brought similar expectations that attributed the power of hierarchical control to the CEO. For example, the Deputy Minister of Education was not happy about the financial state of the board. Shortly after the CEO's appointment she requested a meeting with him with all expectation that he would have a plan to eliminate the deficit. Similarly, parents expected the new CEO to address concerns that they had, and expected that he would have answers within days of assuming the CEO's position. This was particularly relevant to the ongoing school consolidation issues (school closures).

There is no doubt that Driftwood School District had been operating as a bureaucratic hierarchy. While several schools, with the approval of district administrators had been engaged in an organisational learning research and development partnership initiative with university critical friends, this initiative was viewed as a project that might have some implications for school development. It was not viewed as having implications for how the district was led or administered.

### Implementing Emergent Leadership: First Steps

It appeared that the existing structures and norms were barriers to systems thinking and team learning. They perpetuated mental models that inhibited improved practice and limited opportunities for personal mastery. Any shared vision existed at the school level only. The essence of organisational learning—knowledge acquisition, knowledge sharing, and knowledge utilisation would be inhibited if the district did not adopt a more robust structure to facilitate district-wide learning (Barth, 1990; DiBella, Nevis & Gourd, 1996; Dufour & Eaker, 1998; Fullan, 2001; Hargreaves, 1997). Fullan (2001) opined that "If they ever discover how to [get schools to learn from each other] their future is assured" (p. 93). Senge, Roberts, Ross, Smith, R Kleiner, 1994 state that "a new understanding of the process of organisational change has emerged. It is... participative at all levels—aligned with a common understanding of a system" (p. 89).

The CEO was convinced that change was required to improve student learning in the district. Further, he was convinced that the necessary change would not occur without the adoption of an emergent approach to leadership that would foster organisational learning. His challenge was to alter the model of leadership and the organisational structures that would allow for organisational learning in each school and the district when the belief systems and entrenched leadership and organisational models were those symptomatic of top-down hierarchical bureaucracies. Accepting the assumption that leadership success is contingent upon the perceptions of constituents, he concluded that if organisational learning were to occur in the district, it would have to operate within the reality of the hierarchy. The focus would have to be on reducing the negative impacts of that reality by promoting the emergent leadership agenda to the limit of the constituents' level of tolerance. He knew that if he employed a leadership approach that was not within the accepted tolerance levels of the existing "mental models" of the majority of the organisation's Constituents, it would not likely be successful. This would not mean subordinating his perspectives to those held by others, however, just adopting the most common leadership practices to please others would not be leadership.

O'Toole (1996) cautioned that while a leader must consider the fundamental Values and perspectives of followers, he/she must avoid "the too common political practice of pandering to the base wishes of the lowest common denominator—promising whatever the masses think they want" (p. 9-10). He/She must constantly test the limit of public tolerance for change that will inevitably involve trial and error as the limit is pushed beyond that which is acceptable. But the essential value throughout this process must be respect for people (O'Toole, 1996). Similarly, Kouzes and Posner (2003) contend that a leader must have a "clear sense of direction [and] sometimes... should listen to [his/her] conscience and... intuition, instead of [his/her] constituents" (p. 269).

The CEO determined that he would introduce the emergent model of leadership as an innovation. He would mandate the model up while recognising that implementation would occur within the existing hierarchical context, and that it would be a process that would be developed over time (Hall R Hord, 2006). He recognised that the skills involving fundamental new ways of thinking and interacting would take years to master. "Deep beliefs and assumptions are not like light switches that can be turned on and off" (Senge, Roberts, Ross, Smith, & Kleiner, 1994, p. 22). It would be important, therefore, to introduce the model "with sufficient drama and flair that people [would] believe things [were] going to change" (Schlechty, 1990, p, 134). In the process of implementation, the organisation would engage in the domain of action working with guiding ideas, making innovations in infrastructure, and working with theoretic frameworks, methods, and tools that would foster emergent leadership (Senge, Roberts, Ross, Smith, R, Kleiner, 1994). "For a long time it [might] appear that there [was] nothing going on except the surface activity of the [Domain of Action]. People [would] talk about new ideas. They [would] practice the application of tools and methods. They [would] design and implement changes in infrastructure" (Senge, Roberts, Ross, Smith, & Kleiner, 1994, p. 44). This would lead, over time, to the deep learning cycle which is the "Domain of Enduring Change" when new skills, new awareness and sensibilities result in new attitudes and beliefs. Guided by the above-noted assumptions, the CEO determined that he must begin the implementation of the emergent leadership approach through the "Domain of Action". In the first instance, it was essential to clearly articulate the "guiding idea", his vision of leadership and his role as CEO and what constituents should expect, noting, as well, that this vision should be viewed as being key components of the role of other district leaders, including school principals (Schlechty, 1990).

Once the emergent approach to leadership was mandated as the "guiding idea" or vision for leadership in the district, the next step was to begin the implementation process starting with changing administrative structures and introducing the theoretical frameworks, strategies, and methods that would support realisation of the vision. This would include setting up administrative structures in support of team leadership and shared decisionmaking, helping principals to develop skills of emergent leadership, learning about and fostering dialogue, redesigning professional development, developing a shared vision of teaching and learning, redeveloping the strategic planning process, and developing a new strategic plan. We will not discuss all the implementation strategies in the paper.

Instead, we will focus on just one: setting up administrative structures in support of team leadership and shared decisionmaking.

*Changing organisational structures in support of emergent leadership*

The CEO understood that many of the constituents had some involvement in forming the existing structures and, therefore, felt some ownership of them. It was important, however, to make structural changes that would allow for organisational learning and signal to constituents that the CEO's talk was being followed by action. These changes would, nevertheless, leave to remain within the constituents' level of tolerance and there would have to be established a delicate balance between high expectations and accountability for change and the provision of support and capacity building opportunities.

The existing administrative structures included Administrative Council (the CEO and assistant directors), General Advisory Council (selected representatives of programme specialists and principals), Programme Specialists' Meetings, and Principals' Meetings (principals, program specialists, and administrative council). The only administrative structure with decision making authority was the Administrative Council where the model of decisionmaking was one of debate with the final decision taken by the CEO. The General Advisory Council had been constituted to provide advice to the CEO. Program specialists' meetings, chaired by the assistant director of programs, were held bi-weekly. In these meetings, programme specialists made decisions related to teacher professional development and the implementation of new programmes. The model of decisionmaking employed at Programme Specialists' Meetings, similar to that employed at Administrative Council Meetings, was hierarchical. Principals' Meetings occurred approximately four times per year for the purpose of administrative updates and dissemination of materials from district-level personnel. Principals had no formal role in decisionmaking for the district. In fact, there existed no structure that supported participatory leadership at the district level.

### A New Approach to Administrative Council

In the revised structure, the Administrative Council would meet one day per week, rather than twice per month as was the practice, and decisions were to be made by consensus. In the past, the Administrative Council had made most decisions that were disseminated as directives to the followers. As well, the meeting model had been very traditional as manifested by advocacy, debate, and decisionmaking by majority or exercise of authority. Typically, majority support for an idea was sought outside of the meeting and debate was often of a perfunctory nature. The CEO perceived that groupthink (Janis, 1982) was a real danger in the current model of operation, particularly, as individuals tried to gauge his views and to win his confidence. In response to that perception, the CEO presented the concept of dialogue (Senge, Roberts, Ross, Smith, & Kleiner, 1994) as a process that should occur prior to any decision-making process. He explained that

> The intention of dialogue is exploration, discovery, and insight. In a dialogue session people feel involved and welcomed, no hierarchy exists and disagreement is encouraged. Participants feel that it is safe to express and explore ideas or differing views, even those ideas that are not fully developed. While the group may in fact sometimes reach agreement through dialoguing, that is not the primary purpose. (Administrative Council Meeting Minutes, May 31, 2000)

Unfortunately, the concept of dialoguing appeared to be poorly understood by the group and was perceived, at least by several members, as a naïve approach to meetings of senior district administrators, and that it was really not efficient use of time. One assistant director expressed the view that he did not believe that dialoguing could be achieved and that it was not good idea anyway. In spite of repeated efforts to engage in dialoguing through demonstration gild clarification, there were few examples of where such sessions occurred in "pure" form either in the Administrative Council or in any other of the formally structured groups. However, it appeared that efforts to foster dialogue did improve the level of engagement and encouraged the expression of differing viewpoints.

Review of minutes and agendas of the Administrative Council meetings revealed that at the second meeting of the Administrative Council (May 31, 2000), the CEO introduced a discussion related to employing research evidence to inform practice, and presented a power-point presentation of Senge's Five Disciplines of learning organisations. He introduced DiBella, Nevis, and Gould's (1996) definition of organisational learning that focused on knowledge acquisition (the development or creation of skills, insights, relationships), knowledge sharing (the dissemination to others of what has been acquired by some), and knowledge utilisation (integration of the learning so that it is assimilated, broadly available, and can also be generated to new situations (p. 363). Also he introduced evidence from his own research (Brown & Sheppard, 1999; Sheppard & Brown, 1996, 1997, 1995, 1999, 2000a, 2000b, 2000c; Sheppard, 2003a, 2003b) in support of organisational learning and emergent leadership. Additional specific items on that agenda included the need to shift decision-making authority to the school level and to engage school personnel in district-level decisionmaking.

**Establishing General Administrative Council**

A review of minutes of Advisory Council meetings revealed that this group had met only twice in three years and there had been no recent meetings. The outgoing CEO had recommended disbanding it as did the assistant directors and, with the exception of a small minority; programme specialists concurred. As for principals' meetings, the new CEO believed that information could be more efficiently disseminated through correspondence, particularly since district-wide entail software had just been installed.

Both the Advisory Council and the principals' meetings were replaced by a General Administrative Council (GAC) that would have decision-making authority within the district. Membership of GAC included all principals, programme specialists, assistant directors, the controller, the human resources administrator, and the CEO. This group met in six week intervals and as priorities dictated (approximately 10 meetings per year) to engage in dialogue and decisionmaking around key issues in education. This new structure would prove to be a significant structural change in support of the CEO's vision of developing a model of emergent leadership throughout the entire district.

At the first meeting of GAC, the CEO presented a general overview of the new structures that would support the development of organisational learning. During this address, the CEO emphasized the shift in leadership toward emergent approaches that would foster organisational learning. He recognised the bureaucratic, hierarchical context of their work and noted that change would take place over time as GAC worked collaboratively to design and implement changes in structure and practices. He also introduced the concept of action learning as an essential component of organisational learning.

The model of action learning presented was one developed by Sheppard and Brown (2000c) in our work with Pine Wood Alternative School (PWA). Our work with PWA brought us to a new level of understanding of the stages of the implementation process: assessment, planning, implementation, and evaluation (Stoll R. Fink, 1996). While these stages are often presented as a cyclical process, often, in practice, they remain very linear as the planned implementation moves from one stage to another over time irrespective of progress. Whether or not it is presented in a circle graphic or as a straight line, it remains a linear process. Learning from this experience, the PWA Steering Committee approached action learning as a more indepth process. In response to what we had learned, we developed a new action learning model based on the following assumptions:

— Change efforts when treated as established programmes, and not unfolding processes, almost always fail.

— Implementation occurs as a process that is dependent upon experimentation, rather than a prescribed plan.

— Change is a process of action, reflection, and adjusting course on an ongoing basis (not re-evaluating only at specified assessment points).

— Change in complex and multiple learning cycles occur simultaneously around each of the primary foci of assessment, planning, implementation and evaluation.

While the PWA Steering Committee found the new model to be complex and time consuming, they recognised that it contributed to their ability to learn on the basis of ongoing feedback. They no longer equated planning with implementation, or implementation with success. They had come to realise that they needed to employ all action learning cycle for all actions, including information gathering. Each component of the action learning cycle was subjected to multiple learning sub-cycles. Evidence from the PWA study supported previous research findings (e.g., Elden & Levin, 1991; Whyte, Greenwood, & Lazes, 1991) that action research facilitates organisational learning because it provides opportunities for participants to learn flow to learn. As a result of this PWA study evidence, the CEO was convinced that it was essential that he introduce this action learning tool to GAC.

As well, at this first GAC meeting, the CEO introduced another structure that would connect to GAC, the Family of Schools. He noted that each Family of Schools will be linked to the district through a program specialist who will be a "District Champion" for these schools. This will require a change in the role and function of the program specialists who would operate in a mirror image-plus role (Galbraith, Lawler III & Associates, 1993. While they will continue to hold their mandated responsibilities, the new role will help them fulfil that mandate more effectively. The look and feel of the Family of Schools will evolve over time. We are asking that you will begin to set the parameters for that new structure today. (GAC Minutes, September 2000)

### The Families of Schools

The families of Schools were clusters of 6-10 schools of similar grade levels. Each Cluster was facilitated by one or more program specialists. The Families were responsible for teaching and learning, school development, and school councils. GAC members led each Family of Schools and the Families of Schools became the primary operating units of GAC. In GAC meetings, each member of GAC participated in Family meetings. Beyond GAC the Families of Schools provided the mechanism by which teachers and support staff workers were engaged in across-school leadership and shared decisionmaking as they planned learning events, engaged in school development, and learned together.

Both GAC and the Families of Schools were designed to facilitate the needed district-wide engagement of teachers and support staff in decisionmaking and would support the district goal of organisational learning and capacity building. The need to build capacity at the school-level and to include teachers as partners in educational reform has been well documented (For example, Dufour, 1999; Fullan, 2001; Hall & Hord, 2006; Leithwood et al., 2004; Leithwood, Jantzi, & Steinbach, 1999; Hargreaves & Evans, 1997). Hall & Hord (2006) contend that organisations are composed of individuals and only learn as individuals learn. Consequently, while many change processes call be directed toward various groups, in final analysis, it must be recognised that "successful change starts and ends at the individual level" (p. 7). Among district conditions that have been identified by Leithwood et al. (2004) as contributing to improved student learning is having the district structured to facilitate collaboration and professional learning within schools, between schools, and district-wide. Already, there existed a model of in-school learning and school-based decisionmaking through school improvement processes that had been ill vogue for over a decade; however, in this respect, each school operated as an island. There was practically no across-school knowledge sharing and other than the inclusion of teachers or support staff on various ad hoc district committees, there was no opportunity for them to influence district decisions. The district norm for interactions among schools was one of competition and one-upmanship, rather than collaboration. "Schools [were]...terrible at learning from each other" (Fullan, 2001, p. 92); therefore, capacity building was limited.

The learning network that was created and the capacity that was built, through the GAC and the Families of Schools contributed significantly to developing district-wide learning. As capacity grew within the district, not only did the schools within each Family work together, but they included schools front other Families (their Cousins), as well. The Families of Schools implementation facilitated the development of a critical mass of leaders who bean "to think in bigger terms and to act in ways that affect[ed] larger parts of the [district] a whole" (Fullan, 2005, p.27).

**Shared Decision-making Matrices**

While the new administrative structures and changing, roles facilitated shared decisionmaking at GAC, it was just an initial step. Principals, teachers, support staff, programme specialists, and other district-level personnel had heard this before, but there was no culture within the board of shared decisionmaking. The words had often been articulated and promises had been made, but in practice, they had experienced a continuation of the traditional models of top-down management where decisions were made through a hierarchical system of power and authority based on formal organisational roles (Dunlap and Goldman, 1991). They had become quite cynical of ally mention of terms like empowerment and shared decisionmaking, assuming that it was just another case of downloading of responsibility and increased accountability while those at the top made all the important decisions.

In order to advance shared decisionmaking at GAC, the CEO drew on the worn of Wynn and Guiditus (1984) who argued that if shared decisionmaking was to be effectively implemented in an organisation, the powers and rights of the various groups and individuals in respect to decision-making would have to be specifically defined. They proposed that this could be accomplished through the development of decisionmaking matrices. The CEO introduced this concept to Administrative Council and sought their support to introduce decision-making matrix development at GAC. GAC decided that two decision-making matrices would be developed initially: (1) teaching and learning and (2) repair and maintenance.

The process of developing both matrices at GAC proved to be an excellent introduction to shared decisionmaking. It provided an opportunity for GAC members (1) to practise dialoguing as they brainstormed to identify issues and the systems interactions that influence and inform decisionmaking in each area, and (2) to learn about and practice consensus building strategies as they made decisions about the level of power and the rights that were most appropriate for each of the groups and individuals who were included in the matrix. The process helped overcome the scepticism related to the CEO's commitment to shared decisionmaking and improved the level of trust. It also may have contributed to the enhancement of the CEO's leadership credibility as he was called upon to resolve complex problems throughout the process (Gardner, 1990; Kouzes & Posner, 2003). Gardner (1990) has argued that "A loyal constituency is won when the people, conscientiously or unconscientiously, judge the leader to be capable of solving their problems and meeting their needs" (p.28).

The matrices defined the interaction between the district and schools and moved much of the decision-making authority from district-level personnel to GAC members, most significantly, to school principals who engaged teachers and other staff in shared decision-making, within their schools and then act as linchpins between schools and the district at GAC. Within school and across school capacity building and participation in decision-making was facilitated further by a simultaneous shift in both school development and professional learning processes within the district. These aforementioned shifts in school development and professional learning emphasized organisational learning principles and provided increased professional autonomy and decision-making authority to teachers.

## Discussion and Conclusions

The level of public support for education is difficult to gauge, but it is painfully obvious that confidence in public education has declined over the last few decades (Dufour, 2004; Dufour &, Eaker, 1998; Fink & Brayman, 2006; Goodlad, 2001, Hepburn, 1999, 2005; Young &. Levin, 2002; Reeves, 2002; Sarason, 1990; Sergiovanni, 1995). Hepburn (1999) states, for example that, "the Canadian system of public education is inefficient and inadequate [and that] public-opinion polls show that confidence in the system is at a 30-year low. If it is riot to become obsolete, Canadian education needs to be redesigned" (p. 1).

The accumulating effect of this loss of public confidence is increased support for and the implementation of more centralised authoritarian control of the education system by governments (Hargreaves & Fink, 2006). Mulford, Silins &

Leithwood (2004) observe that "the external world of the educational leader is one of increasing loss of control...as education systems in many countries have tightened centralised control mechanisms through accountability devices such as high states (*sic*) testing, performance management and competency frameworks" (p. 1). As a result of such centralised control, politicians and their officials who lack educational expertise have been making key decisions regarding education resulting in the displacement of locally initiated innovation (Giles & Hargreaves, 2006). This trend appears to be counter to current evidence-based leadership models focused on team leadership, shared decisionmaking, and "flattening" the hierarchy (Bennis & Townsend; Kouzes & Posner, 2003; Senge, 1990; Shaker, 2004; Shaker & Grimmett, 2004) leading Giles and Hargreaves (2006) to question whether emergent leadership is sustainable.

Professional learning communities are postmodern organisational forms struggling to survive in a modernistic, micro-managed, and politicised educational world. Where standardised reform practices continue to tighten their grip, as is now the case in North America, the future for schools as learning organisations and professional learning communities that will develop the creativity and flexibility needed in the new knowledge economy does not look promising. (Giles & Hargreaves, 2006, p. 153)

It may be reasonable to assume that Leavitt (2003) is correct that "hierarchies are here to stay" (p. 103) [and while they] are terribly flawed [and] they inevitably foster authoritarianism and its destructive offspring: distrust, dishonesty, territoriality, toadying, and tear, our ability to work effectively in hierarchies depends in large measure on how we deal with those dangers (Leavitt, 3003, p. 98). It appears that rather than rail about common government approaches of accountability exercised through centralised control and the flaws of hierarchy that negatively impact the ability to develop schools and school districts, it is necessary to accept current realities and "work hard to reduce their highly noxious byproducts, while making them more habitable for humans and more productive as well" (Leavitt, 2003, p. 102 ). This can be accomplished if leaders have the complexity to deal with the paradoxes that are inherent in functioning as leaders and administrators in traditional hierarchical structures while employing emergent leadership approaches that facilitate organisational learning. Hooijberg Hunt and Drodge (1997) contend that leaders with sufficient cognitive, social, and behavioural complexity are better able to lead as transformational leaders and better positioned to facilitate team leadership. They suggest that cognitively complex leaders have the ability to view events from multiple perspectives. Those that are socially complex are able to view themselves as performing multiple roles and of understanding political and affective relationships in organisations. Leaders who are behaviourally complex are able to vary their role behaviour depending on the demands of the situation. If there is any hope of being successful in preparing leaders with sufficient cognitive, social, and behavioural complexity (Hooijberg, Hunt, & Drodge, 1997; Kouzes & Posner, 2003) to be the "new theoreticians" (Fullan, 2005), researchers in the field of Educational Administration must be cautious with statements such as "leadership (not leaders) is the key to the new revolution" (Fullan, 2005, xi). Does such a statement suggest that formal leaders are slot required? How does one facilitate or create such leadership?

Our previous work that has focused on developing schools as learning organisations has convinced us that schools, for the most part, continue to operate as traditional bureaucratic organisations that are highly resistant to organisational learning. Often intervention and sustained external pressure and support are required to bring about change (Sheppard & Brown, 2000c). The case study presented herein reveals how strong school district leadership can go beyond an interventionist or support model to one of fostering organisational learning, not only at the school level, but district wide. Perhaps, our moral purpose, as researchers in Educational Administration, should now be to focus on developing the evidence to strengthen leadership at the district level, rather than a continued focus on "strengthening leadership in schools" (Murphy & Louis, 1999, p. xxiv).

## References

Angus, L., (1959), 'New' leadership and the possibility of educational reform. In J. Smyth (Ed.). *Critical Perspectives in Educational Leadership* (pp.63-92), London: Falmer.

Barth, R., (1990), *Improving Schools from Within,* San Francisco, CA: Jossey-Bass.

Bennis, W. & Townsend, R. (1999). *Reinventing Leadership: Strategies to Empower the Organisation,* New York, NY: William Morrow.

Blase, J. (1993), The micropolitics of effective school-based leadership: Teachers' perspectives. *Educational Administration Quarterly,* 29(2), 142-163.

__________, R Blase, J. (1998), *Handbook of Instructional Leadership: How really good principals promote teaching and learning,* Thousand Oaks, CA Corwin.

Bolman, L. & Deal, T. (1997). *Reframing Organisations: Artistry, Choice, and Leadership.* Sun Francisco, CA: Jossey-Bass.

Brown, J., Dibbon, D., & Sheppard, B. (2003, May). The school trustee in a learning environment. Paper presented at the Annual Conference of CSSE, Halifax, Nova Scotia, Canada.

__________, & Sheppard, B. (1999, April). Leadership, organisational Learning, and Classroom Change. Paper presented at the Annual Conference of the American Educational Research Association, Montreal, Quebec, Canada. htt www.eric.ed.gov/. ED431230.

Costa, A. & Kallick, B (1993). Through the lens of a critical friend, *Educational Leadership,* 51(2), 49-51.

Cuban. L. (1988). *The Managerial Imperative and the Practice of Leadership in Schools.* Albany, BY: Suny Press.

DiBella, A. J., Nevis, E. C., & Gould J. M. (1996). Understanding organisational learning capacity, *Journal of Management Studies,* 33(3), 361-379.

Doyle, M. & Straus, M. (1982). *How to Make Meetings Work,* New York, NY: Berkley.

DuFour, R. (1999). Help Wanted: Principals who can Lead Professional Learning Communities. *NASSP Bulletin,* 83(604) 12-17.

Dufour, R., (2004). Leadership is an affair of the heart, *Journal of Staff Development,* 25(1), 67-68.

__________, & Eaker, R. (1998) *Professional Learning Communities at Work: Best Practices for Enhancing Student achievement.* Alexandria, CA : Association for Supervision and Curriculum Development.

Dunlap, D. & Goldman, P. (1991, February). Rethinking power in schools, *Educational Administration Quarterly,* 27(1), 5-29.

Elder, M. & Levin, M. (1991). Cogenerative Learning: Bringing participation into action research. In Whyte, W. F. (Ed.), *Participatory Action Research* (pp. 127-142). Newbury Park, Sage.

Fink, D., R Brayman, C. (2006). School leadership succession and the challenges of change. *Educational Administration Quarterly*, 42(1), 62-89.

Foster, (1989). Toward a critical practice of leadership. In J. Smyth (Ed.), *Critical Perspectives in Educational Leadership* (pp. 39-62). London: The Falmer Press.

Fullan, M. (2001). *Leading in a Culture of Change*, San Francisco, CA: Jossey-Bass.

__________, (2005). *Leadership and Sustainability*, Thousand Oaks, CA: Corwin.

Gardner, J. (1990). *On Leadership*, New York, NY: Free Press.

Giles, C., & Hargreaves, A. (2006). The sustainability of innovative schools as learning organisations and professional learning communities during standardised reform, *Educational Administration Quarterly*, 42(1), 124-1256.

Galbraith, J. (1993). The business unit of the future. In J. Galbraith, J. E. Lawler III & Associates (Eds.). *Organising for the Future: The New Logic for Managing Complex Organisations* (pp. 43-64). San Francisco, CA: Jossy-Bass.

Goodlad, J. (2001). Convergence. In R. Soder, J. Goodlad, & T. McMannon (Eds.). *Developing Democratic Character in the Young* (pp. 1-25). San Francisco, CA: Jossy-Bass.

Hallinger, P. (2005). Instructional Leadership: How has the model evolved? Paper presented at the Annual Conference of the American Educational Research Association, Montreal, Quebec, Canada.

Hall, G. & Hord S. (2006), *Implementing Change: Patterns, Principles, and Potholes*, Totonto: Pearson Education.

Hoy, W & Miskel, C. (2005) *Educational Administration: Theory, Research and Practice*, New York, NY: McGraw Hill.

Hargreaves, A. & Fink, D. (2006) *Sustainable Leadership*, San Francisco, CA: Jossey-Bass.

__________, & Evans, R. (1997). Teachers and educational reform. In A Hargreaves & R. Evans (Eds.). *Beyond Educational Reform: Bringing Teachers Back in* (pp. 105-125). Philadelphia, PA: Open University Press.

Hepburn C. (1999). The case for school choice. Retrieved. February 27, 2006 from http://www.fraserinstitute.ca/.

__________, (2005) Public goals and Private initiative: The Ironic truth behind education for the poor. Retrieved. January 20, 2006 from http//www.fraserinstitute.ca/.

Hooijberg, R., Hunt, J., & Drodge, G. (1997). Leadership complexity and Development of the Leaderplex Model, *Journal of Management,* 23(3), 375-408.

Jains, I.L. (1982), *Groupthink,* Boston: Houghton Miffiin.

Kouzes, J. & Posner, B. (2203). *Credibility,* San Francisco, CA: Jossey-Bass.

Leavitt, H. (2003). Why hierarchies thrive. *Harvard Business Review,* March, 96-102.

Leithwood, K. (1995). Toward a more comprehensive appreciation of effective school district leadership, In K. Leithwood (Ed). *Effective School District Leadership: Transforming Politics into Education* (pp. 315-340). Albany, NY: State University of New York.

__________, Jantzi, D., & Steinbach, R. (1999). *Changing Leadership for Changing Times,* Philadelphia: Open University Press.

__________, K., Louis, K., Anderson, S., & Wahlstrom, K. (2004). How Leadership Influences Student Learning, Retrieved. Nov. 28, 2005 from the Wallace Foundation Web site:

http://www.wallacefoundation/WF/KnowledgeCentre/KnowledgeTopics/EducationLeadership/HowLeadershipInfluencesStudentLearning.htm.

Lord, R., & Maher, K., (1990). Perceptions of Leadership and their implications in organisations. In J. Carroll (Ed.), *Applied Social Psychology and Organisational Settings* (pp. 129-154), New Jersey: Lawrence Erlbaum.

Louis, K., Toole, J. & Hargreaves, A. (1999). Rethinking school improvement. In J. Murphy K. S. Louis (Eds.), *Handbook of Research on Educational Administration* (pp. 251-276). San Francisco, CA: Jossey-Bass.

Maguire, P. (2003), *District Practices and Student Achievement,* Kelona, BC: Society for the Advancement of Excellence in Education.

Marks, H., & Printy, S. (2004). Principal leadership and school performance. An integration of transformation and instructional leadership. *Educational Administration Quarterly,* 39(3), 370-397.

Martella, R., Nelson, R., & Marchand-Martella, N. (1999). *Research Methods,* Toronto: Allyn & Bacon.

Mulford, W., Silins, H., & Leithwood, K. (2004). *Educational Leadership for Organisational Learning and Improved Student Outcomes.* Boston, MA: Kluwer.

Murphy, J. & Louis, K. S. (1999). Introduction: Framing the project. In J. Murphy K.S. Louis (Eds.), *Handbook of Research on Educational Administration* (pp. xxi-xxvii). San Francisco, CA: Jossey-Bass.

Newton, P. & Tunison, S. (2003). Developing Policy for Learning Communities. Paper presented at the Eighth National Congress on Rural Education, Saskatoon, SK, Canada.

O'Toole, J. (1996). *Leading Change,* Toronto: Jossey-Bass.

Reeves, D. (2002) *The Daily Disciplines of Leadership,* San Fancisco, CA: Jossey-Bass.

Sarason, S. (1993), *The Predictable Failure of Educational Reform,* San Fancisco, CA: Jossey-Bass.

Schlechty, P. (1990), *Schools for the 21st Century,* San Fancisco, CA: Jossey-Bass.

*Schools Act 1997,* SNL 1997 Chapters-12.2 (2005).

Senge, P. (1990). *The Fifth Discipline,* New York: Doubleday.

__________, Roberts, C. Ross, R. Smith, B., Kleiner, A. (1994), *The Fifth Discipline Fieldbook,* Toronto: Doubleday.

Sergiovanni, T. (1995), *The Principalship: A Reflective Practice Perspective,* Boston: Allyn & Bacon.

Shaker, E. (2004). More than the sum of its parts, *Education Canada,* 4(3), 13-15.

Shaker, P. & Grimmett, P. (2004) Public schools as public good: A question of values, *Education Canada,* 44(3), 29-31.

Sheppard, B. (1996). Exploring the transformational nature of instructional leadership. *Alberta Journal of Educational Research,* 42 (4), 325-344.

__________, (2000, April). Organisational learning and the integration of information and communication technology in teaching and learning, Paper presented at the Annual Conference of the American Educational Research Association, New Orleans, US. http://www.eric.ed.gov/ ED 42460.

__________ (2003a). If to do in schools were as easy as to know what were good to do, *Education Canada,* 43(4), 16-19.

__________ (2003b). Leadership that Fosters Organisational Learning Proves Critical to the Successful Integration of Information and Communication Technology in Teaching and Learning. *International Electronic Journal for Leadership in Learning.* 7(14). www.ucalgary.ca/-iejll.

__________, & Brown, J. (1996). Taylor High: All emerging learning organisation. *The Canadian Administration,* 36, (3), 1-7.

__________, R Brown, J. (1997, June). Organisational Learning: Connecting Classroom Practices and Team Leadership, Paper presented at the Annual Conference of CSSE, St. John's NF, Canada.

__________, & Brown, J. (1998). Meeting the challenge of information technology through educational partnerships: A case study. *International Electronic Journal for Leadership in Learning,* 2(11).

__________, & Brown, J. (1999, April). Leadership approach, the new work of teachers and successful change. Paper presented at the Annual Meeting of the American Educational Research Association, Montreal, Quebec, Canada. http://www.eric.ed.gov/. ED 431229.

__________, & Brown, J. (2000a). Leadership and the transformation of secondary schools into learning organisations. In K. Leithwood (Ed). *Understanding Schools as Intelligent Systems* (pp. 293-314), Stamford, Connecticut: JAI Press.

__________, Brown, J. (2000b). So you think that team leadership is easy? Training and implementation concerns. *The NASSP Bulletin,* 84(614), 71-83.

__________, & Brown, J. (2000c, April). Pulling together or apart: Factors influencing a school's ability to learn, Paper presented at the Annual Conference of the American Educational Research Association, New Orleans, US.

http://www.eric.ed.gov/. ED443144.

__________, Brown, J., Genge, A. & Walter, L. (1996, June). Building a Learning Organisation: An Analysis of one school district is experience. Paper presented at the Annual Conference of CSSE, St. Catherines, ON, Canada.

Stoll, L. & Fink, D. (1996). *Changing Our School,* Philadelphoa: Open University Press.

Teitel, L. (2006). Supporting school system leaders: The state of effective training programmes for school superintendents. The Wallace Foundation. Date Retrieved. March 20, 2006. http://www.wallacefoundation.org/WF/KnowledgeCenter/KnowledgeTopics/EducationLeadership/SupportingSchoolSystemLeaders.htm

Whyte, W. F., Greenwood, D. J., & Lazes, P. (1991). Participatory action research: Through practice to science in social research. In Whyte, W. F. (Ed.), *Participatory Action Research* (pp. 19-55). Newbury Park, Sage.

Wynn, R. & Guiditus, C. (1984). *Team Management: Leadership by Consensus.* Toronto: Charles E. Merrill.

Young, J. & Levin, B. (2002). *Understanding Canadian Schools: An Introduction to Educational Administration.* Scarborough, ON: Thompson Nelson.

# 5

# The Need and Role of Holistic Education in India

*—Oihika Chakrabariti* and *Sheila Tiwari*

Education in India needs to be reviewed in the light of the goal of national development. In India, the policy on education is primarily focused on academics and is yet to incorporate ways and means aimed at the holistic development of the child — the mental, emotional and physical spheres. Although the National Policy on Education has made some headway from its emphasis on the education of the girl-child, the focus is still primarily on providing useful and relevant elementary education for all children in the 6 to 14 age group by 2010 through the NPE's initiative—Sarva Shiksha Abhiyan. Its goal is to bridge social, regional and gender gaps, with the active participation of the community in the management of schools, through provision of community-owned quality education. There are about 888,000 educational institutions in the country with an enrolment of about 179 millions. Elementary Education System in India is the second largest in the world with 149.4 millions children of 6-14 years enrolled and 2.9 million teachers. This is about 82 per cent of the children in the age group.

The policy also highlights growth and priority areas in education in India that point to the challenges of the future. Increasingly, there is an urgent need to address the challenging issues children face growing up in this changing environment, particularly in urban India. With a view towards this, certain action research art therapy interventions exploring adolescent issues pertaining to growing up were carried out by a social change NGO, Manahkshetra Foundation in partnership with government institutes and schools. A collaborative venture between Manahkshetra and the National Gallery of Modern Art, Mumbai, the initiative was open to children between the ages of 11 /12 and 14/15 years from various schools. The focus of the study was to understand the efficacy of creative arts therapeutic interventions, using a developmental module, 'growing up', which offered a creative platform whereby the children were able to use creative arts therapeutic processes and group dynamics to explore and express visually their understanding of the self, environmental influences, issues related to puberty, sexuality, adolescent behaviours, feelings, attitudes and experience emotional development and change during this phase of growth. The programme enabled children to identify feelings and blocks to emotional growth, express feelings which maybe difficult to verbalise, improve overall communication skills, increase self-esteem and confidence, develop healthy coping skills when faced with a stressful situation and heighten creativity. The focus was in enhancing leadership qualities decision making and problem solving, inculcate an improved body image and overall personality development through various modules such as 'body mapping', 'masks' and the 'heroes module', which explored the self, relatedness and identification of role models through contemporary personalities with children.

A comparative analysis was conducted as children were sourced from private as well as government schools from diverse socio-economic, backgrounds. A staff-training programme in the use of creative arts therapies was also conducted for teachers, counsellors and special educators from 25 schools, wherein the purpose was capacity building within their existent roles to take the programme forward.

Similarly the module was also applied at Bal Bhavan — a government organisation which provides after school extra-curricular activities. The programme was called Bal Pragati — a developmental programme for emotional development of children and was a collaborative venture between Bal Bhavan and Manahkshetra.

We would like to share our significant leanings at the CCEAM conference 2006, 'Recreating linkages between theory and praxis in Educational Leadership', with a view towards contributing and impacting change within the National Policy on Education in India in the future, and the need to incorporate counselling, special education needs and creative/expressive arts therapies, at the school level in India. Currently the scope of counselling is limited to only certain private schools, and we feel there is a strong need to make it available at the larger school level in India.

## Introduction to the Structure and Progress of Education in India

Education in India needs to be reviewed in the light of the goal of national development and priorities set from time to time. In its Resolution on the National Policy on Education in 1968, an emphasis on quality improvement and a planned, more equitable expansion of educational facilities, and the need to focus on the education of girls was stressed.

About a decade ago and a half later, the National Policy on Education (NPE-1986) was formulated which was further updated in 1992. The NPE 1986 provides for a comprehensive policy framework for the development of education up to the end of the century and a Plan of Action (POA) 1992, assigning specific responsibilities for organising, implementing and-financing its proposals.

India's commitment to the spread of knowledge and freedom of thought among its citizens is reflected in its Constitution. Though education is in the concurrent list of the Constitution, the state governments play a very major role in the development of education particularly in the primary and the secondary education sectors.

The focus within the national policy on education is on the broad dimensions and magnitude of the structure, organisation and progress in education. Further it also highlights growth and priority areas in education in India that point to the challenges of the future.

In an effort to universalise elementary education by community-ownership of the school system, the government has launched the Sarva Shiksha Abhiyan. The Sarva Shiksha Abhiyan has been launched throughout the country in the form of a movement in response to the demand for quality basic education all over the country. The SSA programme is also an attempt to provide an opportunity for improving human capabilities to all children, through provision of community-owned quality education. It is an opportunity for promoting social justice through basic education, an expression of political will for universal elementary education across the country. A partnership between the central, state and the local government, it is an opportunity for States to develop their own vision of elementary education, effectively involving the panchayati raj institutions, school management committees, village and urban slum level education committees, parents' teachers' associations, mother teacher associations, tribal autonomous councils and other grass-roots level structures in the management of elementary schools.

The Sarva Shiksha Abhiyan hopes to provide useful and relevant elementary education for all children in the 6 to 14 age group by 2010. There is also another goal to bridge social, regional and gender gaps, with the active participation of the community in the management of schools, through provision of community-owned quality education.

The policy on education which is being implemented through the Sarva Shiksha Abhiyan (Education for All) aims at providing the basic infrastructure and environment, which will provide for holistic development of the child between the ages of 6 and 14 years in the mental, physical and emotional spheres.

## Needs Assessment Study

With a view towards this, it was decided to carry out a study to find out the extent to which the schools in Mumbai (especially those catering to the lower socio-economic group) have been able to meet the requirements outlined in the National Policy of Education. Random samples of 50 schools were selected from across Mumbai for the study (list enclosed in annexures). A questionnaire was distributed to the principals and feedback was invited from them. (Questionnaire enclosed in annexures)

The analysis of the questionnaire has thrown interesting light on the gaps, which are required to be bridged if the NPE has to achieve its desired goals. It is quite clear that even in highly urbanised areas, schools catering to the lower socio-economic group face serious constraints. The findings revealed the following:

— The pupil teacher ratio is 1:65 in about 80 per cent of the schools.

— 60 per cent of the schools do not have either fax or email id.

— In 100 per cent of the schools there is a Parent Teacher Association (PTA) but in 60 per cent of the schools these associations are non-functional.

— 60 per cent of the schools surveyed have lab facilities for teaching the science subjects but the laboratory is not used by students of classes below eighth grade.

— Seventy per cent of the students in these schools are not allowed to handle lab equipment on their own and experiments are demonstrated to them by the teacher or the lab assistant.

— Eighty per cent of the school teachers use teaching aids in the form of charts and specimens. They do not have the time to prepare their own teaching aids, since they are required to complete the syllabus within a given time.

— Almost all the schools contacted, 90 per cent have been provided with computers either by the governments or the local representatives or NGO's and computer classes are conducted in the school but the use of computers is not related to the school subjects

— Ninety per cent of the school's social science subjects, i.e., history and geography are taught through the textbooks, and all the teachers use the map as the teaching aid. Only 40 per cent of the schools had project work for the students.

— All the schools had a visit to the museum on their timetable, however the schools (about 70%), which did not have school buses, advised students to visit the museums on their own.

— Almost all the schools (about 95%) had a physical training teacher on their rolls. Each class was allotted at least two periods for physical training, however only 20 per cent of the schools surveyed had facilities for special coaching in sports. PT Teachers were also given the work of teaching school subjects.

— In the senior schools 65 per cent of the schools utilised the PT period to complete backlog in the academic subjects. None of the schools had gym facilities in their schools.

— In all the schools drawing teachers have been employed to teach drawing to the students up to eighth grade. Visual Arts are not part of the syllabus in the secondary school (grades 9 & 10).

— There is no provision for a special music / drama teacher in any of the schools surveyed. A subject teacher also proficient in music/theatre is requested to train students in music/drama for special functions.

— In about 60 per cent of the schools there is no space for a library. Books are stored in cupboards and the class teacher acts as a librarian. In 40 per cent of the schools provision for a librarian is there but no library space is there.

— About 70 per cent of the schools do have either of the following activities — nature clubs or Scouts/Guides/NCC/SUPW. However 80 per cent of the principals admitted that most of the time their periods allotted to them was utilised for other academic subjects.

— Student counselling, vocational guidance were not part of the school curriculum of any of these schools. There was no post of a counsellor in any of these schools. If the students faced any problem the class teacher acted as a counsellor.

— In these schools needs of special children were not on the priority list.

From the analysis of the questionnaire the education provided by the schools catering to the lower socio-economic groups show that inputs and interventions are required at many levels to help them provide holistic and quality education to their students. Ninety per cent of the principals agreed that they would be interested in providing the following inputs to improve the quality of education in their schools:

— Field trips, project work and site studies activity.

— Use of more teaching aids/technologies, provision of counselling and vocational guidance.

— Art education with inclusion of traditional arts and crafts and music.
— Visits to science centres and museums of antiquity and modern art.
— Community, outreach programmes.
— Specialised sports training
— Increased participation of parents and community

However as the findings illustrate due to the heavy academic pressure of the curriculum with emphasis on exams and marks/percentages, a high pupil teacher ratio and financial constraints this desire for quality does not often translate into concrete steps on the ground. In addition the lack of physical infrastructure, time constraints and the stress of urban life make it even more difficult to provide these inputs and ensure active participation of the parents and community.

## Research Action Art Therapy Intervention The 'Growing Up' Programme

With a view towards bridging these gaps, an initiative was undertaken by Manahkshetra Foundation to address emotional and behavioural issues children are confronted with growing up in urban areas.

It was observed that although the schools under survey were in general providing education to children from the lower socioeconomic strata, residing in the slums (60% of Mumbai's population lives in the slums), it was felt that schools needed to be better equipped in adequately addressing the growing emotional and physical needs of the individual child if schools are to play an important role in the holistic development of the child. However as we have seen, the study unearthed many gaps as majority of the schools focused on academic performance as the benchmark for judging the success or failure of a student.

Increasingly, there is a need to address the challenging issues children face growing up in this changing environment, particularly in urban India. With a view towards this, an attempt was therefore made by the NGMA, Mumbai, in partnership with Manahkshetra Foundation, an NGO committed to the use of the creative arts for psychosocial change, to address these gaps through certain action research art therapy interventions exploring adolescent issues pertaining to growing up.

Various creative stimuli and modules incorporating visual artwork, movement, sound, narration, presentation and role-plays were used to generate awareness and understanding of the self. Art materials used were often unconventional and out of the box, often junk we dispose. Numerous age appropriate creative modules were devised based on research of the adolescent psyche. These included Body Mapping and Body Sculpting to create an awareness of the self at both the physical and emotional levels and its projection *vis-a-vis* others. It was also used as a tool to initiate sex education. A look at contemporary heroes from popular culture supported understanding of childhood dreams and aspirations. The 'heroes module' explored relatedness and identification of role models through contemporary personalities with children. The aim of this module was to see what children today aspire to, whom they admire and desire to emulate. Through the individual task of drawing out their heroes they were made to reflect on the reasons behind their adulation, on the intrinsic qualities they find appealing. Thus, in a way, they were breaking free from what they had been conditioned to say when asked about their idols, such as Mother Theresa or Kalpana Chawla, and unleash thoughts they probably hadn't articulated even to themselves. Leadership qualities such as focus, passion and positive thinking were enumerated.

The development techniques applied were introduced at a latent, unconscious level without the children realising it. They were encouraged to think and be creative, using art as a medium to express themselves. Other modules included keeping a 'ME' diary where they were able to pen down their thoughts and feelings; also a transitional object, which would help them take part of the process beyond the programme. Mask making, role-plays, improvisations and working creatively in teams were other facets of the programme. The module on masks helped them to unearth their hidden selves. For instance, the children from the government school spoke in a formal English but once the masks were on, they reverted to their familiar languages — Hindi and Marathi—in their guise of anonymity.

The programme enabled children to identify feelings and blocks to emotional growth, express feelings which maybe difficult to verbalise, improve overall communication skills, increase self-esteem and confidence, develop healthy coping skills when faced with a stressful situation and heighten creativity. The focus was in enhancing leadership qualities — decision making and problem solving, inculcate an improved body image and overall personality development. The programme enabled children with capacity to work collectively. Important skills like problemsolving, strategising, overcoming conflicts with others and time management were subtly incorporated. Since they had to choose their materials themselves, self-help skills were also instilled. A comparative analysis was conducted as children were sourced from private as well as government schools from diverse socioeconomic backgrounds. In comparison, children from the lower socio-economic strata, from the Government school were initially more timid and formal and responded to it as a classroom experience by simply following instructions. However the transformations in personality from conformity to thinking individuals were incredible during the course of the program as they became more inventive, bolder and experimental in their approach.

It was observed over the duration of the programme, that children went from being self-conscious and unsure to becoming confident, from conforming to copying concepts to becoming more experimental, from naming parents, God and famous personalities as their heroes to believing in oneself. They went beyond the self in connecting and bonding with their peers and working as a team.

In conclusion one must add that the initiative was a small step in the direction to looking at creating alternatives to what most of our schools have to offer today. It was at attempt at facilitating holistic development of children today.

A staff-training programme in the use of creative arts therapies was also conducted for teachers, counsellors and special educators from 25 schools, where in the purpose was capacity building within their existent roles to take the programme forward.

## ANNEXURES

### Mumbai Schools Participating in the Survey

1. Colaba Municipal School, Colaba
2. Holy Name High School, Colaba
3. Marwari Vidyalaya School, Prarthana Samaj
4. Fellowship High School, Nana Chowk
5. Chikitsak High School, Girgaum
6. Wilson High School, C.P. Tank
7. Chanda Ramji Girls School, C.P. Tank
8. Shivai Vidya Mandir, Bhandup (E)
9. Shri Saraswati Vidya Mandir, Bhandup (W)
10. Sahayadri Vidya Mandir Bhandup (W)
11. Maharashtra High School, Bhandup (W)
12. I.E.S. School, Bhandup (E)
13. Bansidhar Agrawal High School, Wadala
14. Central Govt. Employees School, Antop Hill
15. Saraswati Vidyalaya, Bhandup (E)
16. Dyandeep High School, Kanjur Marg (E)
17. Marwari Commercial School, Chira Bazar
18. Seva Sadan School, Gamdevi
19. St. Columba School, Nana Chowk
20. Dyaneshwar Vidylaya, Wadala
21. Ismail Beg Mohammed High School, Mohammad Ali Rd
22. Diamond Jubilee Girls School, Byculla
23. Diamond Jubilee Boys School, Byculla
24. Sharda Vidya Mandir, Gamdevi
25. Nutan Vidyamandir, Trombay
26. Jawahar Vidya Mandir, R.C.F. Chembur
27. Anjuman Takvyatul Islam School, Govandi
28. Unique High School, Govandi
29. Chembur High School, Chembur

30. Maharashtra High School, Girgaum
31. Amolak Amichand High School, Sion
32. Lions Pioneer High School, Sion
33. St. Joseph School, R.C. Church
34. Elphinstone Technical High School, Dhobi Talao
35. Swamy Vivekanand High School, Kandivali
36. Navjeen High School, Bandra (E)
37. I.E.S. High School, Bandra (E)
38. Mahatma Gandhi High School, Bandra (E)
39. Hindi Public High School, Santa Cruz (E)
40. St. Josephs High School, Kalina
41. Sion Municipal School, Sion
42. Santa Cruz Municipal, School, Santa Cruz (E)
43. S.N.D.T. Girls School, Sikka Nagar
44. Modern High School, Sikka Nagar
45. Sane Guruji Vidyalaya, Santa Cruz (W)
46. Sane Guruji Vidyalaya, Mahim
47. Versova High School, Versova
48. G.A. Ranade High School, J.S. Road
49. Sule Guruji Vidyala, Dadar
50. Lalbag Municipal School, Lalbaug

## Questionnaire for the School Principals

1) Name of the School
2) Address,
3) Phone
4) Fax
5) E-mail
6) Name of Principal
7) Medium of Instruction
8) No. of Classes
9) No. of Students

10) Boys /Girls Ratio
11) No. of Teachers
12) Teacher/Pupil Ratio
13) Parent/Teacher Association
14) Facilities for Teaching Science
   => Laboratory, Library, Field Trips Teaching Aids, etc. 15)
15) Facilities for Teaching Social Science
   => Project Work, Site Visits, Visits to Museums, Use of Teaching Aids
16) Sports Activities
   => Sports Teacher, Playground, Gym, etc.
17) Library/Provision of a Librarian
18) Teaching of Art, Music, Drama
19) Use of Computers
20) Other Activities/Facilities Provided by the School
   => Nature Club, N.C.C, Scouts/Guides Community, Outreach

   Program Counselling,
   => In-Service Training for Teachers, Interaction with Parents etc.
21) Would you add the following activities to improve the quality of education in your school
   => Art Education, Music, Theatre
   => Relating Computer Education to Academics
   => Counselling, Vocational Guidance
   => Field Trips, Nature Clubs, Special Training for sports
   => Activity Based Learning, Use of Teaching Aids, Project Work, Community Work etc.
22) What are the possible problems you anticipate in the implementation of these activities?

# 6

# Building Leadership Capacity through Resiliency

—*Annie Henry* and *Mike Milstein*

Leaders constantly face challenges that either stimulate their growth or drain their energies. When choosing, it would be doubtful that leaders would choose to have their energies drained, and yet many find themselves to be depleted. Whether or not leaders are energised or depleted depends upon how they see the world: Is the world full of problems or potential? Each place and individual has both problems and potentials. Is the focus on fixing problems or on developing the health and well being of everyone?

Certainly part of leaders work is solving problems. But problem solving focuses on deficits and how to fix them. Shortcomings and difficulties are the focal point of the mind map of problem solvers that ultimately lead to a fixation on why things don't work. The trap that leaders can fall into is constantly solving problems instead of leading.

In contrast, resiliency is an approach that expands our thinking about students, educators, leaders, schools and communities beyond problem identification and resolution to strengths identification and actualisation. Resiliency concentrates on why things will and do work. Leaders who are resilient and promote resiliency in others make a positive difference in the lives of others around them, sometimes in spite of difficult and challenging environments.

Leaders who shift their mind maps from problem solving and towards resiliency as a frame of reference still reduce or eliminate problems. But a resiliency mentality also increases abilities beyond mere problem resolution and towards creativity, growth and realisation of potential. Resiliency is a powerful path to school and community improvement.

The focus of the paper is on building leadership capacity by focusing on resiliency. Sections include perspectives on resiliency, our six elements resiliency model (Henry & Milstein, 2004), applications for building leadership capacity, strategies that promote leadership resiliency, and resiliency as a powerful path to building leadership capacity.

## Perspectives on Resiliency

When you see a partially filled glass of water, do you see it as half full or half empty? How do you see your world? As leaders, how you see the world will influence many of the people around you. Is your life full of problems to be solved? Or do you see your situations are being replete with positive challenges? If you see the positive challenges then it is more likely that you will be enthusiastic and feel empowered to meet them as they arise. Perceptions and beliefs shape our reality. Leaders who think and behave resiliently think and behave differently from problem-focused people.

Resilient leaders have hardships just as those who do not exhibit resiliency. The difference is how they cope with them. Resilient leaders are like rubber bands; they bounce back from adversities stronger and faster, learn from experiences, gain more self-confidence in the process, and develop new skills. They know what they need to do to bring internal and environmental resiliency building blocks into their lives and get through tough situations.

### Internal and Environmental Protective Factors

Age, ethnicity, gender or culture has little bearings on whether leaders have the potential to respond to life's dynamics with resilience. There is, however, a disparity as to how people react to challenges. Some collapse, others survive, and yet others exhibit resiliency and become stronger.

How is the resiliency capacity built so leaders can become stronger? Partly it is rooted in what the individuals bring and partly in what their environments contribute to the situation. A review of the literature developed by Henderson and Milstein (1996) and adapted by Milstein and Henry (2000) has resulted in a summary of key individual and environmental protective factors that serve as building blocks to resiliency. Table 1 lists the internal protective factors.

Each of us has some, if not all, of these protective factors. They are based on how we respond to life, our personality and genetics. The extent to which these factors exist is affected by our ability to avoid or eliminate dysfunctional habits and learn new and more effective ways of coping.

*Table 1: Internal Protective Factors*

1. Gives of self in service to others or a cause, or both.
2. Uses life skills, including good decisionmaking, assertiveness, impulse control, and problem solving.
3. Is sociable and has ability to be a friend and form positive relationships.
4. Has a sense of humour.
5. Exhibits internal locus of control, i.e., belief in ability to influence one's environment.
6. Is autonomous, independent.
7. Has positive view of personal future.
8. Is flexible.
9. Has spirituality, i.e., belief in a greater power.
10. Has capacity for connection to learning.
11. Is self-motivated.
12. Is "good at something," has personal competence.
13. Has feelings of self-worth and self confidence.

Our environments, e.g., our families, organisations, and communities, can either support our resiliency or deplete it. They impact our ability to cope and bounce back, which, in turn impacts how leaders lead. If our environments are depleting, it may be necessary to consider changing, leaving, or avoiding them for environments that are more supportive of our growth and development. It may also mean that as leaders, our challenge is to change our environments so there is improved health and well being. The environmental protective factors that promote health and well being are listed in Table 2.

*Table 2: Environmental Protective Factors*

1. Promotes close bonds.
2. Values and encourages education.
3. Uses high warmth, low criticism style of interaction.
4. Sets and enforces clear boundaries (rules, norms and laws).
5. Encourages supportive relationships with many caring others.
6. Promotes sharing of responsibilities, service to others, "required helpfulness".
7. Provides access to resources for meeting basic needs of housing, employment, health care, and recreation.
8. Expresses high realistic expectations for success.
9. Encourages goal setting and mastery.
10. Nourishes development of positive connections (such as altruism) and life skills (such as cooperation).
11. Provides leadership, decisionmaking and other opportunities for meaningful participation.
12. Appreciates the unique talents of each individual.

Leaders live in multiple environments that include families, personal and professional friends, neighbourhoods, communities and organisations. These environments can either enhance or exhaust our ability to behave resiliently if the enrichments factors identified in Table 2 are minimal. It is difficult to remain optimistic and motivated when we live in depleting environments. On the other hand, if our environments are responsive to our, as well as others', development needs and our attitudes, beliefs and skills are supported, then there is more likelihood resilience will be built. What might be required is to change our environments in ways that more closely reflect the factors listed in Table 2. It might also require a change of environments or, at least, to minimise exposure to them while seeking out substitutes that support our ability to live and lead resiliently.

Our lives play out differently based on our internal resources and the extent to which our environments are supportive of our ability to bounce back from adversity. As leaders, challenges are a constant. The response to them will vary from loss and submission to growth and success, depending on whether our resiliency capabilities have been honed and the extent to which our environments are fertile soil for rebounding, adapting, and growing. Figure 1 that was adapted from Richardson, Neiger, Jensen, and Krumpfer (1990) visualises these dynamics.

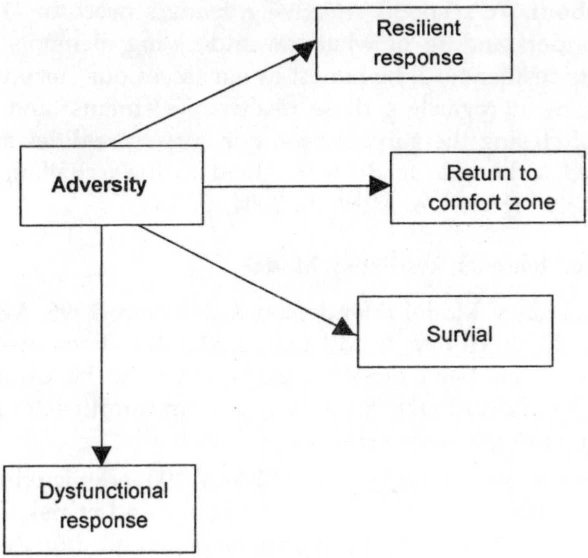


*Figure 1: Multiple Ways to Respond to Adversity*

As seen in Figure 1, there are multiple ways to respond to adversity and stress. Experience, skills, and support change the way in which a response will be given for a situation. If the skills or the environmental support is not there, there will be a feeling of being overwhelmed and withdraw from the situation. This would be a dysfunctional response. Leaders who respond dysfunctionally show up at work but are not mentally and emotionally available to anyone. If leaders learn how to scrape by and respond in ways that are minimally successful, then they will struggle to survive. This is a survival response. If they have relevant and sufficient skills, a willingness to confront issues, and meaningful support from their environments, then they respond to disruptions better. The response is in the comfort zone. If the disruptions result in gleaning new insights, new skills, increased self-confidence, and better support from the environment, then leaders become more resilient than they were at the outset. This indeed is what constitutes a resilient response.

The ability to confront life's challenges in ways that lead to improved capabilities and a better sense of self is what resiliency is all about. To respond effectively, leaders need to: "1) have a clear understanding of what the underlying elements are that promote resiliency; 2) be honest as we assess our current state of development regarding these resiliency elements; and, 3) seek ways of closing the gap between our current realities and what we need to be able to do to respond to life's challenges more effectively" (Henry & Milstein, 2004, p. 252).

**Our Six Elements Resiliency Model**

The Resiliency Model (Henderson & Milstein, 1996; Milstein & Henry, 2000; Henry & Milstein, 2004) has been used for a decade. It has been modified and proven to be durable and useful to individuals, schools and communities to promote growth, strength and well-being.

The six elements (Henry & Milstein, 2004) depicted in Figure 2 summarise key findings of the resiliency and at risk literature. Initially the research focused mainly on youth, but there is an increasing emphasis on resiliency being a key factor in improving the welfare of schools and communities. For example, the New Zealand Ministry of Education has adopted resiliency as a critical part of school improvement (Ministry of Education, 2006). The more these elements are part of our lives and are supported by our environments, the more likely it is that leaders and those they serve will live positive, healthy and meaningful lives.

*Positive Connections:* "People, activities, programmes, institutions, communities, and society, as well as the core values that underlie them, are related in profound ways. These connections, help us know who we are and how we fit in with those around us" (Henry & Milstein, 2004, p. 253).

*Figure 2: Resiliency Model*

With the possible exception of hermits, everyone needs positive connections that are healthy and supportive so our lives can have meaning and value. Supporting our sense of belonging and meaning is done through maintaining and nurturing positive connections and seeking out new ones. When leaders don't have positive connections, then it can truly be lonely at the top.

*Clear, Consistent, and Appropriate Boundaries:* "These include expectations that are communicated in writing, such as laws, policies, and procedures, as well as expectations that are informal but powerful, such as norms and cultural preferences" (Henry & Milstein, 2004, p. 254).

Our behaviours are greatly affected by the expectations of others. If they are clear, consistently enforced, and appropriate to the needs and abilities of those who are expected to abide by them, then they can serve as a safety net that provides guidance for appropriate behaviours. People want to know where they start and stop. Leaders who involve others in setting the boundaries for their schools and organisations, and who also articulate their personal boundaries are stronger and more effective leaders (Bennis, 1989).

*Life Guiding Skills:* "Competencies that are needed to navigate life's twists and turns include goal setting, planning, problem solving, decision-making, communications, conflict resolution and management, and the ability to be reflective and grow spiritually" (Henry & Milstein, 2004, p. 254).

Life skills need to be developed, honed through experiences, and applied flexibly as conditions change and life progresses. Leaders who have undergone formal preparation have been introduced to and practised many of the life guiding skills that are needed to navigate life's twists and turns.

*Nurture and Support:* "We thrive when nurtured and supported by those around us, whether they are relatives, friends, those charged with our care, or others. Life is more worth living when we matter to others" (Henry & Milstein, 2004, p. 254).

We are more fully alive when we experience unconditional regard. Learning how to ask for and receive such attention is important. Being able and willing to give others nurturance and support is also important to our sense of well being.

*Purposes and Expectations:* "When we have clear goals and priorities and the motivation to achieve them, we are more likely to engage with life's challenges. With purposes and expectations, we are motivated to grow and develop" (Henry & Milstein, 2004, p. 254).

*Meaning is the driving energy of life:* Clarity of purposes and expectations and the motivation to achieve them provide the impetus to engage with life's challenges. Leaders who don't have clear purposes and expectations are likely to become alienated, which leaves them adrift and with little drive beyond mere survival. Leaders must ultimately chose and prioritise their own expectations, e.g., to be effective leaders.

*Meaningful Participation:* "As social beings we need to be engaged with our families and friends, as well as with volunteer efforts and the communities we live in. Meaningful participation confirms that we are not alone; that we have something to offer;

and that we have the responsibility to give back to the environments that have nurtured us" (Henry & Milstein, 2004, p. 254).

People may have the time, life experiences, and knowledge to participate meaningfully, but they need to be invited to participate appropriately. Leaders who have strategies for involving appropriate people in discussions that promotes greater understanding and ownership.

**Applications for Building Leadership Capacity**

Teachers, students, parents, support personnel are the fabric of the school. Leaders are the weavers of the fabric of resiliency initiatives. Without active and positive modelling of resiliency, it is unlikely that staff, students, parents and community members will behave resiliently. Leaders who are resilient send a clear message that resiliency is a necessity, not an option. They are in a position where they influence every aspect of the school or institution and community. They monitor the system and the impact it is having on students regularly. They communicate needs and hopes of youth to staff, parents and the community in general.

In order to fulfil these important roles, leaders must understand the importance of promoting resiliency for youth and adults in schools and organisations in the communities. They must also exhibit resiliency in their own professional and personal lives. If they don't, they may even become a major impediment to the resiliency promoting process.

Some leaders face extraordinary challenges daily such as the growing pressure to "produce" better test results, insufficient resources, lack of community appreciation for their efforts, staff that don't have the skills needed for cooperative and collaborative environments, and sometimes, uninterested students. A combination of these challenges can wear down enthusiasm and motivation.

Leaders with many years experience may have had repeated efforts to improve the school or organisation with minimal success or fall short of the mark. They have fought the good fight but have come up short, which can lead to becoming cynical and exhausted, withdrawal, or at least minimise their efforts to improve the school or organisation.

Neither should leaders' understanding of resiliency concepts should not be taken for granted. As leaders progress through their professional life cycle, they tend to fall into one of the three groups identified by Henry and Milstein (2004).

*Leaders Who Remain Resilient Throughout Their Careers.* These leaders figure out strategies to stay engaged and enthused in a variety of ways. They might change schools or levels to lead. They might seek professional development opportunities or volunteer to participate in different initiatives. Whatever activity is chosen, the common denominator is recognition of the importance of growing and developing as human beings. They understand their energy impacts others and their growth.

*Leaders Who Exhibit Low Resiliency at Some Point in Time but Bounce Back.* These leaders have ebbs and flows as they move through their careers. The slippage may be due to any number of factors such as a stressful home life, frustration with navigating the political arena, or not continuing to make the effort to grow as a leader. Reflection and decision making bring leaders to a more resilient state where they commit to re-establish their sense of professionalism and modify the behaviours in ways that they are proud of and enhance their self-esteem. Sometimes they find their way back through support from colleagues or others who care about them. The trigger mechanism might be embedded in individual awareness or it might be environmentally stimulated, but the effort is ultimately based on the clear recognition that they became leaders because they believed that this is a special calling; one that is critically important to the improvement of the lives of their students, staff members and communities.

*Leaders Who Do Not Exhibit Resiliency.* These leaders feel stuck and miserable and make those around them unhappy and frustrated. They avoid risk taking and retire on the job. Their dissatisfactions quickly spill over into the environment. They are poor role models and often road blocks for promoting resiliency.

Leaders who are in the first group manage to become healthier and stronger with the challenges they face. If they are in more supportive situations, they do even better. Leaders in the second group need supportive environments to help them bounce back and regain their enthusiasm. The third group require purposeful attention to help them either overcome their negativity or leave education.

Every effort is needed to develop and maintain resilient leaders so they in turn can strengthen the resiliency of staff, students, parents and ultimately the community.

**Strategies that Promote Leadership Resiliency**

The Resiliency Model (Henry & Milstein, 2004) serves as a framework for developing strategies that can be employed to promote leadership resiliency.

*Positive Connections:* The saying, "it is lonely at the top" captures the typical way leaders are isolated from each other. There are ways of mitigating this situation and promoting positive connections. For example, site-based shared decision making teams, study groups, visits to other schools, and participation in local, regional, national or international professional development can be encouraged. Having a mentor or mentoring another leader is an opportunity to promote positive connections. Promoting norms of cooperation and support can break down isolation that many leaders experience.

*Clear, Consistent and Appropriate Boundaries:* Boundaries provide a modicum of security. This can be promoted by involving educators and students where appropriate, to establish, interpret and implement rules and policies that contribute to deepening their understanding, acceptance and support of these boundaries. Clearly communicating policies in writing and frequently checking for clarity can avoid misinterpretations. This is also true for norms. If norms are clear, understood and share, they can diminish conflict and help new staff members become acquainted with them without undue stress.

*Life Guiding Skills:* New skills are imperative for both those who are relative novices and those who are more experienced. Leaders need to survey their staff members to determine what they think they need from professional development initiatives and activities. Leaders need to model adult learning principles so others will practice them. Learning should be relevant to adult learners so they should participate in what is to be learned. Resources and support for continued learning needs to be provided. Attending conferences or in services is a great start. Follow through is what strengthens implementation. Leaders should also recognise talents that others bring to the school and encourage them to share their expertise with others.

*Nurture and Support:* Leaders who let others know they are valued and supported not only through words but also through actions build resiliency in themselves and others. Purposeful and regular feedback that identifies positive contributions strengthens those behaviours. Mentors can provide feedback for leaders about their leadership and management behaviours, just as leaders can provide feedback on teaching and contributions that staff members make. Celebrations and recognitions of efforts send a strong message of what is valued. Discouraging negative criticism and encouraging positive attention and support of all who are part of the environment is also essential.

*Purposes and Expectations:* Our expectations are significantly shaped by the feedback received. If the messages are negative or critical, safety and low risk taking regarding challenges that are outside our comfort zone will be the norm. Involving others in the development and clarification of the school or organisation's vision, mission and goals promotes a sense of purpose and expectations for achievement. When we participate in the development of purposes we take ownership and are more enthusiastic. Creating ongoing planning and action teams that bring diverse groups together can maintain and expand commitments to purposes and expectations. Communicating progress and problems promotes engagement and commitment to purposes.

*Meaningful Participation:* Leaders who have discovered the value of having people participate in meaningful discussions and decisions promote greater and wider participation in their communities. Teams such as school councils or school improvement teams promote people working together. Leaders must have the skills and motivation to facilitate the process: leaders who convene, intervene, and bring consensus send a clear message that everyone's voice is important and heard. For example, leaders who lead effective meetings ensure the agendas are delivered ahead of time so that everyone can be prepared at the meeting to discuss the issue, provide adequate time for discussion, and that discussions can lead to actions. With experience, cooperative efforts can become a part of the fabric of the school or organisation.

**Resiliency as a Powerful Path to Building Leadership Capacity**

Resiliency can be a powerful path to building leadership capacity for the following reasons:

1. "It is a positive approach that focuses on strengths and potentials" (Henry & Milstein, 2004, p. 248). A great deal of literature emphasizes ways in which leaders can fix problems. There is a plethora of models for decision making and problem solving. The shift to a resiliency approach builds strengths.
2. "It is an easily understood language that can be communicated and shared by everyone—students, teachers, administrators, staff, parents and other community members" (Henry & Milstein, 2004, p. 248). Often leaders use professional educator language that may not be easily understood by others. Using a shared resiliency language and concepts can help bridge the language barrier that often exists among participants.
3. "Resiliency is a holistic framework" (Henry & Milstein, 2004, p. 248). People are encouraged to look at a broader picture instead of simple, magical solutions for complex challenges. Resiliency thinking causes people to inventory current practices and identify gaps that need to be addressed.
4. "Resiliency promotes widespread involvement" (Henry & Milstein, 2004, p. 248). Resiliency research findings (Werner & Smith, 1992) support the contention that people need to participate in meaningful activities to enhance their resiliency. Leaders who involve different facets of their communities for improving their schools and institutions gain greater acceptance and clarity.
5. "Resiliency energises and motivates participants" (Henry & Milstein, 2004, p. 248). The more people are actively involved, experience nurture and care, taught life skills and are challenged to achieve in environments that includes

boundaries to promote safety and security, the more likely there will be an expansion of positive energy directed toward agreed-upon ends.

6. "Resiliency does not require schools and communities to discard strongly held beliefs about specific educational philosophies and programs" (Henry & Milstein, 2004, p. 249). How we communicate, make decisions, and our attitudes shifts the balance between fixing problems to one of thinking about growth and well being.

## In Closing

In brief, resiliency is about encountering disruptive and stressful challenges, learning coping skills and becoming more effective in dealing with life events in ways that promote healthy well-being for everyone. Resilient leaders emphasise potentials and possibilities rather than shortcomings and limitations. Resiliency focuses on adaptability, strengths, development of solutions to problems, and a "can do" attitude.

## References

Bennis, W. (1989). *Why Leaders Can't Lead: The Unconscious Conspiracy Continues*, San Francisco, CA: Jossey Bass Publishing.

Henderson, N., & Milstein, M. (1996). *Resiliency in Schools: Making it Happen for Students and Educators*. Thousand Oaks, CA: Corwin Press.

Henry, D.A., & Milstein, M. (2004). *Promoting resiliency in youth,* educators, and communities in Waxman, H.C., Padron, Y.N., & Gray, J.P. (eds.), pp. 247-263. Greenwich, CT: Information Age Publishing.

Milstein, M. & Henry, D.A. (2000). *Spreading Resiliency: Making it Happen for Schools and Communities*. Thousand Oaks, CA: Corwin Press.

New Zealand Ministry of Education (2006). Interventions for refugee children in New Zealand schools: Models, methods, and best practices www.minedu.gove.nz. 10 March 2006.

Richardson, G.E., Neiger, B.L., Jensen, S., & Krumpfer, K.L. (1990). The resiliency model. *Health Education*, 21 (6), 33-39.

Werner, E.E., & Smith, R.S. (1992). *Overcoming the Odds: High Risk Children from Birth to Adulthood*. New York: Cornell University Press.

# 7

# Developing Leadership Capacity through Mentoring Relationship

—*Ruth Gorinski* and *Vesa Tonder*

The practice of mentoring has become increasingly influential as a mechanism for creating communities of learning that develop leadership partnerships and capability within, and across global educational settings. This study examines the role of mentoring in building such partnerships and capabilities within two discrete contexts: one, amongst students and two, amongst school leaders. The paper provides a broad overview of the mentoring literature within an educational leadership context. It then presents two case studies that highlight the ways in which mentoring builds both leadership capability and agency. A Finnish case study exemplifies the impact of school leaders mentoring senior students to develop leadership capability and capacity. A New Zealand case study highlights how mentoring school leaders has facilitated the building of agentic learning communities with increased social capital.

The research was, guided by a qualitative case study design and used face-to-face interviews, document analysis and focus group discussions as the primary data collection tools. The process of analysis sought to describe the dynamic pattern of relationships between mentors and mentees. The findings are significant for educational leaders who are interested in integrating a theoretical and practical framework of mentoring, to enhance both their own, and their students' leadership capability. There remains abundant scope and reason to continue inquiring into the possibilities of mentoring relationships as a strategy for growing leadership capacity and agency in education contexts.

The desire to enlist mentors in developing leadership in both business and educational contexts has inspired a profusion of research in the areas of mentoring and coaching (Clutterbuck & Megginson, 1999; Gorinski; 1997; Gorinski, Fraser & Ayo, 2004; Hargrove, 1995; Mackay & Johnson, 2002; Parsloe, 1999; Roberston, 2005). There is a range of pertinent literature that aids in clarifying definitions of mentoring from both a business and education perspective. For example, Clutterbuck and Megginson (1999) refer to mentoring as a long-term relationship that aims to help develop the full potential and benefits of all partners — mentee, mentor and organisation. They posit that the mentor is more likely to be an experienced individual who is willing to share knowledge with someone less experienced, and in the process build a relationship of mutual trust.

Gorinski, (1997) describes the relationship of mentoring as a positive, dynamic partnership, through which assistance and support is provided by the more experienced mentor to the mentee. Mentoring may be viewed as a hierarchical vehicle for promoting involvement in learning ...."in doing so, the mentor's role is to encourage and motivate the student/mentee to deepen his/her involvement in learning" (p.41). The mentoring relationship then, is one of collegiality and offers the mentee an opportunity to experiment, with the advice and support of the mentor, in a relatively safe and non threatening environment (Clutterbuck & Megginson, 1999).

## Relationships

Relationships are a dimension of mentoring that is seen to be essential to the overall mentoring process. Stalker (1992, p.3) states: "These relationships define the connections through which interactions occur and outcomes are achieved." Mentoring provides a unique kind of relationship and access to special opportunities (Jacobi 1991). Many components go into the creation of a strong, positive, trusting and effective mentor-mentee relationship. According to the literature, in order for the mentoring process to be positive, a mentor must be more than simply a disseminator of information who perpetuates institutional hierarchy (Angelique, Kyle & Taylor, 2002; Daloz 1991; Rix & Gold 2000; Smit & McMurray 1999). In addition to showing knowledge and understanding and facilitating the integration of theory and practice, a mentor can build a relationship with a mentee, and assist in their growth and development in a variety of ways. The relationship, however, will be based upon constructs of either professional hierarchy or mutuality (Gorinski 1997).

Hierarchical mentoring relationships are most predominantly represented in the literature (Cook 1979; Daloz 1991). Typically, an older, more experienced person guides and acts as a role model to a younger, novice mentee. This activity is a top-down, unilateral (Angelique et al. 2002), "didactic" (Daloz 1991, p.206) one in which "a neophyte academic is chosen .... by an experienced and senior academic" (Stalker 1992, p.3), who has higher professional or organisational status and associated power.

An alternative to such hierarchical relationships is one in which the mentoring relationship is a "mutually enhancing process where the career development of both parties is addressed" (Kram, 1985, p.26) and one in which both should prosper and grow (Angelique, Kyle & Taylor, 2002). This type of conceptualisation necessarily implies a mutually helpful relationship between mentor and mentee. Ideally, hierarchical distinctions between the two are absent in such a relationship. Instead, mutuality is at the hub of this type of mentoring which has the possibility of becoming a two way, interactive, reciprocal process (Daresh & Playko, 1990; Rix & Gold, 2000).

Such reciprocity is demonstrated in the growing body of literature focusing on the study of learning communities. Cochran-Smith (2004, p.127) exemplifies the use of multiple, interactive perspectives in teaching and learning in her description of the "cluster mentors" initiative established across three different educational organisations in Massachusetts. The participants' expressed intention was not only to support new teachers, but also to build a shared body of knowledge from a collective inquiry stance. All involved in the initiative reported increased knowledge of subject material, related pedagogy and day-to-day practice as a result of these collaborative relationships.

## Coaching

Such a mutually enhancing relationship provides an ideal platform upon which leaders can develop their own capability, whilst at the same time contributing to the professional growth and development of their mentoring partner. Robertson (2005) suggests that this is the point at which mentoring and coaching relationships become distinct processes. She argues that mentoring uses the process of instruction to bring the mentee to a point of understanding, whereas coaching develops the skills of reflection to enable the coachee to improve their practice. This notion of improving performance is also discussed by Macky and Johnson (2002) who emphasize two important principles of coaching. First, the coaching process requires the use of feedback and evaluation by both the coachee and the coach. Second, they argue that for coaching to be effective, and hence successful, the relationship between coach and coachee should be positive.

## Challenges

Irrespective of whether the term mentoring or coaching is adopted, positive relationships, built on trust and respect, are a key to increased leadership efficacy. There are however, inherent complexities and challenges in any mentoring or coaching relationship. Generally, the greater the diversity in the workplace, the greater the likelihood that challenges will arise (Holloway, 2003). Issues of cross-cultural mentoring (Johnson-Bailey & Cervero, 2004), gender, age, power inequities (Darwin, 2000), change, and divergent growth within the relationship (Lucas, 2001) create special challenges within mentoring relationships. Clearly, skill and integrity in dealing with interpersonal relationships are necessary co-requisites for any effective and beneficial mentoring relationship (Playko, 1991; Allen & Poteet, 1999).

The literature identifies both explicitly and/or implicitly, a number of outcomes or benefits for participants, from engagement in coaching relationships. These include the creation of professional learning communities, increased critical reflection and the facilitation of agency (Robertson, 2005).

## Professional Learning Communities

Coaching relationships then, can provide a catalyst for the development of professional learning communities. Louis, Marks and Kruse (1996), and Bryk, Camburn and Louis (1999) identified five elements of professional learning communities. These included first, the development of shared values and 'expectations about students' learning, teaching and teachers' roles. Second, professional learning communities develop a collective focus on student learning and achievement, and dialogue around this. Third, collaboration is a key component of learning communities. Leaders, who facilitate collaborative professional cultures, involve staff in goal setting and are committed to shared leadership approaches (Leithwood, 1992). Fourth, professional learning communities are characterised by deprivatised practice involving team teaching and peer observations. Finally, indepth conversations about learning and teaching are part of the normative culture evident in established learning communities.

Within the context of growing leadership capability, as mentors and mentees work together, engaging in critically reflective dialogue about leadership practice they simultaneously work toward facilitating an increased culture of learning in their educational context (Robertson, 2005). In a leadership context, the mentoring relationship provides a potentially powerful mechanism for strengthening individual leadership capability, as welt as relationships within and across schools. The process of critical reflection has an integral role in the mentoring relationship.

## Increased Critical Reflection

Because the mentoring process involves reciprocal processes, leaders can benefit from not only personal reflections on their own practice, but also from reflection on their mentoring partner's practice. When leaders avail themselves of the opportunity to observe other's leadership practice, they can be challenged by what they see. This provides a catalyst for one leader facilitating another leader's critical reflection on their practice.

Reflection can be an individual or collaborative process involving our ability to think about things; to make sense of; and gain meaning from experiences by constructing knowledge from them. Critical reflection is a more macro focused activity, involving the development and construction of specific skills, ideas, understanding or behaviours as a result of reflection (Zepke, Nugent & Leach, 2003). Mentors have a key role to play in this process, as they facilitate a mentee's reflection on their learning process, and on their personal practice and the practices of the educational context within which participants work.

Mentors then, are not only knowledgeable in the basic strategies, procedures and skills of mentoring. They are ideally, also skilled in observing, actively listening and describing interactions (Clutterbuck & Megginson 1999; Robertson, 2005; Rudman, 1998). A mentor is adequately qualified to work collaboratively with a mentee, walking with them through a process of professional reflection and facilitating the development of agentic capability (Bird, 1985; Field & Field, 1994).

## Agency

A key desirable outcome of mentoring relationships is increased agency amongst participants (Fullan, 2001 Robertson, 2005). Mentoring relationships serve "to strengthen the self efficacy and agency of educational leaders" (Robertson, 2005, p. 181). Agency is evidenced in leaders' belief that they have the ability to effect positive change. Such beliefs develop as leaders become increasingly competent in "deconstructing their multiple roles" (Robertson, 2005, p. 182) and challenging their educational assumptions. As a result, they are able to look more critically at the social and political contexts that shape their leadership. Concomitant with such reflection is an increased commitment to, and ownership of, personal and institutional change as a result of critical reflection on their practice (Hargrove, 1995). This leads to more efficacious practice, as leaders involve significant others in problem solving; goal setting and action planning — all critical ingredients of agentic practice (Otero & West-Burnham, 2006; Robertson, 2005).

Fundamental to the notion of agency then, is a belief held by participants, of their ability to effect change, and a strong personal conviction to do so. Mentoring is a powerful strategy for building evidence-based decision making capability amongst leaders; thereby developing agency.

## Research Design

The research design of this project was guided by a dual qualitative quantitative case study. The finer points of the case study approach in qualitative research are detailed by a number of authors (Burns 1994; Merriam 1988; Stake 1994; Yin 1989). The principal reason behind this methodological choice was linked with the focus of the study: to give increased understanding of the ways in which mentoring builds leadership capability and agency amongst school leaders in two distinct global settings. The research question was in part one of measuring how many participant's found mentoring to be a useful leadership tool. It was also about qualitative issues of discerning insights, making discoveries, understanding and interpretation of participant's experiences.

Two situational case studies therefore were employed as the appropriate methodological approach. This facilitated the presentation, examination and interpretation of the specific personal experiences of mentors in tie participating schools. The cohesive collation of all respondents' viewpoints provided a starting point for understanding the contribution of mentoring relationships within a leadership context.

## Ethical Considerations

The data collection processes implemented throughout this inquiry were guided by the ethical principles adopted by the American Anthropological Association. These included discussions with leaders and teachers; making the nature of enquiry overt; and written communication with respondents declaring that their participation was voluntary and confidential and that their anonymity would be maintained (Bogdan & Biklen 1992).

### Selection of Respondents

Respondents self-selected to participate in the research project. They came from a total of ten schools — six in Finland and four in New Zealand. The researchers recognised the importance of credibility and dependability of findings, particularly when working with colleagues, as was the case with the New Zealand case study. To this end, formal mechanisms were implemented throughout the data-gathering process. These included letters to potential respondents (rather than informal conversations); structured questionnaires and structured mentoring meetings in the Finnish case.

Potential respondents included those who were engaged in mentoring activities over the 2004 – 2006 academic years. The initial contact letters explained the nature of the research and sought the cooperation of respondents to participate in either questionnaire completion, or internet inquiry assessment of the benefits of mentoring activities. The purpose of the questionnaires and internet inquiry was to glean both qualitative and quantitative data information about respondent's views and practices in relation to their mentoring experiences.

In total, 97 respondents participated in the research. Five of these were principals, eighty one were teachers and eleven were school helpers.

*Table 1. Respondent Details*

| *#Schools* | *Principals* | *Teachers* | *Helpers* | *Total* |
|---|---|---|---|---|
| 10 | 5 | 81 | 11 | 97 |

**Data Collection and Analysis**

The primary methods of data collection used were questionnaires and an internet inquiry tool. Questions were designed to glean direct responses to the ways in which the mentoring relationship had impacted upon respondent's leadership practice, the benefits of mentoring, and the ways in which participation in a mentoring relationship had facilitated macro level leadership thinking and practice. To enhance the credibility and dependability of the findings (Anderson 1990, the questionnaires and internet inquiry were supplemented with anecdotal notes from informal meetings, and workplace conversations with participants (Bogdan & Biklen, 1992).

The form of analysis for this study was a quantifiable one initially, moving into a qualitative interpretation, where findings were not expected to be conclusive, but rather, a reflection of a perceived cultural situation that warrants further investigation. Essentially, the analysis and interpretation of this data sought to explain and describe the role of mentoring in building leadership capability amongst school leaders, within a set of conceptually specified analytic categories (Huberman & Miles 1994). These categories were developed in two ways. First, the questionnaire responses were examined and analysed, and from this initial raw information, emergent themes or categorisations were identified. Quotes were clustered together based on their similarity and separated from each other according to their incongruity. From the groupings of quotes, elemental meanings were extracted and criteria for each group established. Second, the categorisations were defined in part through the literature review.

## Limitations of the Study

The utilisation of questionnaires may be considered a limitation of this study. Some may argue that insufficient information is gleaned in a single snap shot questionnaire to provide credibility of findings. The aim however, was to capture an initial response to questions asked within a limited timeframe.

Lack of face to face interviews, or focus group discussions may also be seen as a limitation in this study. Interviews or focus groups could have added further dimensions to the study and may have gleaned more indepth responses. A future study could well explore similar questions with some focus groups to aid in triangulation of data collection.

## Findings and Discussion

The findings from this study reveal that mentoring relationships have a key role to play in developing leadership capabilities amongst educators. Indeed, this research has endorsed Clutterbuck and Megginson's (1999) claim that the mentoring relationship is ideally one of collegiality, offering a safe opportunity for leaders to experiment with new and alternative strategies, as they build a shared body of knowledge from a collective inquiry stance (Cochran-Smith, 2004).

Both the Finnish and New Zealand data highlight three key findings. First, mentoring relationships cultivate the building of professional capability. Second, they foster professional learning communities and solidarity amongst leaders. Third, mentoring relationships facilitate the development of a sense of professional identity and cooperation. An area of challenge to the realisation of efficacious mentoring relationships was also identifiable in the data. The following section briefly discusses each of these findings within the context of the relevant literature.

## Building Professional Capability

In both the Finnish and New Zealand contexts, the utilisation of mentors from outside the respondent's school setting was found to be advantageous. The 'unique opportunities' (Jacobi, 1991) or building professional capability, afforded through a the development of a mentoring relationship with an external 'academic' or 'researcher' mentor, was perceived to be advantageous by some respondents.

Consistent with the literature, both case studies illustrated a number of ways in which leaders developed their own professional capability (Gorinski, Fraser & Ayo, 2004; Robertson, 2005) through reflection on their practice. Respondents commented, for example:

> My personal growth [has been] significant
>
> I have learned new ways of doing things through discussion over good practice. I have a wider perspective on leadership.
>
> [Mentoring has] encouraged self reflection and challenged me to problem solve, by steering me and guiding me to discover solutions, or see things in a different way.

Respondents also spoke of the importance of the mentoring relationship (Daloz, 1991; Gorinski, 1997; Kram, 1985; Smit & McMurray, 1999) in building their professional capability, saying:

> This relationship has supported me both personally and professionally.
>
> I would not have the skill or confidence to do this [lead] if 1 wasn't supported through this relationship.
>
> It [mentoring] has enabled me to think ...about strategy, ensuring it's based on strong pedagogical foundations.

The opportunity to discuss professional matters with a mentor either in individual, group or staff settings, wag perceived as valuable by respondents (Macky & Johnson, 2002). The mentoring process facilitated both professional confidence and competence amongst respondents who noted:

> [The mentoring relationship] has provided me with a safe and supportive safety net to take risks and confront issues.
>
> I now realise that multifaceted issues have multifaceted solutions.

In the Finnish context, more teachers found staff (54%) and group mentoring (53%) arrangements useful, compared to individual mentoring situations, which only 32 per cent of teachers found beneficial. Staff mentoring sessions involved all staff working with a mentor to address issues, whilst group mentoring sessions involved smaller clusters of teachers working together to explore shared areas of concern (Cochran-Smith, 2004). In the Finnish case study, the best results in terms of enhanced leader and/or efficacy, were achieved when participants experienced personal, as well as staff and group mentoring relationships. This was consistent with the literature that suggests that mentoring and coaching relationships can provide a catalyst for the development of professional learning communities (Louis et.al, 1996; Bryk, et. al, 1999).

## Professional Learning Communities and Solidarity

The data strongly suggest that teacher efficacy is enhanced through the development of professional learning communities that utilise mentoring relationships as a mechanism for strengthening educational practice and inquiry (Bambino, 2002; Fullan, 2001; Leithwood, 1992). Ninety seven per cent of Finnish respondents identified that a sense of community was cultivated as a result of the mentoring relationship. Similarly, New Zealand case study respondents commented on the benefits of mentoring, in terms of fostering collegiality and collaboration:

> I have developed collaborative approaches to problem solving, taking into accounts all viewpoints... . I am able to challenge colleagues to challenge and address their practice.

> The ability to get together with other school leaders is good for the whole [educational] community.
>
> I am able to share leadership with colleagues. This is all due to the exemplars I have in X [mentor].
>
> The professional knowledge l have gained can be shared through as many mediums as possible

The development of shared values and the solidarity arising from that was highlighted in the findings. For example, respondents commented:

> l believe educational research, debate and decision making needs to be primarily the responsibility of practising teaching professionals.
>
> Decision making always affects the needs of students. It's haw these decisions impact on the lives of stakeholders that we care about.

The data clearly show that mentoring relationships do impact upon the growth and development of leadership capability (Robertson, 2005) as educators work cooperatively together developing their professional identity and agency.

## Developing Professional Identity and Agency

A macro level outcome from the mentoring relationships in both the Finnish and New Zealand contexts, was the development of a professional identity amongst respondents and a corresponding conception of agency (Otero & West-Burnham, 2006; Robertson, 2005). The Finnish case study highlighted the strong sense of inadequacy that teachers and leaders experienced as a result of lack of funding for professional development activities. Despite the limitations in terms of ongoing professional learning, the research identified that Finnish educators articulated clearly defined positions in terms of goal setting, problem solving and action planning, three key ingredients of agentic practice (Otero & West-Burnham, 2006).

In the New Zealand context, respondents spoke of their developed sense of professional identity:

> Working as a mentor has exposed me to the processes behind changes in education. When I was just teaching I simply dealt with the changes as they happened with little thought as to why changes were made or the agenda of those who influenced the change.
>
> I know my ideas are validated and respected, and so I implement them or give my opinion, I have learned to listen to others.
>
> I am confident that I can enter into a discussion/debate an the realities of [schooling experiences].

## Challenge

The contrast between teacher and/or principal demands for professional development through a mentoring relationship, and a lack of prioritised funding to support this, was identified as a barrier to growing leadership capability in the Finnish context. Indeed, axiological issues, that is, issues that deal with the role that values play in a study, appear to provide serious challenges in the Finnish context. The immediate prospects for enhanced professional learning afforded via mentoring relationships, appear to be extremely limited because of municipality financial constraints. This was perceived by some respondents as both a barrier to professional up-skilling, as well as a values-based issue.

In sum, the data illustrate a number of ways in which mentoring relationships support the development of leadership capability. The challenge lies in facilitating the discourse and practice that will build school's receptivity to the implementation of a mentoring based model of leadership.

## Conclusion

This study highlights the ways in which mentoring relationships have the potential to build both leadership capability and agency amongst educators. The findings suggest that efficacious mentoring relationships provide a mechanism for the building of professional capability, professional learning communities and professional identity and cooperation amongst school leaders.

The New Zealand and Finnish education systems are quite disparate. This study however, highlights the similar outcomes emerging from the research in these two differing contexts. Ongoing work will continue to explore the most useful mechanism for defining a mentoring strategy that develops leadership capability.

Education is perhaps the most powerful institution in any society, and teachers and principals are its most powerful agents. Education is also a powerful force for construction. It can produce leaders who are capable of creating communities of learning that transcend international boundaries. There are multiple challenges we as educators face in contributing to the development of such leaders. Mentoring relationships however, provide a strategy for growing leadership capacity and agency in educational contexts. The investigation of its potential remains a challenge to be explored.

## References

Allen, D. & Poteet, M.L. (1999): 'Developing effective mentoring relationships: Strategies from the mentor's viewpoint'. *The Career Development Quarterly* Vol., 48, No. 1, pp. 59-73.

Anderson, G. (1990). *Fundamentals of Educational Research.* London: Falmer Press.

Angelique, H., Kyle, K. & Taylor, E. (2002): 'Mentors and muses: New strategies for academic success'. *Innovative Higher Education,* Vol.26, No.3, pp. 195-209.

Bambino, D. (2002). Critical friends, *Educational Leadership,* March, Vol. 59, No. 6, pp. 25-27.

Bird, T. (1985). From teacher to leader: Training and support for mentor teachers, master teachers and teacher advisors, Cited in N. Zimpher & S. Reiger (1988). Mentoring Teachers: What are the Issues? *Theory into Practice* 27 (3), 175-182.

Bogdan, R., & Biklen, S. (1992), *Qualitative Research for Education: An Introduction to Theory and Methods.* (2nd Ed.), Boston: Allyn & Bacon.

Bryk, A., Camburn, E., & Louis, K.S. (1999). Professional community in Chicago elementary schools: Facilitating factors and organisational consequences. *Educational Administration Quarterly,* 35 (Special Issue), pp. 751-781.

Burns, R. (1994), *Introduction to Research Methods,* Melbourne: Longman House.

Clutterbuck, D. & Megginson, D. (1999), *Mentoring Executives and Directors*. London: Kogan Page.

Cochran-Smith, M. (2004): 'Preparing teachers for the 21st century: Research and teacher learning'. *Teachers as Learners: Challenges and Strategies from Global Perspectives*. Hong Kong.

Cook, M.F. (1979): 'Is the mentor relationship primarily a male experience?' *Personnel Administrator*, Vol.24, No.11, pp.82-86.

Darwin, A. (2000): 'Critical reflections on mentoring in work settings'. *Adult Education Quarterly*, Vol.50, No.3, pp.197-212. Retrieved May 3, 2004, from http:web15.epnet.com

Daloz, L. (1991): 'Mentorship', in Galbraith, M. (ed.), *Adult Learning Methods*. Malabar: Kreiger, pp. 205-225.

Daresh, J.C. & Playko, M.A. (1990). 'Mentoring for effective school administration'. *Urban Education*, Vol. 25, No.1, 43-53.

Field, B., & Field, T. (1990. *Teachers as Mentors: A Practical Guide*. London: The Falmer Press.

Fullan, M. (2001). *Leading in a Culture of Change*. San Francisco: Jossey Bass.

Gorinski, R. (1997). Beyond Mentoring: A Model of Transformative Discipleship in Christian Teacher Education. Unpublished PhD Thesis. The University of Waikato, Hamilton New Zealand.

Gorinski, R., Fraser. C., & Ayo, L. (2007). Mentoring as a key strategy in the development of a community of reflective practitioners in tertiary education. In O. Kwo & M. Mason (Eds.). *Teachers as Learners. Challenges and Strategies from a Global Perspective*. Hong Kong: Springer Publications.

Hargrove, R. (1994). *Masterful Coaching*. San Francisco: Jossey-Bass.

Holloway, J. (2003, March). 'Mentoring for diversity'. *Educational Leadership*. 88-89.

Huberman, A., & Miles, M. (1994). Information management and analysis methods. In N. Denzin & Y. Lincoln (Eds.), *Handbook of Qualitative Research*, 428-444. London: Sage Publications.

Jacobi, M. (1991). Mentoring and undergraduate success: A literature review. *Review of Educational Research*, 61 (4), 502-532.

Johnson-Bailey, J., & Cervero, R. (2004). 'Mentoring in black and white: The intricacies of cross-cultural mentoring'. *Mentoring and Tutoring*, Vol. 12, No. 1, 7-22.

Kram, K. (1985). *Mentoring at work: Developmental Relationships in Organisational Life*. Glenview, FL: Scott Foresman & Co.

Leithwood, K. (1992). The move toward transformational leadership, *Educational Leadership*, Vol. 49, No. 5, 8-12.

Louis, K., Marks, H., & Kruss, S.D. (1996). Teacher professional community in restructuring schools. *American Educational Research Journal*, 33 (4), 757-798.

Lucas, K. (2001). 'The social construction of mentoring roles'. *Mentoring and Tutoring*, Vol.9, No. 1, 23-47.

Macky, K., & Johnson, G. (2002). *Managing Human Resources in New Zealand*. Sydney: McGraw-Hill.

Merriam, S. (1988). *Case Study Research in Education: A Qualitative Approach*. San Francisco: Jossey Bass.

Otero, G., & West-Burnham, J. (2006). *Educational Leadership and Social Capital*. Course Readings paper PROF 580-06A. The University of Waikato, Hamilton.

Parsloe. E. (1999). *The Manager as Coach and Mentor*. India: Universities Press.

Playko, M. (1991). 'Mentors for administrators: Support for the instructional leader'. *Theory into Practice*, Vol. 30, No.2, 124-127.

Rix, T., & Gold, J. (2000). "'With a little help from my academic friend': Mentoring change agents". *Mentoring and Tutoring*. Vol.8, No. 1, 47-62.

Robertson, J. (2005). *Coaching Leadership: Building Educational Leadership Capacity through Coaching Partnerships*. Wellington: NICER Press.

Rudman, R. (1998). *Human Resources Management in New Zealand: Contexts and Process* (Fourth edition). Auckland: Longman Paul.

Smit, A., & McMurray, D. (1999). 'Mentoring as a tool of the modern learning organisation'. In Zepke, N., Knight. M. Leach, L. & Viskovic, A. (eds.), *Adult Learning Cultures Challenges, Choices and the Future*. Wellington: Wellington Polytechnic.

Stake, R. (1994). Case studies. In N. Denzin & Y. Lincoln (Eds.), *Handbook of Qualitative Research*, 236-247. London: Sage Publications

Stalker, J. (1992). 'Athene in academe: Women mentoring women in the academy'. *International Journal of Lifelong Education*, Vol. 13, No. 5, 361-372.

Yin, R. (1989). *Case Study Research: Design and Methods*. Beverly Hills, California: Sage Publications.

Zepke, N., Nugent, D., & Leach, L. (2003). *Reflection to Transformation*. A Self Help Book for Teachers. Palmerston North: Dunmore Press.

# 8

# Empowering Women for Educational Leadership

*—Hemlata Talesra*

The last hundred years may rightly be called the age of women awakening in the world. In every part of the world equality of the sexes has been ensured, various laws have been passed to improve the status of women. But on the contrary, in spite of all changes women cannot be regarded as being emancipated from orthodoxy, the old traditions and customs determined to the flowering of their personalities.

This paper makes an attempt to analyse the status of women and suggest strategy for their empowerment in educational leadership.

The social and religious attitude towards the role of women in the family and society, which still have a strong hold on the minds of the people, are the main hurdles in the way of social progress of women. In India and some other countries, society is still male-dominated. The double standards of morality graciously provide more social freedom to men than to women. The major burden of adjustment and the household work falls mainly on the women.

Age-old attitude and customs have made women accept their position, which in the words of Bertrand Russel, means 'mental prison'. Women's position in the home and outside of it is so closely interlinked that it is very difficult to separate them. The position of a woman in the home would refer to two aspects of a person: social position role and status—role, referring to obligations and duties, and status referring to rights, privileges, power prestige.

Women are perceived to be weak and in need of protection and to be confined to home. A woman's role may be that of daughter, wife or mother. In the name of protecting them, they are exploited. They have problems like malnutrition, exploitation, rape, dowry, violence and repeated childbirth which they have had to face. On the basis of data collected for my Ph.D work on 'Higher Education among Women' (1985), in Rajasthan Mewar, the erstwhile princely state there was a strategy to keep the women away from awakening. The feudals created a kind of social structure within their princely states that had an inbuilt resistance to female education. Short of insecurity compelled the masses to keep the movements of their young daughters restricted only to their courtyard or to the close vicinity of the house. The practice of marriage, including child marriage, female infanticide, seclusion of widows in the dark corners of the house and the overall law status assigned to women kept them far in the background all through the period of feudal history. The women were required to toil in the fields or house day in and day out without expecting anything beyond what was needed for mere subsistence. People from the lower sections of the feudal society often stand in need of borrowing money from the moneylenders and this compels them to agreements of bonded labour offering the services of females to the moneylender. These services are normally in lieu of payment of the interest for the loan borrowed.

The Maharanas and the jagirdars practice polygamy. They had a number of wives and concubines in their rajmahals and ravalas. Quite a large number of concubines passed a miserable life in the palaces. They were at the mercy of the will and honour of the rulers. The practice of polygamy, a status symbol was also imitated by the higher caste Hindus. This practice consequently pulled the status of women down in general. Women living in the palace or havala could not be approached by any male except the ruler or the thakur. Even the teenagers were not allowed to see behind the curtain or the beauties of the palace. The purdah system was meant to keep the movement of women restricted to the four walls of the house. It denied them all opportunities of widening their views and outlook of the world. Though the custom is now on its last legs, yet it has its hold among the conservative sections of the society.

The Rajputs who belonged to the ruling class had a tendency to look down upon women. According to them it was difficult to maintain their virginity. They were the warriors and therefore they did not want to take the responsibility of protecting women. This gave rise to institution of female infanticide. This practice definitely lowered the status of women in the society.

By the end of the nineteenth century there came some awakening among the people of the different states of Rajputana. Whatever little efforts were made regarding women awakening and development were all in the interest of the oppressors.

My study reveals that higher education is a strong factor to empower the women and in moulding her total personality. But in theory it is open for all. It has a reality become a privilege of the few. In a sample of 500 students 30 per cent belong to Baniya caste, 27 Brahmins and 11 Rajputs. About 75 per cent of women students who go to college belong to the higher caste. The professional courses (medicine, agriculture, home science, etc.) are grabbed by the top high caste Hindus. Weaker sections of the society are losers in getting higher education. I would say that structurally speaking women's higher education today is for high caste, rich class, urban people and higher income group. Only high caste and higher class women are being empowered.

My study shows that there has come some social change among the educated women — strangely enough about 80 per cent of women like to live in a joint family. About 62 per cent of women stand for higher age at marriage whcih is 18 years. Strangely enough educated women do not stand for the eradication of dowry. This seems due to lack of empowerment.

## Empowerment of Women for Educational Leadership

Education for women has gradually gained increased recognition from the time our country has won her freedom. Literacy campaigns have indeed raised women's hopes and desires to achieve freedom from ignorance and economic dependence particularly when these are oriented towards socio-economic development. Even the rural and the urban under-privileged women, though small in number but significant as a group, have now begun to articulate and act as a pressure group to demand justice and fairness in all dealings that concerns them most, whether it is in obtaining drinking water or access to health schemes or public distribution system or education or participation in employment generation programmes of the government.

At the grassroots level eventful and appreciable success stories are being reported about the achievements made by women groups from different parts of our country. They are *jathas* or *yatras*, *rallies* and street plays with major thrust on important select themes like legal control overland, anti-arrack movement, anti-dowry and injustices, ill tratement of women, environmental protection campaigns (Chipko movement), like Jungle Bachao Yatras, Save Narmada agitation and so on besides demands for basic needs like drinking water, health services, etc. These movements are probably the ethos or the spillover effect of the education and conscious group of women spread over in different parts of the country.

Despite widespread illiteracy and ignorance, women in recent years have gradually become conscious of the need for liberating themselves from male suppression and economic dependence. A large number of women in different parts of the country are making significant moves to struggle for empowerment. Progress of women in terms of literacy over a period of four decades is satisfactory. In 1951 it was 8.86 per cent and in 1991 it was 39.41 per cent. The importance of women's education is perpetually emphasized in full measure by the government, and special provisions are being made to educate them and also to improve their socio-economic status.

Today women have acquired new dimensions, educated and armed with knowledge and skills. They has entered formal work-setting delinking themselves from their social structure and network of relationships, like their male counterparts; they have entered in the world of occupation, career, profession, competition and achievement in their own right and created the need to experience themselves and be accepted as automous beings.

Woman now aspires and struggles to establish a professional status or career and economic independence. Previously the main occupations open to women were those of teachers, doctors and social workers. Now a whole panorama of careers has opened up before them. They has entered the fields of science, engineering and arduous and strenuous jobs, like men have done. They are successfully performing the tough and hard jobs of military and police.

Bringing about a profound social change through new networks of female solidarity, drawing spiritual sustenance from her identification with the goddess, the collective heroine has the potential to accomplish on the global scale what she has humbly been doing at the family and the village level nurturing, energising and redeeming. Invested with the power as well as the responsibility, she seems to incorporate a new vision of 'Shakti' and 'street hero'.

Equal opportunities for education and development are imperative to empower women. They have shown their worth in myriad fields. Ms.Tarjani Vakil, the Chairperson and the Managing Director of the Export Import Bank of India, Ms Kiran Bedi, Bachendri Pal, Dicky Dolma—the list is endless—have shown that given an opportunity, women can excel men in any field. A large number of urban and educated women are enjoying the facilities providing for their educational upliftment. They are giving leadership to make the masses conscious about women's education. But all these educational provisions, developmental support and assistance have made trivial impact on rural and tribal women. Even the legitimate right to education accorded to a girl is hardly ever used by those who have remained by hereditary non-educated in the rural and tribal areas.

A large variety of socio-economic and development generation programmes for women in rural and tribal areas which are aimed at developing their status in the society have been introduced but with lesser or least impact on them. It is a stark reality to witness women as a major group remaining educationally and economically exploited by their own counterpart. A case in point is the introduction of Development of Women and Children in Rural Areas (DWCRA). Various evaluate studies of the socio-economic programmes like IRDP, Nehru Rozgar Yojana, etc., discovered that women were seldom included as beneficiaries. In 1985, for instance, only 9 per cent of

IRDP beneficiaries were females against a target of 30 per cent. It is certain that rural women are not aware of several programmes offered to them and even so, they have no means of knowing how to utilise these opportunities to their own benefit.

International development have been challenged in recent decades. Different studies (Agrawal 1988, Bakar 1987, Bala Krishnan 1990, Pietella, 1990) indicate that families and households have been viewed as the best and most efficient. Negative impact on women, if such occurred, was thought to be temporary. National policies affected development programmes and opportunities for women and families to participate in and benefit from development. The status and position of women have increased and technology changes have led to role shifts in families.

Urbanisation is a mark of development that may increase women's isolation or increase their networks, education and job access. Women reshape their traditional roles and create viable new ones. Modernity has emphasized Western values. Professional efforts have fostered an orientation to Western lifestyles, economic development and facilitated transfer in Western perspectives.

### Strategies for Empowerment of Women for Educational Leadership

What are strategies for empowerment of women for educational leadership? Strategies are based on a belief that resources and choices have not necessarily or successfully 'trickled down' as a result of opportunities afforded to women in development efforts. The following recommendations were presented at a forum sponsored by the International Federation of Home Economics which preceded the 1990 meeting of the UN Commission on the Status of Women.

— The potential economic values of girls to parents should be established. Income-generating training to adolescent girls which will require literacy training and primary education should be given.

— Increase income available over the long term for food, health care and education, so that goods and services are in sufficient supply for distribution at household levels.

This strategy may entail increasing women's income to meet family needs.

- It is urgent for communities and governments to work together to resolve the 'double-day' syndrome (ever-increasing time pressure on women to balance and contribute to both household and market work). Both men and women must be involved in this dialogue and in experiments and incentives for reducing the double day. The key message should be delivered by mass communication and traditional media using local people to sensitise families and societies in this effort.
- It is important to encourage and document men's increase towards family work and parenting responsibilities in households where women work to pay. It is important to identify discrepancies between societal and male support system expectations and family expectations which may militate against changes in work, resource allocation and child socialisation responsibilities among family members. Educational programmes should formulate strategies to overcome these inconsistencies and support men wishing to participate in emerging family roles.
- Coalitions of women and men allies can be promoted to press for change in men's family roles and privileges through a combination of strategies, i.e., focus on rightness and fairness of men's full participation; emphasis on comprehensive family management for all members; and education in the process or give and take in exchange for mutually satisfactory benefits.
- A consensus is needed on an developmental framework which identifies, assesses the priorities and needs reflecting accurately women's conditions relative to poverty, lack of education, overwork and their position relative to men in families.
- Gender equity and empowerment may be facilitated not only by socialisation but by education of girls as well as boys to perceive themselves as productive persons in family setting, and to perceive the economic and social worth of both reproductive and productive work in families.

— Families life courses should be promoted, so that men and women students, as part of the general education, study families in their own and other countries and issues of gender in international and national development, and have opportunities to become sensitive and aware of equity and empowerment issues.

Besides the above strategies the Programme of Action for the Naitonal Policy on Education 1986 guides that by 1995 every educational institution should take up a study and awareness of the women's predicament, and promote a strong self-image among women.

Miss V. Ushasri's study on conditions and problems of women perceived by women students suggests that each woman should fight bravely the problem she faces. Educated women should lend support to the illiterate women to build up greater self-confidence and courage.

In Baroda a school exclusively for women, Manasi, offered different programmes from cooking to sex education, from art and culture to computers, and from fashion designing to finance and many other things to make a complete woman in other words to empower women in different fields; improve her personality, give basic knowledge in health and beauty care, home management, general etiquette, table manners, child care, English conversation and about her legitimate rights in property and inheritance.

9

# Educational Reforms and Their Impact on Leadership

*—Joy G. Nkukwana*

After 1994 South Africa became a democratic country. The African National Congress (ANC)-led government came into power, following an era of colonialism and apartheid. Several educational reforms were made as an effort to redress the imbalances of the past, to make education accessible and equitable to all its citizens, and to promote democracy in schooling. It is, therefore, imperative to recreate linkages between theory and practice in order for the transformation to be successful.

The theoretical framework of this paper is founded on contextual realism. The main question addressed by this paper is: "What impact do educational reforms have on educational leadership?" The arguments presented in this paper are derived from a survey conducted on 20 principals and 30 Bachelor of Education Honours students in Educational Management. The qualitative data gathered in the survey indicated that respondents found that most of the reforms had a negative impact on educational leadership, compared to those which had a positive impact. The most cited reforms that they perceived as impacting negatively on leadership are the curriculum changes, the abolition of corporal punishment, the introduction of school governing bodies, the no fee schools, the inclusive education policy, the redeployment of educators and the language policy. Reviewed literature confirmed some revelations made by respondents that some theories impacted negatively on leadership. Literature also revealed that there was a gap between theory and practice and also between policy and praxis, that some policies were driven by political imperatives to the exclusion of practical considerations, based on the ideal and not the real.

The main theme of this conference is "Recreating linkages between theory and praxis." This paper addresses this theme from the perspective of educational reforms and their impact on leadership. The focus is on school reforms and school leadership, which refers to the Principal and the Heads of Departments (HoDs).

The motivation to conduct this study is my observation, with concern, at the rate at which educational reforms are made and changed in a short period and given out to schools to implement without involving all stakeholders involved in education in their design or in the adequate training of all implementers.

When theory is not linked to practice and policy to praxis, this creates a gap (policy practice 'gap') or becomes symbolic as Jansen (2002:199) puts it, or the 'distance between policy and practice'.

In order to close the gap between theory and practice, transformational leadership is necessary. For leadership to be catalyst of change, they need to be involved or else well informed about the envisaged change. They need to be part of the designing process of the intended reform in order for them to own the results, and thus be able to communicate it to their subordinates and monitor its proper implementation. By so doing the contextual realities will be addressed in order to try to reach the ideal situation. The gap that exists between theory and practice or policy and praxis is due to the absence of participation in designing and the knowledge of the reforms, and most likely the rationale behind the design of such reforms. A conclusion arrived at, drawn from the findings, was that contextual, realism was over looked in favour of idealism in the passing and implementing of these policies.

## Background

Since South Africa's first national democratic elections in 1994, the Government of National Unity issued several curriculum-related reforms intended to democratise education and eliminate inequalities of the past colonial and apartheid education systems.

Educational reforms are generally designed to improve the quality of schooling. This was very crucial to South Africa in particular, because of its colonial and apartheid history to promote transformation.

Formal education during the colonial era was introduced by missionaries whose main aim was to convert "heathens or slaves" (Van Zyl in Lemmer & Badenhorst, 1997:53-54). According to Van Zyl in Lemmer & Badenhorst (1997:52-53):

> The British, too, played a role in establishing separate education. They ruled the Cape from 1795 to 1803 and annexed it again in 1806. Apart from their efforts to anglicise the Cape in terms of the medium of instruction in order to make it worthy of the British Empire they also played a significant role in establishing separate education.

Consequently, separate education came to a climax in 1953. The Nationalists Party (NP), who coined the term 'apartheid,' came into power in 1948. The Nationalist Party consisted of predominantly Afrikaners. The Bantu Education Act No 47 of 1953 based on the recommendations of the Eiselen Commission of Native Education was designed to promote apartheid education. This Act made formal education for Black people a state affair; until then it was provided mainly by mission schools. This education was geared towards meeting the demands of semi-skilled labour in the expanding factories. Although the Blacks were to serve the economy, they were not considered full members of the elite (White) society. The intention of securing hegemony for Whites was clear from the views of the NP. There were 19 departments of education in South Africa.

The then Nationalist Minister of Native Affairs, Dr. H. F. Verwoerd, argued:

> When I have control of native education I will reform it so that natives will be taught from childhood to realise that equality with Europeans is not fit for them...People who believe in equality are not desirable teachers for natives (Troup, 1976:22).

Dr Verwoerd later maintained that there was no need to teach Blacks mathematics and science, arguing that what is the need to show them greener pastures in which they will never graze. Apartheid education was thus characterised by segregation, along racial and ethnic lines, and the education for Blacks was the most inferior compared to that of other racial groups, the Coloureds, Indians and Whites. This reform impacted negatively on Blacks. Even today the country lacks Black teachers to teach these subjects. The country is dependent on expatriates to teach the said subjects.

It is believed that when one wants to relegate a people to subservience, education is the best weapon to do that. This is evident from the past two eras. This history has negatively impacted on the majority of the indigenous people's education and their socio-economic status, because they were disadvantaged and marginalised by both the colonial and apartheid laws. This, in turn, has had a negative effect on the development of the country. Hence, South Africa is still regarded and rated a developing country because education is regarded as key to development. Hence, after the 1994 elections in South Africa, when the democratic government came into power, this paved, way to a flurry of policies to 'purge' the ills of the past. The following section gives a brief account of the reforms which were made.

## Educational Reforms in South Africa

The energies of the Minister of Education during the first period of democratic rule were applied to creating a sound legislative policy framework for educational transformation. Key policies and legislation in this phase included:

- The South Africa's (SA) Constitution, Act No. 108 of 1996, which required that education be transformed and democratised in accordance with values of human dignity, equality, human rights and freedom, non-racism and non-sexism.
- The National Education Policy Act No.27 of 1997 (NEPA), designed to inscribe in law the policy, legislative and monitoring responsibilities of the Minister of Education and formalise the relations between national and provincial authorities.

— The South Africans Schools Act No. 84 of 1996 (SASA) to promote access, quality and democratic governance in the schooling system.

— The Further Education and Training Act (1998), Education White Paper 4 on Further Education and Training (1998) and National Strategy for Further Education and Training (1999-2001), which provides the basis for developing a nationally coordinated Further Education and Training system, comprising the senior secondary and technical colleges.

— The Higher Education Act (1997), which makes provision for a unified and nationally planned system of higher education which provides advice to the Minister responsible for quality and assurance and promotion.

— The Adult Basic Education and Training (ABET) Act (2000), which provides for public and private adult learning centres, funding for ABET provisioning, the governance of public centres, and quality assurance mechanisms for the sector.

— The SA Qualifications Authority Act No.58 of 1995 that provides for the creation of the National Qualifications Framework (NQF), which establishes the scaffolding of a national learning system that integrates education and training at all levels.

— Curriculum 2005 which was envisaged for a general education which would move away from a racist, apartheid, rote learning teaching, to liberating nation-building, learner-centred outcomes based one.

— A range of legislation, including the Employment of Educators Act (1998), to regulate the professional, moral and ethical responsibilities and competences of teachers.

All the above stated reforms are cited from a range of policy documents issued by the Department of Education (DoE), and were "a first attempt to purge the apartheid curriculum of racially offensive and outdated content" (Jansen, (1997).

One of the most plausible reforms made was the infusion of the 19 different departments of education into one national department of education catering for the different racial groups

(Harber, 2001:12). Thereafter, the most comprehensive of these reforms was the Curriculum 2005 underpinned by the outcomes-based education (OBE) approach. This is said to be the most ambitious curriculum policy since the Government of National Unity. No wonder that it is the most cited reform which impacts negatively on leadership, as will be discussed later under the findings.

Reforms entail transformation, which is change for the better. However, change is not easy. Change threatens the status quo; change needs one to move away from one's comfort zone, and to explore new avenues. There is uncertainty of whether the expected outcomes will be achieved.

> All real change involves loss, anxiety and struggle... Ambivalence will pervade the transition (Fullan, 1991:31)

Change is coupled with resistance, especially if change has not been well managed. Managing change includes, orienting people about the change, proper advocacy, preparing people for change and over and above all, involving key people in the designing and preparation for implementation, shared decision-making so that people can own the decision taken, and thus they will enthusiastically and willingly implement and monitor for the achievement of desired goals.

The period between the announcement of the reform and its actual implementation is the period of transition. Transition is not trajectory or transient. There are no short-cuts to educational transformation. Transformation in education, in particular, does not take a short time as planners usually anticipate, especially where humans are involved. There is a lot that is at stake, most seriously the child's mind. Damage done in the child's mind is irreparable.

Educators and principals are regarded as agents of change, but while some are receptive to change, others resist change. Change deskills. This is particularly true to leadership whose main function is to influence the people to change.

Some of the people in leadership position were taught during the apartheid era, when education was teacher-centred, now all of a sudden the approach has to be learner-centred, quite a paradigm shift, without being adequately prepared. Some claim to have attended a few hours' briefings, not proper workshops. Some claim to have attended workshops for only a day or two days or a week, and are expected to implement with immediate effect. At times some do not even attend these workshops claiming that the facilitators admit not knowing what they were doing themselves.

For South Africa to successfully implement the reforms, it needs transformational or transformative leadership that which involves "building a shared vision, improving communication, developing collaborative decision-making and problem-solving processes" (Huber (1998:14). As Rail (2004) puts it, "Leadership is coupled to change; it makes change real." This is true if the leadership embraces the change.

This also applies to the instructional leadership, which on the other hand, focuses on the so-called first order changes: improving the technical, organisational, instructional activities of the school, for instance, through close monitoring of educators' and learners' classroom work (Oduro, 2005:7). Leithwood (1992:9) explains that a transformational leader empowers those who participate in the change process. A pertinent question is: "How can leaders be transformative when they are ignorant of or uncomfortable about the very changes they are expected to implement, facilitate and monitor?" When there has been inadequate preparation of the leadership, it is obvious they will have negative attitudes towards the reforms and there will be no successful implementation. In such a case, there will be a knowledge gap that will further result in a gap between theory and practice and policy and praxis.

My main claim is that the educational leadership should fully understand these educational reforms in order for them (leadership) to be able to facilitate the successful implementation of the reforms, because the educational leadership should be catalysts of change. They can only have true knowledge of these policies or reforms if they are involved in their development and participated in designing them, in order to own them and be able and willingly put them into practice, otherwise the gap between theory and practice and policy and praxis will remain there or will widen instead.

## Methodology

This study sought to understand what impact educational reforms have on educational leadership and subsequent questions; how educational reforms impact on leadership and; which educational reforms impact on leadership. The study was guided by an interpretivist paradigm, which aimed at capturing the lived experiences and perceptions of the participants in their natural setting. The interpretive tradition of social enquiry, according to Carr & Kemmis (1986:83, 87), assumes that actions have meaning in relation to understanding, purpose and intentions of the actor, and the actor's interpretations of the significance of the context of the action. It is descriptive, with the view to try to understand human action; interpretive to present reality of participants from their own viewpoint (,cabbie & Mouton, 2003:28-33; Henning, van Rensburg & Smit, 2004:19-22. It enables the researcher to put himself in the shoes of the individual and by so doing, learn through the process of interaction what perceptions, interpretations and meanings the individual attaches to his actions (Adler & Adler, 1987; Catrell, 1993; Denzin & Lincoln, 2000). The interpretive research offered me the opportunity to work in a natural setting, thereby creating a congenial atmosphere for the participants to talk about their work.

## Population and Sampling

The 20 Principals who were participants in this study were conveniently selected and the 30 postgraduate students in Educational Management were opportunistically and conveniently sampled. This sample may appear to be limited or small but, in addition to the two samples, the researcher had the opportunity to interact with principals, Hobs, while supervising Teaching Practice students since 1999. Discussions were held with postgraduate students studying for the Bachelor of Education Honour Degree (B. Ed. Hons) in Educational Management, since 2001. The researcher became aware of some of the challenges they are faced with regarding the educational reforms. In addition, the challenges the Teaching Practice students, the lecturers as supervisors, and the subject teachers as well at the schools in which they were practising, were faced with before the National Curriculum Statement (NCS) was implemented in Grade 10 in

2006. The samples added or confirmed what had been established from the other groups.

## Instrument Used for the Study

This article used evidence obtained from qualitative data collected by using a questerview, a questionnaire consisting of open-ended questions (Adamson et al., http://www..../query.fcgi-cmd) in Gwarinda (2006:2). The questerview was given to 20 principals and 30 B. Ed. Hons students. The latter composed of a mixed group consisting of principals, Heads of Departments (Hobs) and educators in schools from the neighbouring locations of the Butterworth Education District.

The questerview enabled the participants to respond to questions in writing. This also allowed them to respond in their own free time without the researches causing any unnecessary or additional pressure during their school ,time. The questerview also takes care of the validation and reliability of the date gathered. There is no need to go back to the participants to check whether what the researcher had captured or reported was what the participant had communicated. The questerview is an open-ended questionnaire which is used for collecting qualitative data (Adamson et al. as cited by Gwarinda (2006:3). Gwarinda further motivates the use of the questerview by explaining that "the use of open-ended questionnaires enables respondents to provide deeper and well thought-out answers than may be collected in a live interview." He also cites Postlethwaite (2005:5), who argues for the use of questionnaires in non-probability samples. A couple of closed questions were also included.

## Findings of the Study

There was a 75 per cent response rate including both samples, of the principals and the B. Ed. Honours students.

### Presenting and Discussing Findings

1. Do you thick linkages need to be recreated between theory and praxis? Yes or No.

   All replied with a "Yes"

2. If "yes". How?

The implementers should receive thorough in-service training.

3. Can educational reforms impact on leadership? Yes or No.

   All responded with a "yes".

4. Give reasons for your answer.

   i) When the leadership is left out and only educators are work-shopped, this creates a knowledge gap between that of the leadership and that of the educators, thus making it difficult for the leadership to monitor and mentor educators.

   ii) Once the policies change and there is no emphasis on the full participation of all stakeholders in the education arena the leadership style is bound to change.

   iii) Full external environment participation affects the leadership style.

5. Which educational reforms impact on leadership?

**i) Curriculum Changes — Curriculum 2005**

All (100%) respondents cited that the curriculum changes impact negatively on leadership. They feel that they had been left out in the whole process of designing, capacity building and implementation. They find it difficult to monitor because of inadequate advocacy and training. Some claim that in most cases the workshops for principals are not workshops *per se*, but just two hour briefings the most. They also complained that they are confused because there are so many changes to the curriculum that they are not sure as to which curriculum is actually being followed. One principal from the GET Band stated that he was not sure whether they are following the RNCS or the NCS.

At the time of this study, which was conducted in March, most educators had not attended any workshop for the NCS. The NCS workshops were only held during the June school holidays, yet the NCS for Grade 10 FET Band had already been implemented at the beginning of the year (2006). Therefore, the majority of educators, including the principals, had not had any training for the NCS, except for those who participated in the ACE Life Orientation (LO) and Mathematical Literacy (ML) Programmes from 2004 to 2005. The question is: What did the leadership and other educators teach between January and June when the NCS workshops had not been held? They say that the lack of empowerment make them feel powerless to monitor the successful implementation of the changes in curriculum. They say that in most cases they feel embarrassed because at times the educators, who are supposed to be their subordinates, know more than they do, there is a knowledge gap between the leadership and the educators.

What is worrying also is that some workshops which were to be held in June were disrupted by some logistical problems and these did not take place. The question is: What are the affected educators teaching in their classes? Even the two weeks which were scheduled for the workshops were not sufficient to adequately prepare the educators for a major curriculum change.

The majority of principals are not office-bound; they have classes that they teach, some teach Grade 12 classes. They complain about the short notice they are usually given to attend to meetings or workshops. This interferes with and disrupts their daily routine. This negatively affects the learners, as this takes them out of the classroom, and at the end of the year, they are expected to account for the failure rate.

The non-involvement and communication of the said workshops had some impact on the institutions of higher learning as well, because block sessions and examinations for educators who are pursuing higher qualifications, are normally scheduled to be held during school holidays. If institutions of higher learning are informed in good time of the intended changes and developments, they would be able to design programmes on time and schedule their timetables accordingly, to accommodate the changes. This would also assist the DoE in the training of the educators.

The anticipated positive effects of the new curriculum had been widely heralded with little criticism of these proposals, given the social and educational context of South African schools. It was envisaged that a good education system will produce the skills necessary for the country (The Education Policy, Act No. 27 of 1996). This is a system of education that will give everyone an equal opportunity to develop one's talents, accepts responsibility concerning the organisation, governance and funding of schools by all stakeholders (The South African Schools Act No 84 of 1996) (SASA).

The Curriculum had to be structured to reflect the country's new democratic society (Department of Education, 1997). A number of principles to guide the curriculum design were agreed upon:. Learner-centredness: Relevance: nation-building and non-discriminatory. Learning programmes had to encourage the development of mutual respect for diverse religions and value systems, cultural and language traditions, multilingualism and informed choices regarding the languages) and learning; cooperation, civic responsibility and the ability to participate in all aspects of society; an understanding of national, provincial, local and regional development needs.

Curriculum 2005 is not synonymous with outcomes-based education (OBE) as it is loosely referred to. OBE is the approach used in Curriculum 2005. Curriculum 2005 derived its name from the notion that if it will be phased in at Grade 1 level and Grade 7 in 1998, and the planners envisaged that by year 2003 it would have been implemented at Grade 12. The years 2004 and 2005 were considered for a provision for fundamental review of the new curriculum with a view of improving and refining the achievements of our curriculum goals (Bengu, 1997:18). The phasing in of the new Curriculum is illustrated in Table 3 below.

Table 1 NB: 2000 and 2001 are put in brackets to indicate a presumed correction; 2001 was inserted for Grades 3 and 9 and 2000 for Grades 4 and 10; 2003 was for phasing in Grades 6 and 12. This Table is adopted from the *Curriculum 2005: Lifelong Learning for the 21st Century* (Bengu, 1997:18).

*Table 3*

| *Grades* | *Year of Implementation* |
|---|---|
| 1 and 7 | 1998 |
| 2 and 8 | 1999 |
| 3 and 9 | 2000 |
| 4 and 10 | [2001] |
| 5 and 11 | [2002] |
| | 2003 |

According to Professor SME Bengu, the first Education Minister of the Democratic South Africa, "all teachers will be introduced to the outcomes-based approach in 1997. Facilitators will be trained in each province and will then be responsible for conveying the information to the teachers." He further states:

> Teachers of Grades 1 and 7 will be targeted for in-depth training and a field test will be run in the second half of 1997 in order to assess needs and pre-empt problems which might arise. The field tests will be managed in such a way that all types of schools will be included to give a clear picture of how the new curriculum will impact on schools across the board. The field tests will be extended to Grades 2 and 8 in 1998 and so on in the relevant grade every year thereafter, until full implementation has taken place.

As can be seen the theory looks good but the pertinent questions are: Was this theory successfully put into practice? If not, why? Was there enough consultation and involvement of envisaged implementers? Were the facilitators adequately trained? What was the duration of their training? Were Principals included in this training? Were college and university lecturers included in this training? Harber (2001:53) reveals that throughout 1996 and 1997, as the policy was being developed, there were regular complaints of lack of consultation and insufficient time to prepare and retrain. He cites, for example, the South African Democratic Teachers Union (SADTU) which said that the process was being driven by the bureaucracy and that there should be greater involvement of teachers and students and more time before it was introduced (Kgobe, 1996); Professor Danie Schroeder of Stellenbosch who described the lack of teacher involvement as a flaw, quoting him as saying, "Without teacher involvement is like the top management of a car manufacturing company designing a new model in the boardroom while on the factory floor workers are still manufacturing a 1954 model" (The Teacher, January 1997).

Further, Harber (2001:54) states that a study of 39 schools in KwaZulu Natal (KZN) revealed that:

— most Black schools had not implemented Curriculum 2005;

— most White schools believe that they have been doing OBE anyway and do not have to change anything; and

— White teachers had accumulated resources and support materials well beyond the short informal sessions provided by the provincial department of education, while Black teachers had very few support materials.

Harber (2001:54) maintains that 20,000 primary schools in rural areas had not implemented Curriculum 2005, for reasons such as lack of teacher preparation, lack of resources. Conversely, in many former Model C schools, teachers had resisted attending workshops or implementing the new curriculum, dismissing it as 'simplistic', 'repetitive' and 'watering down standards'. Across the country, most teachers expressed similar views. He argues that those teachers who had begun to implement OBE realised that there are particular practices that are required in order to make OBE work. (It should be noted that OBE is used synonymously with Curriculum 2005 in this study at times.)

A Report on research carried out by the Presidential Education Initiative, published in 1999, indicated that OBE is succeeding in the ideological domain, with teachers embracing its main intentions. However, many teachers did not have the conceptual resources to give effect to it in the classrooms. Some researchers observed significant contradictions between teachers' verbal support of the learner-centred pedagogy of Curriculum 2005 and the actual practices of these teachers.

The Presidential Education Initiative report stressed the importance of pre and in-service education programmes in helping teachers to develop a sound conceptual framework.

Harber (2001:54) states that local studies of the implementation of OBE in schools had also been conducted by students doing dissertation for higher degrees. He cites Russell (1998), his study of the introduction of OBE in thee primary schools in Durban, found that teachers were positive about OBE and felt that the learners were generally benefiting from the change. The teachers were beginning to alter their classroom practices but they also identified a range of important problems such as the top-down nature of the reform and the confusing speed of change, using the OBE approach with large classes of over 40 learners was problematic, and the increased administration caused by the routine of recording marks for continuous assessment.

The idea of all teachers to be introduced to the OBE approach was a very good one for collegiality and collaboration purposes. Principals and HODs are mentors and instructional leaders; they should have been the first to be trained for the implementation of the new curriculum. College and university lecturers are trainers of teachers they should have been involved in the planning, or if not, in being trained together with the facilitators.

Some critiques targeted the piecemeal implementation of OBE, they felt that it should have been introduced across the board (Mqingwana, 1998), and Harber (2000:47) also echoes these sentiments when he expressed his concern which was more on the process of assessment, arguing "...if OBE is to succeed, then school assessment at all levels, including the senior certificate, will have to be reformed." The researcher also shared the same sentiments.

Generally, the reception of the new curriculum was mixed. Some critiques in the media reported that OBE had failed in Britain and elsewhere, did not understand why South Africa had to adopt it. "If it had failed in developed countries, how will it succeed in a 3rd World country such as South Africa?" (Anecdotal evidence). Jansen (2000) was also a big critique of OBE. He mentioned ten reasons why OBE will fail in South Africa.

Most of the *Ten Reasons Why OBE will Fail* given by Jansen were related to the fact that the policy makers were driven by political imperatives, and the pressures for delivery. The planners were thinking about the ideal situation only without taking into consideration the contextual realities of the majority of schools which are in disadvantaged communities. Harber (2000:52) quotes Jansen who concludes by arguing "OBE should be seen as an act of political symbolism in which the primary preoccupation of the state is with its own legitimacy, particularly in terms of a political need for the Ministry of Education to be seen to be doing something towards school transformation." Harber (2000:23) echoes this by citing Dyanti (1999), a teacher who said, "How can we expect to teach our children about realities of a national crisis, when we want to ignore these realities"? Dyanti said this when teachers walkout of an HIV/AIDS lecture organised by the Gauteng Department of Education as a project to educate teachers/educators as part of the Government's Curriculum 2005 reform.

In February 2000, the second Minister of Education, Professor Kader Asmal, established a Review Committee, chaired by Professor Linda Chisholm of the University of Natal, following the criticisms and complaints from teachers. The report of this Committee was: "While there was an overwhelming support for OBE, Curriculum 2005 was too complex and confusing for most teachers to use and that implementation had been hampered by inadequate teacher training, lack of good quality support materials, policy overload and shortage of staff and resources. The Committee recommended a reduction in the number of learning areas from eight to six, scrapping of the 66 specific outcomes (but the critical outcomes) and also simplifying other complex assessment and performance measures" (MacGregor 2000b).

The researcher's greatest cause for concern is the various drastic changes which have been made to the Curriculum 2005 since 2000 and are still currently being made. These cause great confusion. Curriculum 2005 was implemented up to Grade 9 in the General Education and Training Band (GET) by 2000. The GET curriculum has already been reviewed and improved, and in 2004 Foundation Phase learners and educators started implementing the streamlined and strengthened Revised National Curriculum (RNCS). The RNCS was phased into the rest of the GET band from 2004 to 2008 (Eastern Cape Department of Education (ECDoE), 2005:2). Learners passing the GET band before OBE was phased in at Grade 10 (FET) were confronted with the traditional method after being exposed to OBE, from learning areas to subjects, and from the RNCS to the National Education Report (HATED) 550, an interim curriculum established in 2001, which still used the traditional method of teaching. It had also been very frustrating to lecturers, teacher trainees and subject teachers. Teacher trainees were being prepared for the New Curriculum, but when they were on Teaching Practice at High Schools, they had to observe subject teachers who were still using the traditional method. When their lecturers came to supervise them, they expected the teacher trainees to practise what they had taught them, the OBE approach. The subject teachers, who are expected to mentor the teacher trainees, still had no idea of OBE. There was this knowledge gap between the subject teachers, who are supposed to be mentors of the teacher-trainees. They did not bother to familiarise themselves with OBE because it was to be implemented in high schools only in 2000, which was later rescheduled to be implemented in 2006.

When 2006 came, the learner: educator ratio is still very high in certain schools in the townships in particular, some classes have over 100 learners, there is hardly any space for the educator to stand and write on the chalkboard. The rearranging of desks to suit the group work which is characteristic of the new curriculum is impossible. There is no space for the facilitator, as educators are referred to, to move between groups. In fact it is very impossible for the lecturer to get into the classroom to supervise the teacher trainees during Teaching Practice. Some learners sit in fours in a desk meant for two learners. In some schools where plastic chairs are used with desks, what one finds are more three-legged broken chairs or the steel chair frames used with the loose desk top to sit on. How much more to the educator who has to be in class at least two periods a day? The morale of the educators at the schools is very low. There is uncertainty, and even the leadership feels helpless. Only the Life Orientation and Mathematical literacy teachers got two-year training sponsored by the DoE, other educators including principals (managers) have not been work shopped for the National Curriculum Statement (NCS) which has been implemented at the beginning of the year (2006). Educators for Grade 10 will only attend a workshop for a week during the June 2006 school holidays. All the above information is given to draw a picture of the situation in disadvantaged communities — the contextual realities.

The latest development is that the GET Band is also now doing the NCS since last year, no longer the RNCS, which was supposed to have been phased in up to 200$ in this Band (B. Ed. Hons students who are educators in the GET Band).

As the Further Education and Training (FET) is the final gateway to higher education and the workplace, it became important that the changes be extended to FET learners. The policy framework had been in place for some time and learners in the FET band have been on the NATED 550. In this curriculum the language and content of the old syllabi had been 'cleansed' of offensive and racist and gender biases. Bigger changes in the form of the NCS has now put the FET curriculum more fully in line with the GET curriculum and the needs of the country (ECDoE, 2005:2).

Data reveal that the various changes that have taken place since the curriculum change in South Africa are a cause for concern and are causing such confusion and frustrating to the leadership who have to implement them, especially if they have not been involved in the planning nor had been adequately and timeously trained. They claim that it is frustrating in the sense that while one had just comprehended a change today the following day one had to study the new changes. It has also been very frustrating to trainers of educators (lecturers), how much more to the people who have to implement these changes daily? It is no wonder that all the participants cited the curriculum reforms as having a negative impact on them.

**ii) School Governing Bodies (SGBs)**

Ninety-nine per cent of the respondents felt that the introduction of SGBs is negatively impacting on leadership. According to the responses, this is so, because, firstly, there is no clear defined line of demarcation between the roles of the governors and those of management. Secondly, the parent governors are illiterate or semi-literate and cannot understand and carry out the functions that are prescribed for them by SASA Section 20. Thirdly, they claim that the parent component want to be paid for being SGB members and claim that they are doing work that is supposed to be done by educators who are paid. Fourthly, they claim that there is no means of communication or it is difficult to communicate effectively with the SGB parent governors. There is no effective means of communication. There are no telephones in most rural schools, and parents do not have telephones in their homes nor do they have cellular phones. Learners do not give notices of meetings to parents. As a result parents do not attend meetings. Fifthly, there are no roads, and transport is poor as a result, making it difficult for some parents to come to the school, especially when it is raining and wet. Sixthly, some principals do not have transport to transport SGB members to workshops. Finally, even when some parent SGB members are at the workshops, because of their literacy standard, they do not comprehend all the proceedings at the workshop.

In May 1997 all public or state schools elected the first SGBs. This marked a shift of power and authority from the principal to other stakeholders, such as the parents, educators, non-educators, learners who are in Grade 8 and above and co-opted community members. This is the second most-cited reform which most principals are not happy about. Some state that the roles of SGBs are ill defined and overlap with professional functions which thing causes friction and conflicts in most schools. Others add that the SGBs are illiterate, especially the parent component, and are unable to function as stipulated by the SASA Sections 20 and 21. They feel that the SGBs had not been properly empowered to take up the responsibilities imposed upon them by the SASA.

For education to be in line with the democratic Constitution of the country and to democratise education, the SASA introduced the concept of school governance, to devolve power and control from the state or national level, macro level, through the province, meso level, to the school, micro or local level. Beckmann (2002:156) refers to this as "concurrent and exclusive legislative power". He explains that, because both the province and the schools do not set their own laws and policy *per se*, these have to conform to those set by the state. He calls this 'disguised centralisation'.

Beckmann (ibid) further refers to what he states as 'some political realities'. He explains "decentralisation implies as both the letting go and the embracing of power, and that this process is often complicated by an unwillingness to let go of power and or a reluctance to assume responsibilities. Pseudo or pretended devolution is not uncommon" (Beckmann, 2000).

Further on, Beckmann (2002:156) makes a claim that moving from centralised to a decentralised system is complicated by what the National Education Policy Initiative (KEPI) (1993:160), termed 'structural continuity', that is, the tendency for largely decentralised systems to remain largely decentralised, while the largely centralised systems tend to remain largely centralised despite 'countervailing' tendencies. He explains that this tension implied above are made worse in South Africa by political realities in the sense that legal provisions on education are as a result of a negotiation process which led to a political settlement in South Africa in 1994. If this scenario prevails at higher levels, then it would not be surprising for the same to prevail at lower levels, taking into consideration micropolitics in schools, that is the politics of the school, especially, since the SGBs have disturbed the status quo, that is the locus of control being solely on the principal now being removed from him to shared decision-making.

The respondents argue that the notion of SGBs is a good one and is ideal for decentralised decision-making or devolution of power to schools. It operates well in affluent communities, where most parents are even more knowledgeable than educators. They understand their roles, they have great ideas to fund raise and have money to support the fund-raising drives. But when considering the contextual realities in disadvantaged communities, this becomes problematic. SGBs in disadvantaged communities are faced with a lot of challenges. A lot needs to be done to bring them on par with those in affluent communities.

**iii) Abolition of Corporal Punishment (Bill of Rights)**

This reform has been equally cited as that of the SGBs, cited by all respondents, following the curriculum change.

Ninety nine per cent of the respondents expressed their concern regarding this policy, saying that learners have become very unruly and it is difficult to maintain discipline at schools, because there are no alternative measures stipulated by the policy makers. Learners do not do tasks given by educators, tasks such as homework, writing of tests and projects, and others. They come late to school, do drugs and other substance abuse. They are rude to educators and show insolence because they over-emphasize their rights, such as right or freedom of expression, to the total disregard of the responsibilities or obligations that go with these rights. This state of moral degeneration demotivates educators, and this in turn has a rippling effect on the leadership and on the effectiveness of the school. Some respondents argued that more emphasis should be put on school improvement rather than on school effectiveness.

Data also reveal that most respondents perceive that discipline can only be maintained in schools through the use of corporal punishment. They state that it is the most effective punishment 'our learners' respond to. They quote from the *Bible* as well: 'Spare the rod and spoil the child'. They say they will not stop using corporal punishment because they are the ones who have to decide on the most effective form of punishment that forces learners to do their work. They say that they are the ones who have to account for failures at the end of the day, while policy makers are not there.

Anecdotal evidence also revealed this when a principal meted corporal punishment to a learner for coming late to school. Unfortunately the learner died immediately thereafter, and a criminal case was opened for murder. It was unfortunate for this principal. Perhaps, he had not established the reasons why this learner came late, maybe the learner was not feeling well. But the media capitalised on the inflicting of the corporal punishment as the cause of death.

Respondents expressed that maybe the principal could have used other forms of punishment. Though the other forms of punishment that could be used to maintain discipline, such as detentions during break time or after school or weekends, to do manual work or school work, depending on the nature of the offense. Educators also argue that these could also be interpreted as amounting to abuse and this also means additional work for the educators who have to monitor or supervise the detained or punished learner to do the manual work. They maintain that some educators as well as learners live far from school and have contracts with their transport, so detentions after school affects other co-travellers in such contracts. If anything could happen to a learner that was detained after school and has to travel long distances home, the educator will be held responsible. On the other hand, locking of the gates when the school time starts, even after warning learners and parents of habitual late coming to school, this is regarded as denying learners the right to education, and this contributes to a high failure rate for which educators have to account for as well, because the lessons missed are usually not be made up again by the learner(s). They argue that detentions could be a suitable form of punishment for boarding schools but not for day schools. These are what educators express as frustrating; they feel that learners have more rights than teachers.

Frustration can lead a person to skewed reasoning. For example, a teacher forced learners to stand on their desks for more than an hour because they failed to stand up to greet him when he entered the classroom (Prega Govender, 2006, April 9, Sunday Times). This form of punishment angered parents, who demanded that the teacher be expelled.

Respondents reported that learners come to school with dangerous weapons, drugs, and other intoxicating substances. Educators are scared to search or confront them for fear of contravening their rights. Some learners come to school pregnant. Pregnant learners are a bad example to other learners and have a poor effect on discipline. They fall asleep in class. Some are moody and cheeky. Some miscarry in class or get labour pains in class during a lesson. The poor educators have to run around seeking for help because they are not midwives. They say this is a violation of the rights of others; the educator's right to teach, and also the right of other learners — the rights to be taught and to learn. Seeing a learner bleeding could be traumatic to other learners as well as to the educator. Obviously, this is not what parents send their children to see! This is not in the educator's job description to be act as midwives.

Section 12 of the South African Constitution states that everyone has a right not to be treated or punished in a cruel, inhuman or degrading way. The SASA Section 10 has also made corporal punishment in schools illegal. Parents may not give the principal or teachers permission to use corporal punishment. Anyone who ignores this regulation and applies it at a school commits an offence and can be charged in a court of law and can be punished.

**(iii) No-fee Schools**

Ninety-five per cent of the respondents stated that this is a very noble reform as it is meant to take into consideration the socio-, economic situation of learners in order to ensure that no child is denied education because the parents cannot afford to pay school fees. But what puzzles them is that schools in the same locality or community are not treated the same; one school is identified as a no-fee paying school and another in the same community is not identified as no-fee paying school. They state that they do not know how the DoE is identifying or the format used in categorising schools into the quintiles. They say this is negatively affecting those schools that charge fees, whilst positively affecting those which have been identified as no-fee paying schools. Their experience is that learners are flocking to the no-fee paying schools, and the fee paying schools are getting depleted of learners. Educators and the leadership are worried because this is negatively affecting the numbers of learners in the schools which are not identified, or have been categorised in the wrong quintile. This will result in the redeployment of teachers and possible closing down of certain schools. One other problem that they are reporting is that parents of the no-fee paying schools are demanding the money the state is paying to the school for the learners.

Schools in each province are classified into five groups or quintiles, from the poorest to the least poor. For example, Quintile 1 is a group of schools in each province catering for the poorest 20 per cent of schools. Quintile 2 caters for the next poorest 20 per cent of schools while Quintile 5 schools represent the least poor. Quintile 1 receives the highest allocation per learner, while Quintile 5 receives the lowest.

Every year the Minister of Education determines the national quintiles for public schools which must be used by the Member of the Executive Council (MEC) to identify and publish a list of these schools in their provinces.

The parents and the entire community must know in which quintile their school is, and the amount of money the school will receive. Provincial offices should communicate this information through their District Offices to schools in writing.

Should parents and the SGB think that their school has not been classified under the right quintile, they have the right to lodge a dispute. The Provincial and District offices must inform parents and schools of the dispute procedures to be followed.

It would be a good thing for the government to make education compulsory and free up to Grade 12 in order to solve all these problems.

**v) Redeployment of Educators**

Ninety per cent of the respondents expressed their concern about the way this reform is applied. They claim that the DoE is uses the Morkel Model which considers only the teacher:pupil ratio and not the curriculum offerings in the school. This means that when educators are redeployed from one school to another the subject specialisation is not taken into consideration. This results in some subjects having redundant staff or the opposite. This adds more stress on leadership and other educators.

This reform was effected as a government restructuring initiative to deploy educators who were more in some schools with small numbers and visa versa. This also was done to check on schools with inflated numbers. Some principals are said to have inflated learner numbers in order to get more teachers and higher ranking for promotional purposes.

### vi) Language and Religion Policies

Seventy-five per cent respondents regard the language and religion policies as contentious. The Bill of Rights states clearly that there are 11 official languages and anyone is free to choose the language of instruction of his choice where practicably possible. This is not such a problem in the rural areas because learners are homogeneously Xhosa speaking. The only problem cited is the fact that English is the medium of instruction whereas learners do not understand the English language, and this affects their pass rate. Most of the time educators teach in the vernacular but assess learners in English. When it comes to Grade 12 examinations, the papers are set in English and Afrikaans only and not in English and in IsiXhosa. This has a negative impact on the leadership who has to account to the DoE when the pass rate is low.

Although the Religion policy is not much of a problem to some respondents, there are those who seem to think that learners, especially at high schools, either want to abuse this right by using it as an excuse for smoking dagga or wanting to come to school in Rastafarian dreadlocks and smoking dagga, maintaining that it is their religion. This impacts negatively on discipline.

### vii) Inclusive Education

Seventy per cent expressed concern about having physically challenged learners in their schools where the educators are not skilled to attend to such learners. They are aware of the Bill of Rights, which stipulates that no learner should be denied the right to learn and that there should be no unfair discrimination. It is human nature to think of the extremes or the worst of cases, such as, the deaf and mute, or the blind and other cases of gross disability. Their main concerns are that the facilities for the normal learners are not sufficient in the schools, and how much more is required for learners with special needs (LSN); there are no trained educators in our schools to handle learners with very gross disabilities.

According to the *Newsletter*, 2005 October, a significant number of children who currently fall outside the formal education system—those with severe intellectual disability and/or multiple disabilities—are provided for by specialised daycare centres across the province, with minimal subsidy from the Department of Health. Early intervention programmes are crucial to assist the development of such children with such disabilities, and to prevent secondary difficulties in later life. Their educational needs are very specialised and in most developed countries are met through special schooling or specialised units attached to other schools.

Their resource centre has been contacted by various medical practitioners in public health services. They seem to be really struggling to access education for young, especially Xhosa-speaking patients with multiple (not necessarily intellectual) disabilities. It is stated that there seems to be an urgent need for special schools to access additional support to enable them to include such learners who end up being at home. The Western Cape Forum for Intellectual Disability has lobbied long and hard for such children to receive their rightful slice of the education budget.

According to the above information it appears as if this avenue needs to be explored, especially in our District in Butterworth. There are special schools in Bizana and Mthatha only, in the Transkei part of the Eastern Cape Province. No such schools exist, yet the District is very wide.

## Recommendations and Conclusion

### i) Curriculum 2005

Data reveal the various reforms the respondents expressed as negatively impacting on leadership. The curriculum reforms being the most cited, especially the rate at which the curriculum changes were introduced, the short time given to training or at times implementation without training at all. The findings seem to be backed by the criticisms of critiques of the Curriculum, although these criticisms are reasonable, but the timing the critiques voiced their criticisms was premature. These criticisms were made even before the implementation of Curriculum 2005 in 1998, and shortly thereafter, is a cause for concern on the part of the researcher. Others conducted research as early as 1998, 1999. Some of the criticisms might have had a negative influence on the full and successful implementation of the new curriculum. For example, Jansen puts forward an argument that is predictive as early as 1998, "Ten Reasons Why OBE will fail". This statement, in my opinion, is both predictive and provocative. Perhaps, the statement could have been constructed differently, for example, instead of using "will", "may" or "might", could have been used. As much as the ten points made are valid, they came out too soon, in the very year of the implementation of the new curriculum. These criticisms could have incited most teachers who are resistant to change to find reasons not to be receptive of the new curriculum. These reasons should not have been for public consumption but they should have been directed straight to the planners before the actual launch of the new curriculum. This causes one to wonder what these researchers or critiques would have done if they were in the shoes of the Ministry of Education, knowing the political pressures on the Minister to deliver.

My strongest criticism is the lack of participatory decision-making and training of the leadership (SMTs) as implementers of the reforms, who need to mentor and monitor the educators, and the trainers of educators, who are supposed to work in partnership with the DoE in the policy making, decision making or in the development of the curriculum, to be in line with the democratic principles of the country. It is also a cause for concern to note the time when the wokshops were held for the NCS, a curriculum which had already been implemented at the beginning of the year. Workshops were only held during the June 2006 school holidays this year, for the NCS which was implemented at the beginning of the year.

Educational reforms are good but discourses and interrogation of the reforms between the various stakeholders need to be undertaken ahead of introduction and implementation. The proper and adequate advocacy and orientation of all stakeholders, say two or three years before the actual launch and implementation of the reform is recommended. Institutions of higher learning should be part and parcel of the design of the reform, or be informed and given the same time which is given to writers and publishers of books for the new reforms. The curriculum changes should not be effected without the proper and adequate training of all implementers including trainers of educators. The duration of the indepth training for each teacher is not stated. It is assumed that the first half of 1997 was for the training, and the second half, as stated was for field testing (Bengu, 1997:18). It is not clear what would happen after the field testing.

Control measures need to be put in place by the DoE to monitor workshop attendance and to check whether the proceedings are proper and have been understood. Then follow up to check whether the desired curriculum reforms have been implemented and also establish whether there are implementation problems, and remedy where possible.

Evaluation of the degree of successful implementation of whatever new reform passed. Follow-up strategies after workshop attendance should be put in place and the monitoring of workshop attendance.

**ii) School Governing Bodies (SGBs)**

Data reveal that the SGB reform has also a negative impact on leadership due to various reasons, and the most cited reasons include the fact that there is no clear defined line of demarcation between the roles of the governors and those of management, and the illiteracy rate of parent governors, who find it difficult to play their roles as stipulated by the SASA, especially the Section 20 and 21 compulsory and allocated functions respectively, and others.

What the leadership loses sight of is that they are responsible for the capacity building of the SGBs, as stipulated in SASA Section 19. The lack of involvement of all stakeholders is at variance with the principles of democracy.

The DoE should move the elections of SGBs forward to March or April; establish effective strategies for capacity building of SGBs as soon as the elections have been completed, especially in schools which have a high parent's illiteracy rate. Such schools should be encouraged to open ABET centres, make sure that these are effective with relevant programmes, are run properly, and the ABET educators are paid properly and on time.

The co-opted members should be granted voting status especially if that particular member has high skills, especially in financial management and fund raising skills, and should stay for the full term. The expectations of SGBs should also be considered, not only what the school expects them to do. Volunteering without any form of incentive when one is poor is not easy especially in remote rural areas where the transport and the means of communication are a problem.

**iii) Abolition of Corporal Punishment (Bill of Rights)**

Concerning the abolition of corporal punishment, data also reveal that all respondents perceive that discipline can only be maintained in schools through the use of corporal punishment. They state that it is the most effective punishment 'our learners' respond to. Some even quoted from the *Bible* as well: 'Spare the rod and spoil the child'. But contrary to this, the SASA Section 10, states in no uncertain terms that corporal punishment is a criminal offence. Therefore, leadership and educators should use more humane forms of punishment to maintain discipline with the help from the DoE. Perhaps the more humane forms of punishment to be used should be recommended by the DoE for the schools to use.

The DoE should consider providing special schools for pregnant learners with midwives, or attach a special unit at the maternity hospitals for learners, or provide special classrooms for pregnant learners and a school nurse.

The DoE should provide with guidelines for alternative forms of punishment for schools and review the policies regarding the excessive rights of learners which may lead to moral degeneration.

It is worth noting that, due to the latest sprees of violence in our schools during the last week in September, where a learner shot a principal fatally wounding him, and other incidence of learners shooting each other, the DoE will be installing some devices at schools to detect dangerous weapons brought in by learners, and the Minister of Education was shown on E-TV News and SABC 1 News, 2 October 2006, saying that the educators have a right to search learners for drugs and dangerous weapons without violating human rights. Data revealed that this was one of the main concerns by educators.

**iv) No-Fee Schools**

The DoE should do away with all the present strategies and provide free and compulsory education for all schools in the disadvantaged communities, especially in rural areas or else do a proper categorisation of school quintiles. This move might take care of the high rural-urban migration which causes overcrowding in townships schools.

**v) Redeployment of Educators**

The DoE must be more vigilant by constantly checking the numbers of learners before deploying educators. DoE officials should go to the affected schools to do a proper skills audit of educators and head count of learners, to check against the habit of leadership of inflating learner numbers and to check again for "ghost educators".

**vi) Language and Religion Policies**

The Bill of Rights states clearly that there are 11 official languages and anyone is free to choose the language of instruction of his choice where practicably possible. Therefore, examination papers should cater for all by recognising the language most in use by the majority of the learners in that particular province or area and English since it is the medium of instruction in order to accommodate all official languages

**viii) Inclusive Education**

The Butterworth District does not have specialised schools as revealed by the *Newsletter* for those learners with gross disabilities. This needs to be given serious consideration as many physically challenged people are neglected, especially in the rural areas where poverty thrives. They are open to severe abuse. Some do not even get the Disability Grant, or if they do it is not used for its purpose. In the meanwhile a lot of advocacy for inclusive education needs to be undertaken so that leadership could understand and embrace it.

**Idealism Versus Realism**

The term 'ideal' is a conception of something that is perfect or something existing only as an idea. Vos & Britz (1990:4), quoting Sir Michael Sadler (1861-1943), a former director of the London Board of Education, in his sensational article "How far can we learn anything of practical value from the study of foreign systems of education?" (1900) declared, "In studying foreign systems of education we should not forget that the things outside the school matter even more than the things inside the school, and govern and interpret the things inside". Sadler used the following example to elucidate his statement:

> Just as one cannot wander at leisure among the education system of the world, like a child strolling through a garden and picking a flower from one bush and some leaves from another, and then expects that if one sticks what has been gathered into the soil at home, one shall have a living plant, one cannot transplant foreign systems of education or parts thereof to a national system of education and expect it to flourish.

Sadler regarded the education system as being rooted in the national life, national character, national history and traditions of a people, the contextual realities. The term 'real' means that existing or occurring in the physical world. Reality is the state of things as they are rather than as one might wish them to be, the ideal.

Planners and policy makers should make informed decisions, by taking into account the contextual realities rather than the ideal. Moving from theory/policy to practice/praxis is a difficult process and proves to be problematic. This necessitates the recreation of the linkages between theory/policy and practice/praxis which is the key theme of this conference. The linkage between contextual realities should be taken into consideration when theories are developed and policies formed. Political imperatives, in the case of South Africa, were at the forefront without taking into considerations the contextual realities — the situation existing on the ground, especially in the majority of communities, the indigenous people of the country.

The leadership is supposed to be catalysts of change. If there is a knowledge gap in the leadership, there is bound to be a theory and praxis gap. South Africa, during this period of transition from the past paradigms to the new paradigm shift needs both transformational leadership as well as instructional leadership in order to create linkages between theory and practice and policy and praxis.

## References

Adler, P. & Adler, P. 1987. *Membership Roles in Field Research.* (Vol. 6). Beverly Hill: SAGE.

Babbie, E. & Mouton; J. 2003. *The Practice of Social Research.* South Africa: Oxford University Press.

Beckmann, J. 2002. The Emergence of Self Managing Schools in South Africa: Devolution of Authority or disguised centralism. *Education and the Law,* Vol. 14, No. 3, pp 153-166.

Bush, T. 1995. *Theories of Educational Management.* London: Paul Chapman Publishing Ltd.

Cantrell, DC. 1993. 'Alternative Paradigm in Environmental Education Research: the Interpretive Perspective'. In Mrazek, R. (ed.) *Alternative Paradigm in Environmental Research.* Troy Ohio: NAAEE.

Denzin, N.K. & Lincoln, Y. S. (Eds) *Handbook Of Qualitative Research. 2nd Edition.* Thousand Oaks: Sage Publications.

Carr, W. & Kemmis, S. 1986. *Becoming Critical: Education, Knowledge and Action Research.* London: Falmer Press.

Department of Education. 1995a. *White Paper on Education and Training.* Pretoria

__________, 1995b. *National Teacher Education.* Pretoria.

__________, 1996. *South African Schools Act.* Pretoria.

__________, 1997x. Pretoria. *Understanding the Schools Act.* Pretoria.

__________, 1997b. Curriculum 2005. *Lifelong Learning for the 21st Century.* Pretoria.

__________, 1998x. *Norms and Standards for Teacher Education.* Pretoria.

Eksteen, FRLN, Naude, CHB., Miller, HR. & Eksteen, FRL. 1988. *Business Economics Standard 10: Higher Grade and Standard Grade.* Cape Town: NASOU.

Fataar, A. 1999. Localisation, globalisation and compensatory legitimation: School curriculum policy and politics in South Africa. Paper presented at the Comparative and International Education Conference, OISE, university of Toronto. Canada. 14-18 April 1999.

Fullan, M. 1991. *The New Meaning of Change.* London: Cassell.

Govender, P. 2006. Pupils forced to stand on desks for an hour. *Sunday Times,* April 9, p.10.

Gwarinda, TC. 2000. *Socialism & Education: An introduction.* Zimbabwe: College Press Publishers (PTY) Ltd.

__________, *Using Questerview in Case Study Research: A Justification.* A discussion paper presented at the PhD Seminar on 12 May 2006 at the School for Post Graduate Studies, Faculty of Education Fort Hare. Alice.

Harber, C. 2001. *State of Transition.* United Kingdom: Symposium Books.

Henning, E., van Rensburg, W. & Smit, B. 2004. *Finding Your Way in Qualitative Research.* Pretoria: Van Schaik.

Huber (1998) in Oduro. G.K. 2005. Cultural and Political Factors that Influence School Leadership Practices in Africa: Perspectives from South Africa and Ghana. Paper presented to the Education Management Association of South Africa (EMASA) 8th International Conference 11-13 March... Gauteng (Johannesburg): Mathew Goniwe School of Leadership.

Jansen, J.D. 1997. Curriculum Reform in South Africa: a critical analysis of outcomes based education, *Cambridge Journal of Education,* Vol. 28, No.3, 1998 pp.321-332.

__________, 2002. Political Symbolism as Policy Craft: Explaining Non-reform in South African Education After Apartheid. *Education Policy.* Vol. 17, No. 2, pp 199-215.

Leithwood (1992) in Oduro. G.K. 2005. op.cit.

MacGregor, K. 2000b. Baffling Curriculum Dropped. *Times Educational Supplement,* 23 June.

Oduro. op.cit.

Rail, J. 2005. Managing Leadership Through Change Or Leading Management Through Change? Does It Matter Which? *Executive Business Brief.* April/May, Vol. 10, No. 2, p.27.

Troup, F.1976. *Forbidden Pastures: Education under Apartheid.* London: International Defence & Aid Fund.

Van Zyl, A. in Lemmer, EM. & Badenhorst, DC. 1997. *Introduction to Education for South African Teachers: An Orientation to Teaching Practice.* Kenwyn: Juta & Co. Ltd.

# 10

# Emerging Teaching Practices

*—Linda L. Lyman*

This paper presents an analytical interpretive evaluation of the success of a doctoral leadership seminar in changing participants' definitions of leadership and thereby affecting their leadership practices. The seminar design grew from a deceptively simple concept: definitions are central to both the practice and the power of leadership. Lambert (2003) articulates the same idea in these words, "How we define leadership frames how people will participate in it" (p. 4). Whereas more typical leadership courses may rely on secondary sources and focus on the historical evolution of leadership theory, this seminar focused on theoretical perspectives that have emerged in the past thirty years, and used primary source readings. The goals of the seminar were stated on the syllabus:

> Through dialogue with each other, seminar participants will review the mental models surrounding the traditional conceptions of leadership and will explore emerging ideas about leadership that have the potential to reculture schools. This seminar is designed to give participants the opportunity to develop further their own understandings of leadership through reflection and indepth reading of ground-breaking books about leadership. Attention will be given to practical applications of the ideas explored, controversial topics, end issues associated with research on leadership.

The opportunity for indepth reading and discussion of primary sources, processes of reflection required by the writing assignments, exploring the paradigm of constructive postmodernism, and focusing on developing and articulating one's own definition of leadership were key to the seminar's success.

Participants' pre-seminar definitions of leadership highlighted getting others to do the leaders' wishes, focused on achieving goals, and featured linear processes; but their end of seminar Synthesis Papers contained definitions that highlighted the moral imperatives of leadership, focused on reciprocal relationships, and suggested organic processes. In this paper, data from the Synthesis Paper and a Follow-Up Survey will be presented to substantiate that the seminar approach was successful in changing participants' definitions of leadership and thereby affecting their leadership practices.

## Emerging Leadership Theories

Designing a seminar around emerging leadership theories makes sense because "past understandings of leadership from a paradigm of power and dominance are not equal to the challenges of today and have in fact contributed to the challenges of today" (Lyman, Ashby, & Tripses, 2005, p. 143). There is no agreed upon definition of the concept of leadership (Leithwood & Duke, 1999) or postmodern leadership (Chapman, Sackney, & Astin, 1999; Furman, 2002; Willower & Forsyth, 1999). The goal of the seminar was not to advance a particular definition of leadership, but to contribute to developing authentic leaders whose practices are connected with and reflect their beliefs. Begley (2004) calls authentic leadership "a metaphor for professionally effective, ethically sound, and consciously reflective practices in educational administration" (pp. 4-5). Works considered were: servant leadership (Greenleaf, 2003); leadership as adaptive work (Heifetz, 1994); constructivist leadership (Lambert, Walker, Zimmerman, Cooper, Lambent, M. D., Gardner, & Szabo, 2002); relational leadership (Drath, 2001); a post-industrial· leadership paradigm (Rost, 1991); and leadership in a quantum age (Wheatley, 1999). Each offers a different approach to defining leadership.

Greenleaf's (2003) essay *The Servant as Leader*, published as part of a collection of his essays in 1977, featured a story about how "leadership was bestowed upon a person who was by nature a servant" (p. 21). Greenleaf's new paradigm has had enormous direct and indirect influence. Although he articulated no actual definition of leadership, he implicitly offered a redefinition of leadership as service and stewardship. The closest he comes to a definition is: "The very essence of leadership, *going out ahead to show the way* [emphasis added], derives from more than usual openness to inspiration" (p. 28). He also wrote "Leadership by persuasion and example is the way to build — everywhere" (p. 98).

Heifetz (1994) acknowledges that "the way we talk about leadership betrays confusion" (p. 13). His position is "Rather than define leadership either as a position of authority in a social structure or as a personal set of characteristics, we may find it a great deal more useful to define leadership as an activity" (p. 20). In particular, he articulates the concept of adaptive work as the essence of leadership: "Adaptive work consists of the learning required to address conflicts in the values people hold, or to diminish the gap between the values people stand for and the reality they face. Adaptive work requires a change in values, beliefs, or behaviours" (p. 22). He frames leadership as a process of education: "Leadership is a special sort of educating in which the teacher raises the problems, questions, options, interpretations, and perspectives, often without answers, gauging all the while when to push through and when to hold steady" (pp. 244-245).

Lambert et al. (2002) focus on leadership in schools, charging that many preparation programmes are still based on outdated ideas about leadership. Lambert addresses the transformative power of leadership, writing, "Leadership as critical social and intellectual transformation is achieved through reciprocal, purposeful learning in community" (p. xviii). She defines constructivist leadership as "the reciprocal processes that enable participants in an educational community to construct meanings that lead toward a common purpose of schooling" (p. 36). This is a redefining that situates leadership in "the processes among us rather than in the skills or disposition of a leader" (p. 42), with equity "deeply embedded in these patterns" (p. 44) of relationships. A central process in building patterns of relationships is conversation. Lambert explains, "The conversation is the major approach to constructivist change as conversations host mean-making .... A primary role of the constructivist leader is to lead the conversations. In so doing, a leader opens, rather than occupies, space" (p. 64).

Drath (2001) addresses the confusion surrounding our understanding of leadership: "At the heart of our current confusion about leadership is the persistence of a taken-for-granted idea about leadership .... I propose that this persistent central idea is that leadership is something leaders possess as an individual attribute and, therefore, leadership is given by, created by, leaders. This is the idea of leadership that is causing our confusion" (p. xiv). Rather than a definition of leadership he advances three principles of leadership — "deeper than a definition, and . . . deeper than a leadership style" (p. 11). The principle of personal dominance reflects "a way of understanding leadership as the personal quality or characteristic of a certain kind of person called a leader" (pp. 12-13). The principle of interpersonal influence is "a way of understanding that leadership happens when a group of people agree and disagree, ally and contend, concur and argue, plan and negotiate until someone emerges as the most influential person and thus claims the role of leader" (p. 13). Finally, the principle of relational dialogue reflects "a way of understanding that leadership happens when people who acknowledge shared work use dialogue and collaborative learning to create contexts in which that work can be accomplished across the dividing lines of differing perspectives, values, beliefs, and more generally what I will refer to as differing world views" (p. 14-15). Which knowledge principle a person holds influences whether or when the person recognises leadership as happening. Drath believes that all leadership is a process of shared meaning-making.

Rost (1991) presents an exhaustive history and discussion of leadership definitions from 1900 to 1979. He concluded after extensive study that leadership and management have essentially been equated with each other. In fact, he writes that "leadership as good management is the twentieth century [industrial] paradigm of leadership" (p. 94), featuring "those great men and women with certain preferred traits who influence followers to do what the leaders wish in order to achieve group/organisational goals that reflect excellence defined as some kind of higher-order effectiveness" (p. 95). Rost shares in the book the reasoning behind elements of his definition: "Leadership is an influence relationship among leaders and followers who intend real changes that reflect their mutual purposes. Every word in that definition was carefully selected to convey very specific meanings that contain certain assumptions and values which are necessary to a transformed, postindustrial model of leadership" (p. 102). He issues this challenge: "Leadership scholars in the future are going to have to think new thoughts about leadership, using post industrial assumptions about human beings, organisations, societies, and the planet Earth" (p. 183).

Wheatley (1999) writes, "As we let go of the machine model of organisations . . . we begin to see ourselves in much richer dimensions, to appreciate our wholeness, and hopefully, to design organisations [schools] that honour and make use of the great gift of who we humans are" (p. 14). In the original edition (1992) of her groundbreaking book, Wheatley provided a different way of thinking about organisations as living systems that is clearly postmodern, even if she does not use that term. Her work focuses on the implications of the new science for organisational practices and leadership. Quantum physics, in particular, leads to the understanding that we live in a world of relationships, that "even organisational power is purely relational" (p. 39). Rather than defining leadership she offers insights about leadership processes that derive from the new sciences and believes that principles from science can contribute to a 'new' science of leadership. Stating that leadership has been defined in the past in terms of its control functions, the closest she comes to a definition of leadership is this passage:

> These ideas speak with simple clarity to issues of effective leadership. They recall us to the power of simple governing principles: guiding visions, sincere values, organisational beliefs—the few self-referential ideas individuals can use to shape their own behaviour. The leader's task is first to embody these principles, and then to help the organisation become the standard it has declared for itself. This work of leaders cannot be reversed, or either step ignored. In organisations where leaders do not practise what they preach, there are terrible disabling consequences. (p. 130)

## Seminar Participants and Processes

The seminar was held in fall semester, 2005, at an off-campus location for students in an Illinois State University doctoral cohort. The 12 participants included three elementary principals, five secondary administrators,. and four central office administrators. The four women and eight men were from a variety of school districts in terms of size and type, including both large and small districts in suburban, urban, and rural areas as well as small towns. The seminar met 11 times from September 1 to December 1.

At the first meeting of the seminar, participants were given time to write their definitions of leadership. Then as an opening activity they divided into three groups, shared the definitions they had written, and came to consensus on a definition of leadership. The first class concluded with an introductory lecture titled *Comparing Traditional and Emerging Conceptions of Leadership*. Both historical perspectives and categorical perspectives for defining leadership were presented, as well as examples of traditional and non-traditional definitions.

Subsequent reading assignments allocated either one or two nights for each author with participants writing three-five page reflection papers for five of the six books. Each reflection paper centered on practical implications for educational leaders of two-three major ideas from the book under discussion. Varied seminar activities were built around the practical implications generated by the participants in these reflection papers. For example, after a video about Greenleaf (2003) provided a context for his ideas, participants wrote reactions to assigned passages from the readings, then compared responses in small groups, followed by a general discussion of Greenleaf's concept of servant leadership. Problems in the participants' schools and districts were categorised according to Heifetz's (1994) adaptive versus technical challenges distinction, followed by group problem solving. Lambert et al's. (2002) constructivist leadership ideas were explored using an adapted World Cafe format (Brown, 2005). Drath's (1991) three leadership principles were used to categorise the group consensus definitions from the first night and the participants' own evolving definitions. Then the principles were used to analyse two case studies. Rost's (1991) work provided a historical context and overview of the evolution of leadership definitions. His distinction between management and leadership provoked much discussion as did his comprehensive explication of his own definition of leadership. Finally, Wheatley's (1999) ground-breaking insights about organisations and leadership arrived at by analogy moved the conversation directly into the meaning of leadership in a post-modern or quantum age.

## Research Findings

Data to establish changes in definitions of leadership come from the Synthesis Papers, an assignment due on the final night of the seminar:

> In a well-organised final Synthesis Paper (approximately 10 pages) each seminar participant will address what she/he learned about leadership from the seminar. Compare and contrast the ideas about leadership with which you began and ended the class, and present an indepth analysis of how and why your ideas did or did not change. Conclude with your unanswered questions about leadership, and make recommendations for how the course could be strengthened. A scholarly APA style (5th edition) paper with references to a minimum of 10 sources (including the 6 required course books) is expected.

Data to establish effects of the changed definitions on leadership practices come primarily from the Follow-Up Survey completed five months after the seminar ended. The seminar participants received an email invitation in May 2006 to participate in the Follow-Up Survey. Although all 12 participants replied they were willing to participate in the research, only 11 completed the Follow-Up Survey. The survey was sent as an email attachment following receipt of their intent to participate and they returned their completed surveys by email. The survey contained the three questions. Only responses to the first two questions are considered in this paper.

1. Would you define leadership today in the same words you used in your final paper? If the answer is 'yes,' please explain why in the space below. If the answer is "No," please state your current definition of leadership in the space below and explain the reasons for the change.

2. How has your December 2005 end-of-class definition of leadership influenced your leadership practices in the past five months? Please explain and use examples.
3. In what ways have other experiences affected your leadership practices in the past five months? Please explain and use examples.

**Changes in Leadership Definitions and Leadership Practices**

All 12 seminar participants reported changes in their pre-seminar understandings or definitions of leadership as a result of studying the work of selected leadership scholars from the last 30 years. Six identified the changes as "profound" or "significant". Ten of the eleven who responded to the Follow-Up Survey reported effects on their leadership practices. The thinking of each participant is presented first, followed by a summary and discussion of the changes to their definitions of leadership and their leadership practices as reported in the Synthesis Paper and Follow-Up Survey. All names used in the paper are pseudonyms.

**Elementary Principals**

*Amanda:* "Amanda" concluded the final Synthesis Paper, "My perspective of leadership has changed throughout this course. The readings have given me impetus to continue to question my definition and let it evolve as I continue to work in an administrative position .... I certainly will be more open to promoting shared leadership and valuing the constructs that come from this relational leadership." At the end of the seminar she still felt comfortable with the initial definition she wrote in the first class exercise: "Leadership is promoting vision, creating consensus and goals for that vision, and facilitating a path to realise those visions and goals." Amanda's pre-seminar definition reflected her belief that the focus of leadership should be on the outcome or product. Saying that this "initial concept of leadership . . . still stands true to me with some additions," she articulated the following revised definition: "Leadership is a process promoting vision and creating consensus and goals for that vision through sustained trust in the facilitation of a path of change that realises those visions and goals with equitable collaboration."

Amanda was the only participant to offer a revised definition in the Follow-Up Survey. In her post-seminar definition she added the words "and awareness of stakeholders as we build community" following the phrase equitable collaboration at the end of the definition. She wrote that this addition was a direct result of the policy analysis class taken by the cohort the semester following the leadership seminar. "The language or linguistics of leadership should include this awareness of stakeholders. The idea of building community regardless of race, ethnicity, ability, etc. has affected my definition of leadership." This addition highlights her developing understanding of the importance of relationships and reflects attention to a moral imperative. The definition is clearly reflected in what she writes about its effects on her leadership practices. She used as an example the processes she is using to lead the opening of a new school for 2006-07. This confident experienced principal stated, "I am relying on facilitation of a good transition and the setting of goals. I have learned that I cannot do it all! Putting out a team collaboration and providing equitable opportunities are of paramount importance. We will be building community." Her example is an illustration of how the seminar effects are reflected in her handling of a complex task.

*Stephanie:* "Stephanie", a first year principal, did not actually offer a pre-seminar definition of leadership in her Synthesis Paper. She did say, "As a result [of my strong educational background and learning experience from my master's program], I have always realised that top-down hierarchal leadership is insufficient to meet the needs of today's information overloaded society. What I didn't realise is that top-down decision making is necessary in certain rare situations and that leadership is more than shared or collaborative decision making." Her pre-seminar view of leadership is implied in these words: "My views regarding collaborative or shared leadership or continuous improvement have not changed. Rather, they have been heightened to new levels of understanding." She elaborated how the ideas of Drath, Heifetz, and Wheatley had the most influence on her end-of-seminar definition: "Leadership is a social concept that transpires when there is a collective desire for continuous improvement leading to purposeful action that ensues as a result of relationship building and collaboration." The definition reflects what was her struggle as a first-year principal — to cultivate a collective desire for continuous improvement that would lead to purposeful action on the part of her staff. Her concluding words included these, "I sincerely gained a better sense of leadership and have come to a better understanding of my own role as a leader, influenced by various evolutionary perspectives. Defining leadership has been a powerful exercise for me."

Reporting in the Follow-Up Survey on the effects of the definition, Stephanie wrote, "I would have to say that learning the concepts of questioning, leading the conversation and reciprocal learning [Lambent et al.] have influenced my leadership practices significantly in the last five months." Having spent the first half of the year building trust and relationships, she was at a turning point in January and was able to use those skills "to move the staff closer to a professional learning community. Staff members are taking a more active role in building decisions. Individuals are feeling more empowered to have voice during faculty meetings." Her example illustrates the effects of the seminar on her handling of complex tasks through enhanced cognitive processes.

*Dave:* "Dave", the third elementary principal, wrote, "As I read the assigned texts, my own definition [of leadership] was impacted by them. It has not changed drastically. However, certain elements have been added and others reinforced." He offered as his initial definition these words, "Leadership is promoting a vision for an organisation, building consensus for that vision, and developing others to assist in realising that vision." Dave, as did Amanda and Stephanie; revised his definition by adding to it. He discussed how "the readings significantly affected all three elements of his initial definition" and then offered this revised definition of leadership: "Leadership is the shared development and promotion of purpose for an organisation, developing collaborative relationships toward that purpose, and developing each other to achieve that purpose." Generalising, he wrote: "Most importantly, in each element [of the definition] a multidirectional characteristic has emerged, reflecting a perception of leadership as shared. It is important to recognise the distinction between a definition emphasising collaboration and one emphasizing shared meaning and purpose. They are not the same. My definition has changed chiefly in this shift from collaboration to shared leadership as a common thread." Throughout, the word 'purpose' has replaced the word 'vision'.

In reporting effects of the definition on his leadership practices Dave wrote in the Follow-Up Survey, "I recently revised my approach to my building leadership team, working with them more as a member than chair. Previous discussions had a structure of I introduce a topic, they discuss and offer input, I make the ultimate decision. Now, we discuss and consensus rules most of the time anyway." He also reported, "I just completed a several-week process leading a strategic action planning team where I took a shared approach, rather than being more directive, which I would have done a year ago." He offered a third example, "And in the last few weeks I selected a new assistant principal and wrote several new questions into the interview process, including one asking for the candidate's understanding of 'servant leadership.'" His examples illustrate two themes: effects on leadership style and handling of complex tasks.

**Secondary Administrators**

*Sam:* In the Synthesis Paper "Sam", a middle school principal, wrote the following about his experiences in the seminar:

> In the beginning of my journey, like many, I believed leadership to be a simple series of traits one had or could acquire to gain influence over others. I understood that leadership could be easily defined. Although I believed there must be followership, I did not consider the moral imperative a necessary feature when defining true leadership .... My definition of leadership continues to evolve and transform as my experiences and knowledge develop .... I now believe the power of a leader is more greatly seen in the questions they ask, not the answers they facilitate. I have moved from a linear model of leadership to a non-linear one. Both the top-down and bottom-up approach leave me unsatisfied. Today I strongly support a moral imperative to leadership. The journey of leadership is a cultivation of ourselves to become understanding human beings.

Toward the end of the paper Sam wrote, "I have profoundly changed my view of what leadership both is and is not. In August

I believed leadership was a linear, definable, tool which some came to possess and others would never find." He elaborated a new understanding of what leadership is by highlighting the concepts that are now part of it. These were the idea of the power of adaptive challenges to give the questions that need to be addressed by all the members of an organisation; the role of relationships in leadership ('One might even say that leadership is relationships'); and "The responsibility to transform leadership, to compassionately move towards a relationship-centred model which nurtures the human condition and is self-reflective in nature, can and must begin to benefit us all." Sam did not respond to the Follow-Up Survey.

*Chad:* In the final paper "Chad", principal of a freshman centre, presented a working definition of leadership, stating,

> I refer to this as working because it has changed significantly since my enrolment in EAF 583 and most likely will evolve in the future. My prior view of leadership was leader and goal focused. I also discovered my expectation for the follower was too passive. I viewed leadership as something I did 'to' and 'for' people. While I did embrace communication via conversation with followers, I may have been too manipulative in my intent, using dialogue to advance my mission or goal.

In concluding the paper Chad restated his working definition succinctly: "'Leadership is a reciprocal relationship of influence between leaders and followers creating common synergy toward shared outcomes.' It is clearly evident to me how far I have travelled with my views on leadership. Gone are goals and objectives; and 'in' are relationships and shared outcomes. This is a significant paradigm shift."

In the Follow-Up survey Chad gave several examples of how his definition had affected his leadership practices. He mentioned being more confident when critiquing the leadership style of others. When faced with an issue, his definition has assisted him in "being able to decipher problems and impediments to change and interpret conflict more clearly." He also described his attention to having his public communications be congruent with his definition, saying he used the definition as a litmus test when framing communications. He reported that the definition helped in his role as co-leader of a boundary committee where selecting the boundary for the proposed new school was "very contentious, heated along racial lines, and was the reason the referendum failed miserably." Throughout the process, "My definition grounded me and became my personal base," he wrote. Although it was challenging he actually enjoyed the process. "Truth be told, my coping statements included my leadership definition. I kept telling myself remember this is a reciprocal process," and "a good leader is a good listener." He said, "As school administrators you do not often have the opportunity to stand up publicly . . . for something as important as equity." His examples illustrate all three themes found in the data: effects on leadership style, handling of complex tasks, and cognitive processes.

*Cindy:* "Cindy", a high school department chairperson wrote, "At the beginning of this class, I viewed leadership as *the ability to both facilitate and/or manipulate a group of people toward one common goal* .... Based on the many readings I have encountered thus far since the start of this semester, my definition has been greatly modified. This new definition of leadership that I have developed has a few different components, which were difficult to compile into one short definition, so I defined leadership with a listing of characteristics. My current definition of leadership is:

> Leadership is a skill that is learned through experience. It is the ability to lead a group of people toward mutual purposes while keeping oneself open to new ideas and finding solutions to adaptive problems while utilising the groups' opinions. Leadership depends on reciprocal learning that will produce real change between a leader and followers' mutual purposes.

Cindy concluded the Synthesis Paper,

> My thoughts on leadership have definitely been modified throughout the course of this semester. I have appreciated the exposure to a variety of different leadership definitions. My thoughts on leadership have enlightened my perspective on how to approach different situations .... Personally, I have tried Drath's three principles and have found that allowing leaders to emerge within the different levels of solving an adaptive problem is actually less stressful than trying to solve it by myself as a leader.

In responding to the Follow-Up Survey Cindy wrote in some detail about her experiences:

> I truly feel that my understanding of this definition has helped me grow over the past few months. I have accepted a new position as an administrative assistant, which will provide me with a wide range of opportunities as we get ready to open two new high schools in the next three years. The part of the definition that has helped me as a leader is in the second sentence — 'Leadership is the ability to lead a group of people toward mutual purposes while keeping oneself open to new ideas and finding solutions to adaptive problems while utilising the groups' opinions.' I truly enjoy finding solutions to problems while receiving input from the teachers.

Cindy then described how she is working with the person who will replace her as department chair, "encouraging him to seek the mutual purposes we have worked on in the department and helping him transition from the follower to the leader as I make the transition to a follower of the assistant principals that I will follow." Her example illustrates the effects on handling of complex tasks and cognitive processes.

*Eric:* "Eric", chairperson of a large high school division containing several departments, resisted defining leadership. He wrote in the Synthesis Paper, "The concentration of this class has been our journey into the understanding of leadership . . . . Though I did not enter this journey with any preconceptions, I do believe I have gained a different view of the topic .... I had no clear defined definition of leadership. My earliest examples of leadership are those taken from the lives of the saints." He then framed his definition in terms of the essence of leadership, writing, "I refer to the essence of leadership rather than a definition of leadership because I do believe that more needs to be taking place in leadership than a definition can equate. Members who are part of dynamic organisations would agree that components, which may be more spiritual in nature, are present in these organisations. These spiritual components are also almost indefinable." He continued,

> In retrospect, my original view of leadership based on personal dominance [saints as models] is not so far in reality

> from where I have journeyed. Those leaders who are the exemplar of what is good and right may have already made the journey. Their self-sacrifice and integrity has put them in touch with themselves and has allowed them to form a vision of what they wish to accomplish. These leaders were trying to make the world a better place, where all individuals are able to reach their potentials. I see leadership now as the responsibility of the leader to create an environment where survival is not an issue .... I believe Wheatley quite eloquently describes how the process we follow in our work is more important than the product..

Eric's definition — "the essence of leadership as a spiritual connection among members of dynamic organisations" — appears influenced by his early veneration of the saints as leaders to emulate, and also by the experience of twice being part of a dynamic instructional team where a high level of mast resulted in attaining impressive results. He articulates clearly how this spiritual connection serves as a source of energy:

> I believe in such a state [of spiritual connection], fluidity of thought and dialogue between the members drive discovery of new options. Mainframes of individuals tap into a group consciousness, where neither a leader nor a follower exists for long periods. The reciprocal interaction eliminates expertise or power centers since individuals learn and adopt strengths from those sharing in this interconnection.

Examples Eric gave in the Follow-Up Survey of the definition's effects on his leadership practices are both about creating new options to strengthen faculty teaching through collaboration. He requested from his administration an alternate schedule so that division staff could meet once a week. The board approved the request and the state granted a waiver creating first hour on Wednesday every week as time for such meetings. He also argued for the course instructional teams to meet once a month. He has met with each team and "we created a list of top 10 accomplishments we wished to attain over the year. My only other direction to the teams was to survey the effectiveness of the curriculum according to state standards and to create an instructional guide utilising a curriculum template that the team leaders created." Reflecting on these actions, Eric said, "In retrospect I believe my performance was more in line with constructive transactional leadership. I hope this will be more of a transformational initiative that will develop leadership from within the building and provide more instructional opportunities for our students." He found these actions to have been quite successful.

> Since this experience — I would agree even more with my original assertions. A quarter of the teams performed adequately and met a competent level. Most of these had minimal participation by the members and the leader took on most of the labour. However the vest majority of the teams congealed and met not only during the assigned meeting times but requested to be subbed out or met on their own times. These were very dynamic groups that often had major disagreements but who created very innovative instructional units.

One of our few veterans commented that she actually feels that we are in "it" together. Eric's examples illustrate how a definition can inspire handling of complex tasks in ways that create new options.

*Tom:* "Tom", a high school assistant principal, wrote about his interest in political leadership, and about the ideas of leadership he had been exposed to in administration. Great leaders from history, players in the political world, were the basis for his beliefs about leadership. Also considered in the paper were ideas from leadership books his superintendent had "assigned" to him. He stated,

> Going into this course, my definition of leadership would, if I could articulate one, be based on trait theory and history. If I were forced to write down my definition of leadership, I would say it is the ability of a person or persons to articulate a positive vision for an organisation and to convince the stakeholders in that organisation to join in moving the organisation towards that vision. This definition takes into account the historical events I read about and taught while a classroom teacher and the 'qualities' I was exposed to during the past few years I have been an administrator.

Toward the end of the paper Tom wrote, "I feel safe in saying my definition of leadership is changing. I know as my graduate studies continue my definition will continue to change; it will never be finished because learning is a lifelong pursuit. After reading so many definitions, I don't know if I will ever be able to develop one of my own." He quoted Wheatley (1999) to summarise the new definitions of leadership: "We must interact with the world in order to see what we might create. Through engagement in the moment, we evoke our futures" (p. 39). He continued, "This idea is carried through all the books discussed here regardless of the author or who assigned it. . . . If anything is going to be synthesized in this paper it is that because of all the common threads between leadership definitions, a set of common beliefs about leadership is taking shape and this set of beliefs halls great promise for the future of education."

Tom did not report any clear effects on his leadership practices in the Follow-Up Survey, offering this discouraged explanation:

> I don't know if my definition has had any impact on my leadership practices over the last 5 months. Due to the nature of my job, I am often swamped by petty details. I spend a great deal of my time performing a clerical function. When I do attempt to offer leadership on an issue important to me, I am often unable to follow through because so much of my work day is consumed by scraps of paper.

**Central Office Administrators**

*Larry:* A central office assistant superintendent for business, "Larry" observed with reference to the course readings, "Based upon the study of their theories and observations regarding the essence of leadership I refined my definition [of leadership] and reshaped my opinions about authority and power, the change process, leadership style, and worldview." In the Synthesis Paper he presented his pre-seminar definition, "Leadership is the ability to use one's knowledge, skills, and experiences to positively or negatively influence others in a manner that will allow for the attainment of the goals of the organisation." Toward the end of the paper, he presented his end-of-seminar definition of leadership: "Leadership is the relationship between individuals who influence each other to accomplish real changes through adaptation for the common good of the organisation." Larry discussed the influences of particular authors on the revised definition, and mentioned identifying with Greenleaf's 'leader as servant' metaphor rather than his previously favoured 'leader as coach' metaphor. In concluding the paper, Larry offered a dramatic conclusion about his district:

> As a result of this seminar I have revised my definition of leadership as I have broadened my worldview. I have gained many interesting and useful ideas presented by the authors studied and have been able to not only change my definition of leadership, but also apply much of what was discussed in my current position. I have come to the realisation that I no longer agree with my current district's beliefs about effective leadership.

Writing in the Fallow-Up Survey about the effects of the course on his leadership practices, Larry explained why he still holds the definition of leadership he developed in the seminar: "I realised through course readings and class discussions that leadership is a two-way, multifaceted relationship, between many individuals working toward a common goal or theme. Leadership is not an individual making independent decisions in a void and then passing them down to the workers below." As a result he is now "involving more people in making the decisions that affect my department." He continues, "This has allowed for free flow of information from multiple levels often providing a better solution than could have been generated alone." Two additional examples he shared were using the World Café technique successfully to facilitate work of a district facilities improvement committee to develop a 10-year facility improvement plan. He also allowed staff to decide whether or not to upgrade the district's computerised financial system. "They decided yes and there was 100 % buy-in when it came time to implement the new software." He offered the following observation: "I have found that the changes I made in my approach to leadership [requiring more involvement from others] provided positive results, thus reinforcing my newly held understanding of what leadership is. Success breeds success." Larry's examples illustrate the effects of his end-of-seminar definition on his leadership style and his handling of complex tasks.

*John:* "John", a first-year superintendent, prior to the class had "always viewed the leader as a manager." In the Synthesis Paper he reviewed the definition he had written at the first clasp, "Leadership is defined as having a vision and being able to get others to follow you and accomplish tasks necessary to see the vision completed. It could also be described as the ability to develop team work through the buy-in of others." John explained that he tackled the readings for the course reluctantly at first, but "As the author read the books a little light would go off in his mind. He would often think about how the writings of the books could be applied to his everyday job as Superintendent of a small school district .... the author often catches himself doing something that was influenced by one of the authors read in the class." He concluded the paper:

> This author's definition of leadership would now closely match that of Joseph Rost (1991), who defined leadership as; 'an influence relationship among leaders and followers who intend real changes that reflect their mutual purposes' (p. 102). In fact, Rost is responsible for this author realising that his old ideas of leadership came from an industrial definition of management, that is, a factory driven definition that was reinforced by this author's background in industrial arts and his work experience in industry.

John's end-of-seminar definition, "Leadership is a relationship between leaders and followers who seek change for a common cause," reflected a significant shift in thinking for him.

As a result of this leadership definition process, John reported in the Follow-Up Survey that he is "becoming more self motivated to step up and claim the leadership role that is rightfully mine as superintendent." He gave as an example stepping in to help correct a bullying situation at a school, setting up counsellors and arranging for a bullying prevention expert to come in and work with the students to turn the situation around when that was not happening just through the efforts of the principal. Another reported effect of the definition was selecting others to help with the school improvement process and turning them loose to work, rather than thinking he had to do everything himself. His examples illustrate effects on leadership style, handling complex tasks, and cognitive processes.

*Madeline:* "Madeline", a superintendent in a challenging district, explained in the Synthesis Paper, "My initial definition of leadership was completely centered on the leader. Leadership is the ability to direct a group of people to achieve goals within a specific timeline. The rationale for this definition was based on my work experience." For her the biggest challenge presented by the readings was to distinguish leadership from management. She was particularly struck by the concept of servant leadership, calling it "quite a paradigm shift for me. I began to reflect on how I could be a servant to my staff and set a goal to put this in practice at least once a day." Commenting on Drath, she wrote, "Personal dominance, interpersonal influence and relational dialogue are concepts that served as a catalyst in the transition of my definition of leadership." She wrote, "Upon reflecting on the transition of my understanding of leadership, I am much more aware that the vision of an organisation can be undermined by the structure of the organisation." Madeline stated, "Building relationships is the single most important task of any leader," and discussed how relationships develop trust and encourage collaboration. Finally, she presented this transformed definition of leadership: "Leadership evolves in an ethical organisation as trusting relationships are formed. These relationships enable team members to design creative and ethical solutions. Leadership is fluid and not necessarily centered in a single person." She observed, "My definition transitioned from one based on management by a lone leader to one based on relationships within an organisation in which listening is the most important skill. It has changed my practice in my professional life and in my personal life as well."

On the Follow-Up Survey, Madeline described how the seminar set in motion an evolutionary process for her.

"My view of leadership changed and my definition described leadership as fluid. I transitioned from a manager to a leader of a different type. It is still my obligation to direct people to achieve the goals of the organisation, but there is a much deeper sense of my obligation to the people of the organisation. My realisation of the concept of servant leader has caused me to reflect not only on my practice, but generated some ideas for further research in school organisation .... The challenge of merging the manager and the servant leader caused me to reflect on and to make changes in my leadership style and practice. Taking time to build relationships, engage all employees involved in a project in the decision-making process and in the management of that process not only completed the tasks, but the projects were completed with more efficiency and with happier employees."

She gave three specific examples. The first involved group interviews with employees, where she did very little talking herself but spent the time listening. "It was apparent they gained a new level of respect because I listened to their responses and wrote every one of them down as a valued response. One particular comment made really caused me to reflect on that practice and my future practice. 'Know what? No one ever asked us before.'" A second illustration involved playing a facilitative rather than a directive role in working with a food service director and building custodian to solve a problem. She brought them together by being spontaneous aid flexible herself, put the custodian in charge of the task and the timetable, and let the two managers work together to accomplish the task, which was done by morning. "In the past I would have met with him in my office, directed him to complete the task by the deadline and made sure it was completed on time," she explained. A third example was forking differently with the secretaries on the summer schedule, asking them to take care of it. "In a much shorter time they completed the work and had it typed up and distributed. The support staff is working together in a much more cooperative way," she said. Her examples illustrate effects on leadership style, handling of complex tasks, and cognitive processes.

*Matthew:* "Matthew" is an experienced superintendent nearing retirement who has always wanted to earn a doctorate. He began the class with this definition: "Leadership is the act of providing a change in inertia through emotional support, social acceptance and a psychological safe harbour by modelling the expected future behaviour so as to initiate a change in another person. Inculcation of one's personal values and ethics must colour the expressed behaviour and attitudes of the leader." In the Synthesis Paper he wrote, "There were several concepts that have expanded my current definition of an educational leader. Suffice it to say, my definitional vantage point in this respect is continuing to shift to a systems vantage point. I have begun to think in terms of leadership from a global perspective with a values-driven system .... Clearly there has been a sea change in my ideas, perceptions and implications for leadership in the future." In concluding the paper he wrote, "Currently, I favour the leadership definition provided by Rost — 'leadership is an influence relationship among leaders and followers who intend real changes that reflect their mutual purposes'." He noted that he would expand that operational definition "to include Greenleaf's thoughts about choosing service over self-interest in our approach as leaders."

On the Follow-Up survey Matthew answered "yes" and "no" to whether his end-of-seminar definition of leadership is his current definition. He did not offer any alternative wording for his previous definition. He said he is clearly still trying to integrate into this thinking the concepts from a policy analysis course the cohort took the semester following the leadership seminar. "These diversity studies have added another dimension to my 'white, male, conservative' thinking," he wrote. Having been exposed to Freire's dichotomy of the oppressor and the oppressed, Matthew wrote with poetic conviction: "A realisation of and empathy for the oppressed throughout the world will create a 'soft' palate far painting the realities of those who lead and are led. Further, empathic feelings for all sides of the leadership conundrum will heighten the depth and breadth of conversation to resolve issues that arise in everyday leadership followership discussions." That having been said, he reported three influences of his end-of-seminar definition of leadership on his leadership practices. These were: "a more relaxed leadership style", "confidence in my leadership precepts and frame of reference", and "comfortable with my self-defined leadership reality." He added a qualification to that comfort, saying "so long as the authors are recognised for leading-edge ideas and remain recognised as the most important current thought on leadership practice I feel comfortable." He concluded by saying "continued enlightenment by the endless dichotomies described by Freire and numerous other authors of the same ilk will help me to continually re-define leadership with the times." His continuing insights into leadership are affecting his leadership style and cognitive processes.

**Summary and Discussion of Changes in Leadership Definitions**

Participants made changes in their leadership definitions as a result of the seminar and reported these changes in the final Synthesis Papers. Two themes emerged through analysis of the pre-seminar definitions participants presented in the Synthesis Papers. These themes were: (1) having personal influence, and (2) achieving goals. Representative phrases to illustrate the theme of having personal influence include: traits that "gain influence over others" (Sam); ability "to facilitate or manipulate a group" (Cindy); "being able to get others to follow you" (John); and "initiate a change in another person" (Matthew). Phrases that illustrate the theme of achieving goals include: move group "toward one common goal" (Cindy); "attainment of the goals of the organisation" (Larry); "to see the vision completed" (John); and "to achieve goals within a specific timeline" (Madeline).

Analysis of their end-of-seminar definitions, also presented in the Synthesis Papers, revealed quite different major themes: (1) a focus on the moral imperatives of leadership, and (2) building reciprocal relationships. Representative phrases to illustrate the theme of focusing on the moral imperatives include: "Leadership is a social concept that transpires when there is a collective desire for continuous improvement leading to purposeful action" (Stephanie); ". . . emphasising shared meaning and purpose" (Dave); "Today I strongly support a moral imperative to leadership" (Sam); "Members who are part of dynamic organisations would agree that components, which may be more spiritual in nature, are present in these organisations" (Eric); and "These relationships enable team members to design creative and ethical solutions" (Madeline). Phrases that illustrate the theme of building reciprocal relationships include: "developing collaborative relationships toward that purpose [of an organisation]" (Dave); "One might even say that leadership is relationships" (Sam); "Leadership is a reciprocal relationship of influence between leaders and followers creating common synergy toward shared outcomes" (Chad); "Leadership is the relationship between individuals who influence each other to. . ." (Larry); and "Building relationships is the single most important task of any leader" (Madeline). Table 1 displays the two sets of major themes.

*Table 1*

*Themes in Pre-Seminar and End-of-Seminar Definitions of Leadership*

| *Response Frequency** | *Themes* |
|---|---|
| | *Pre-Seminar Themes* |
| 11 | Having personal influence |
| 8 | Achieving goals |
| | *End-of Seminar Themes* |
| 11 | Focus on the moral imperatives of leadership |
| 11 | Building reciprocal relationships |

*N = 12

A minor theme was a stated or implied movement from leadership using linear processes to a different worldview resulting in leaders using organic and more fluid processes. Representative comments from six participants include: "I have moved from a linear model of leadership to a non-linear one. Both top-down and bottom-up leave me unsatisfied" (Sam); "I have begun to think in terms of leadership from a global perspective with a values-driven system" (Matthew); "I have revised my definition of leadership as I have broadened my worldview" (Larry); "In each element [of my definition] a multidirectional characteristic has emerged" (Dave): "I believe in such a state, fluidity of thought and dialogue between the members drives discovery of new options. Mainframes of individuals tap into a group consciousness, where neither a leader nor a follower exists for long periods" (Eric); and "Leadership is fluid and not necessarily centered in a single person" (Madeline).

Nine of the 11 who completed the Follow-Up Survey, in responding to the question "Would you define leadership today in the same words you used in your final paper?" affirmed their end-of-seminar definitions for a variety of reasons, including that holding the definition in practice had reinforced its "truth" for them. Several explanations offered are representative. For example, Chad said that his definition would possibly change in the future, but he currently still professed it. He explained that he had thought long and hard before formulating his definition, and was now engaged as a principal in walking the talk. "I have trust in my creation and like a child that must go off into the world to find itself, I too armed with my leadership theory must go forward," he wrote. Dave, also a principal, wrote, "If anything, I believe even more strongly in this definition. Shifting both semantically and in practice from 'collaborative' to 'shared' has had some wonderful initial results for me as a principal." Cindy, the high school department chairperson, wrote, "My definition of leadership has not changed, but given me more of a personal motivation to lead others towards a common goal." Not everyone was so definitely positive. For example, Tom, the assistant high school principal who can always be counted on to be a voice of realism, wrote, "I am still clinging to my words from December. My world is so hectic. I have not really thought much about leadership in recent weeks." As previously reported, only Amanda had made an addition to her definition, and Matthew answered "yes" and "no" to whether his definition had changed since the end of the seminar.

**Summary of Changes in Leadership Practices**

In the Synthesis Paper, five of the 12 participants noted effects of their changes in definition on their leadership practices. The effects noted were: "I will certainly be more open to promoting shared leadership" (Amanda); "Personally I have tried Drath's three principles and have found that allowing leaders to emerge within the different levels of solving an adaptive problem is actually less stressful than trying to solve it by myself as a leader" (Cindy); "I have gained many interesting and useful ideas. . . and apply much of what was discussed in my current position" (Larry); "The author often catches himself doing something that was influenced by one of the authors read in the class" (John); "I began to reflect on how I could be a servant to my staff and set a goal to put this in practice at least once a day" (Madeline). These unexpected suggestions of changes in practice interested me in finding out whether there would be any long-term effects on leadership practices as a result of the seminar. That curiosity was the genesis of this research. Analysis of participants' responses to the Follow-Up Survey question of how the end-of-seminar definition of leadership had affected their leadership practices in the ensuing five months revealed three themes: effects on leadership style, effects on handling of complex tasks, and effects on cognitive processes.

Representative descriptors of the effects of the seminar and their leadership definitions on leadership style include: approached building leadership teams and leading a district strategic action planning team differently (Dave); relied on concepts of questioning, leading the conversation, and reciprocal learning to move staff closer to professional learning community, with them taking more active roles and letting their voices be heard (Stephanie); appointed a school improvement process group and turned them loose to work (John); conducted employee group interviews by asking questions and then mostly listening rather than talking, and turning problems over to those involved to solve (Madeline); changed decision making in department to involve more people and allow for free flow of information (Larry); and have a more relaxed leadership style (Matthew).

Representative descriptors of the effects of the course and their leadership definitions on the handling of complex tasks include: provided mindset for process of opening a new school (Amanda); gave framework for handling co-leader role of boundary committee that became contentious and heated along racial lines (Chad); modified hiring process by adding new questions, including asking about concept of servant leader (Dave and Eric); requested and had approved by the state an alternate schedule to make more frequent staff meetings possible and initiated monthly course instructional team meetings, required appointed team leaders, gave teams two tasks, and left them free to work with largely positive results (Eric); used World Cafe technique with district facilities committee to generate a 10-year facility improvement plan (Larry); moved staff closer to a professional learning community (Stephanie); problem solving with input from others (Cindy and Madeline); and resolving a situation involving bullying at a district school (John).

Representative descriptors of the effects of the course and their leadership definitions on cognitive processes include: used as litmus test for framing communications and helped me decipher problems associated with issues (Chad); made me more willing and able as first-year superintendent "to step up and claim the leadership role that is rightfully mine" (John); gave me "confidence in my leadership precepts and frame of reference," and I became "comfortable with my self-defined leadership reality" (Matthew); learning and applying the concepts of questioning, leading the conversation and reciprocal learning (Stephanie); and merging the attributes of a manager with the concepts and practices of the servant leader (Madeline)

Table 2 summarises the themes in responses to how the seminar and developing their leadership definitions have affected the participants' leadership practices. Response frequency refers to the number of persons whose responses fit each theme. Taken as a group the responses represent experiences of 10 of the 11 participants who completed the Follow-Up Survey. One person reported no effects on his leadership practices (Tom).

*Table 2*

*Themes in Response to Question about Seminar's Effects on Leadership Practices*

| *Response Frequency** | *Themes* |
|---|---|
| 6 | Affected leadership style |
| 9 | Affected handling of complex tasks |
| 5 | Affected cognitive processes |

*N = 11

## Connecting Leadership Theory and Practice

"Some of the scholarship associated with post-modern leadership focuses on redefining the essence or meaning of leadership, given the world's pluralism and new scientific understandings of the nature of reality; other scholarship focuses on implications for practice" (Lyman, Ashby, & Tripses, 2005, p. 146). If we have as a field been disappointed in efforts to link leadership theory with practice, perhaps the fault is twofold: the content selected for study and the processes of that study. In the inaugural issue of the *Journal of Research on Leadership Education*, Cambron-McCabe (2006) writes, "Our understandings of traditional leadership are rooted in organisational theory that is focused on rationality, effectiveness, and efficiency of bureaucratic institutions, defining the education of leaders, for the most part, in terms of specific skills and performances that can be quantified" (p. 1). She refers to widespread calls for a different kind of school leader — "one whose actions embody justice, respect, ethical values, care, spirituality, and equity" (2006, p. 1). I certainly concur. The content selected for study in leadership courses needs to move out of the industrial paradigm and display the post-modern complexity and diversity characteristic of the twenty-first century.

Brown's (2006) discussion of transformative andragogy suggests that the instructional processes of leadership courses must feature attention to beliefs, create experiences, and give opportunities for reflection. She writes, "Transformative learning is a process of experiential learning, critical self-reflection, and rational discourse that can be stimulated by people, events, or changes in context which challenge the learner's basic assumptions of the world. Transformative learning leads to a new way of seeing" (p. 2). Individual reflection and rational discourse with colleagues must be key components of courses aiming for transformative learning, for changing beliefs about what leadership is and is not. From my perspective, the seminar sessions became for the cohort members "extended and repeated conversations that evolve[d] over time into a culture of careful listening and cautious openness to new perspectives" (Brown, 2006, p. 3). Confronted with the challenges of their positions of leadership, this openness to new perspectives coupled with their new definitions led them to see and enact new possibilities in their leadership practices.

As documented, the content and processes of the leadership seminar featured in this paper were successful in leading participants to a new way of seeing, to changes in beliefs that affected their leadership practices. A recurring criticism of current programmes is that they are not preparing administrators for the challenges facing them. This research suggests that a leadership seminar with multiple opportunities for reflection and dialogue, and based on emerging leadership theories, rather than what has been the conventional managerial wisdom of the field, can be successful in affecting leadership practices and enabling administrators to confront the challenges of educational leadership in a post-modern world.

## References


Begley, P. (2004). Understanding valuation processes: Exploring the linkage between motivation and action. *International Studies in Educational Administration,* 32(2), 4-17.

Brown, J. (2005). *The World Cafe: Shaping our Futures through Conversations that Matter.* San Francisco, CA: Berrett-Koehler Publishers Inc.

Brown, K. M. (2006). A transformative andragogy for principal preparation programs. *UCEA Review,* 45(2), 1-5.

Burns, J. M. (1978). *Leadership.* New York: Perennial.

Cambron-McCabe, N. (2006, April). Challenging the current organisation of schools. *Journal of Research on Leadership Education,* 1(1), http://www.ucea.org.

Chapman, J. D., Sackney, L. E., & Aspin, D. N. (1999). Internationalisation in educational administration: Policy and practice, theory and research. In J. Murphy & K. S. Louis (Eds.), *Handbook of Research on Educational Administration* (2nd ed.) (pp. 73-98). San Francisco: Jossey-Bass.

Drath, W. (2001). *The Deep Blue Sea: Rethinking the Source of Leadership.* San Francisco: Jossey Bass.

Furman, G. (2002). Postmodernism and community in schools: Unravelling the paradox. In G. Furman (Ed.), *School as Community: From Promise to Practice* (pp. 51-75). Albany, NY: State University of New York Press.

Greenleaf, R. K. (2002 - 25th Anniversary Edition). *Servant Leadership.* New York: Paulist Press.

Heifetz, R. A. (1994). *Leadership without easy answers.* Cambridge, MA: Harvard University Press.

Lambert, L. (2003). *Leadership Capacity for Lasting School Improvement.* Alexandria, VA: Association for Supervision and Curriculum Development.

_______________, Walker, D., Zimmerman, D. P., Cooper, J. E., Lambert, M. D., Gardner, M. E., & Szabo, M. (2002, 2nd ed.). *The constructivist Leader.* New York: Teachers College Press.

Leithwood, K., & Duke, D. L. (1999). A century's quest to understand school leadership. In J. Murphy & K. S. Louis (Eds.), *Handbook of Research on Educational Administration* (2nd ed.) (pp. 45-72). San Francisco: Jossey-Bass.

Lyman, L. L., Ashby, D. E., & Tripses, J. S. (2005). *Leaders Who Dare: Pushing the Boundaries.* Lanham, MD: Rowman & Littlefield Education.

Rost, J. C. (1991). *Leadership for the Twenty-first Century.* Westport, CT: Praeger.

Wheatley, M. J. (1999, 2nd ed.). *Leadership and the New Science: Discovering Order in a Chaotic World.* San Francisco: Berrett-Koehler Publishers.

Willower, D. J., & Forsyth, P. B. (1999). A brief history of scholarship on educational administration. In J. Murphy & K. S. Louis (Eds.), *Handbook of Research on Educational Administration* (2nd ed.) (pp. 1-24). San Francisco: Jossey-Bass.

# 11

# Ethics Education in Educational Administration: International Perspectives

—*Keith Walker* and *James Green*

## Introduction

In this paper we present our preliminary findings from two on-line surveys of graduate-level ethics education in educational leadership programmes. The first survey, Ethics Education Survey, was intended for directors, heads, and chairs of educational administration and leadership programmes in a number of countries. The second, Graduate Ethics Education Survey, invited instructors of courses providing ethics education to participate. Despite the disappointingly low response to the two surveys, we believe the data are valuable as a stimulus to dialogue on ethics education in graduate programmes of educational administration and leadership. After a brief orientation to historic and contemporary perspectives on ethics education, we outline our methodology and present the responses to each survey, in turn. Finally, we provide a short discussion of our preliminary findings and introduce our next steps in this project.

## Perspectives on Ethics in Preparation Programmes

The idea that leaders of educational institutions should be ethical is not new. Historically we have assumed that leaders of educational institutions represented the highest moral standards of our society (Beck & Murphy, 1997). Moreover, the notion that ethics should be incorporated into the curriculum for preparing leaders in education dates to the earliest programmes in educational administration (Elias, 1989). However, recent scandals occurring in some of society's leading institutions have raised awareness for the importance of professional ethics, and increasingly graduate education programmes worldwide are responding with more explicit instruction in ethical standards. For example, in the USA state standards for programmes that prepare educational administrators typically include provisions for education in ethics.

### Historical Perspectives on Ethics in Educational Administration Programmes

Administrators in public education during the nineteenth century were responsible for establishing and nurturing the moral climate of the school community (Tyack & Hansot, 1982). At the heart of administrator preparation programmes was the expectation that leaders would embrace the values and ideals of their culture, and formal efforts to prepare administrators for their roles of moral leadership were influenced by two scholar-practitioners of the day: William Howard Payne and William Torrey Harris (Culbertson, 1988.) Payne and Harris developed a set of "ethical maxims" that were intended to guide administrators. In addition, these maxims were grounded in religious beliefs, clearly Judeo-Christian in origin.

Early in the twentieth century the social sciences began to replace religion as the foundation for educational thought, and decision-making skills needed by school administrators began to be defined by efficiency, rather than morality (Campbell, Fleming, Newell, & Bennion, 1987). Preparation programmes began to emphasize the management of economical, productive, and efficient institutions. In the 1930's a convergence of social forces and political issues became the impetus for another shift in the philosophy of administrator preparation programmes, giving rise to a "human relations" movement (Campbell et. al., p. 51). As a consequence, the ethics education that was grounded in moral absolutes during the late nineteenth century and the cult of efficiency during the early twentieth century, focused on social norms during the 1930's and 40's. In the 1950's and 1960's another pattern began to evolve as scholars deliberately attempted to define the field of educational administration built upon the idea that theories derived from value-free inquiry could produce a scientifically supported professional knowledge base (Crowson & McPherson, 1987). This conscious attempt to distance the professional education of administrators from social philosophy was viewed as a way to elevate the status of educational administration to that of the other historic professions, such as medicine and law.

During the 1970's and 1980's several studies on the curriculum of programmes in educational administration were conducted, and conclusions uniformly revealed that ethics education was given little, if any attention by this time (Silver & Spuck. 1978; Farquhar. 1981; Norton & Levan, 1987).

**Contemporary Perspectives on Ethics in Educational Administration Programmes**

Beck and Murphy (1997) observed a revival of interest in ethics education among programmes for preparing educational administrators. Although, they reported that only 60 per cent of the institutions responding (N=42) characterised their programmes as giving "somewhat" or "a great deal" of attention to ethics. The other 40 per cent of the participants indicated that the attention they gave to ethics education was "very little" or none. Beck and Murphy further reported several themes on ethics education that emerged from their analysis. First, professors of educational administration viewed ethics as an aid to problem solving. Second, ethics was a distinct part of the knowledge base of educational administration. And third, professors of educational administration viewed leadership as a fundamentally ethical endeavour.

Recognition of the moral dimension of leadership (Willower, 1988; Shapiro & Smith-Rosenberg, 1989; Hodgkinson, 1991: Slater, 1991; and Sergiovanni, 1992) continues to give impetus to ethics education in the preparation of school administrators. Consequently. We felt another update on prevailing methods for implementing ethics education in administrator preparation programmes was warranted.

Heightened interest in ethics education has resulted in a wide range of approaches. Therefore, the purpose of our larger project is trifold. First, we seek to describe the state of ethics education in graduate programmes that prepare educational administrators. And thirdly, the investigation seeks to provide professors in educational administration programmes with a much needed map of the ethical theories that are utilised worldwide in the decision of instruction in ethical decisionmaking. The focus of this paper is on the preliminary investigation of the first of these three purposes.

## Our Methods and Data Sources

The project investigation utilises mixed methods that combined two surveys of education administration programmes from a number of English-speaking nations with content analysis of course syllabi from those responding. The survey yielded descriptive data on the nature and extent of ethics education, as reported in this paper, and the content analysis will yield further information on the theoretical frameworks used in design and delivery of the courses. A mixed method approach was selected because it allows simultaneous analysis of quantitative data on the frequency and type of instructional delivery along with qualitative data on the theoretical frameworks that are represented. Content analysis is particularly well suited to the examination of curriculum materials, including course syllabi.

*The sample:* A convenience sample was utilised. Six strategies were used to invite participation in these two surveys (See Appendix A). Electronic mail addresses listed in public directories maintained by professional organisations for colleges and universities and professors of educational leadership were used to identify participants (this was limited to Canada and the United States). Due to the difficult access to electronic mail addresses for directors, heads, and chairs outside of Canada and the United States of America, we conducted web searches, country-by-country. These searches yielded e-addresses for colleagues in eight nations: Australia, New Zealand, England, Scotland, Republic of Ireland, Hong Kong, Israel and South Africa. Third we contacted the executive officers of a number of national and international educational organisations (BELMAS, ACEL, NZEAS, and ATEE) to solicit help in obtaining addresses, contacts, and posting invitations on their websites or including our invitation on their listserv to members. Fourth, we directly invited members of the Division A (AERA) listserv to consider participation in one of two surveys. Fifth, for the second survey (instructors), we invited heads, directors and chairs to directly nominate or refer persons who would be able participants. We did this through items on the Ethics Education Survey. Finally, the public directories (limited to Canada and the United States) were used to identify professors of educational leadership who might provide ethics education, as indicated by their recognised areas of interest. We estimate that approximately 1,000 persons received our invitation to participate (in one form or another). We suspect that some of our participant may have responded to both surveys. We have confirmed participation from the United Kingdom, Israel, Hong Kong, Canada and the United States. Figure 1 decpicts the distribution of respondents by their national and international professional affiliations.

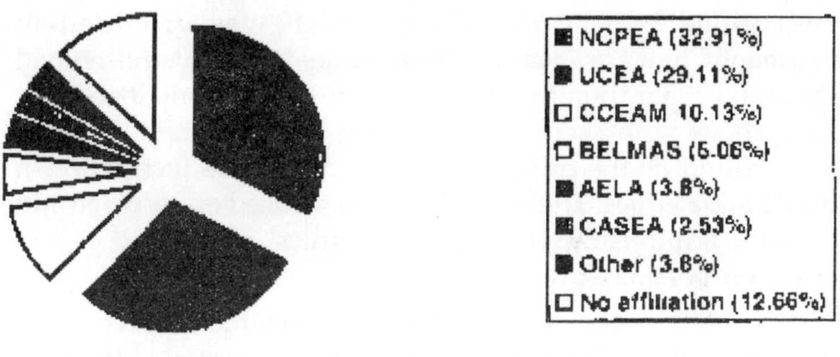


*Figure 1*

*Distribution of Respondents' Professional Affiliations*

*Data gathering procedures:* E-mail messages explaining the investigation, with the URLs for two online questionnaires, were sent to the participants. Questionnaires were returned to the investigators via online responses. Face validity for the questionnaires were established in a beta test during the spring, 2005.

*Data analysis:* The data were analysed using basic descriptive statistics for the survey items. These frequency and percentage statistics were tabulated to determine the extent that ethics education is incorporated into programmes for the preparation of school administrators, as well as the prevailing curriculum models and instructional methods that are utilised.

*Comment on limitations of methodology:* As indicated, our experiment with international on-line surveys was somewhat disappointing (perhaps 10% response rate). While we were pleased to receive the responses we did, the effectiveness of our methodology was limited. We were hoping to broaden the reach of our inquiry beyond Canada and the United States but failed to do so in meaningful ways. Our experience provokes us to wish for a more global database of professors of educational administration and leadership, including an inventory of graduate programmes.

## Presentation of Data: Survey of Programme Administrators

This segment of our paper reports the responses of 58 participants to the Ethics Education Survey which was provided to Department Chairs or Heads in Educational Administration and Leadership preparation programmes. The survey contained three major sections with each section having sub-questions. The first section centred on the provision of curriculum and instruction in administrative ethics. The second section focused on research and writing on administrative-leadership ethics. The third section centered on personnel-related questions.

*Ethics learning opportunities:* The extent to which the reporting departments offered learning opportunities concerned with ethics is expressed in Table 1, with 3.5 per cent of the participants specifying that their departments did not offer learning opportunities relating to ethics at all. About 12 per cent indicated that their departments offered very little, while 37.9 per cent of the participants maintained that they somewhat offered these opportunities. The highest percentage of the participants, 46.6 per cent, responded that their departments offer a great deal of learning opportunities concerned with ethics.

*Satisfaction level for ethics education:* Table 2 shows the extent to which participants were satisfied with the degree to which their departments offer learning opportunities in ethics. About 22.4 per cent were very satisfied, 41.4 per cent were satisfied, 20.7 per cent were neutral, 12 per cent were dissatisfied, and 3.5 per cent were very dissatisfied.

*Table 1*

*Extent of Learning Opportunities Concerned with Ethics*

| | | |
|---|---|---|
| Not at all | 2 | 3.5% |
| Very little | 7 | 12.1 % |
| Somewhat | 22 | 37.9% |
| A real deal | 27 | 46.6% |
| Total Respondents | 58 | |

Some of those who do not offer ethics as a course in their departments responded that the subject has been interwoven into the curriculum of some other courses such as educational leadership, organisation of public schools, finance, and school law. As a respondent said, "In the past year, we have infused issues of character and ethics more purposefully throughout our preparation programme." Some participants also identified lack of expertise, and financial limitations which hindered the offering of ethics as a separate subject in their department.

*Table 2*

*Participants' Satisfaction with Ethics Learning Opportunities*

| | | |
|---|---|---|
| Very Satisfied | 13 | 22.4% |
| Satisfied | 24 | 41.4% |
| Neutral | 12 | 20.7% |
| Dissatisfied | 7 | 12.1 % |
| Very Dissatisfied | 2 | 3.5% |
| Total Respondents | 58 | |

*Availability of ethics education by programmes:* Table 3 shows the availability of specific courses or modules on the subject of administrative or leadership ethics in participants' programmes. About 17 per cent of the participants reported that there were no specific courses or modules on administrative/leadership, ethics in their certificate programme, 32.1 per cent responded "not applicable," while 50.9 per cent responded there were specific courses or modules in their certificate programmes. Excluding the population of those who responded that the question was not applicable to them (those who have no certificate programmes in their departments), the percentage of those who said there were specific courses or modules on the subject of administrative or leadership ethics in their certificate programmes was 75 per cent, while about 25 per cent said there were no specific courses or modules on the subject of administrative or leadership ethics in the certificate programmes.

In the case of postgraduate diploma programmes, about 19.6 per cent of the participants answered that there were no specific courses or modules on the subject of administrative or leadership ethics in their programmes. On the other hand, 56.5 per cent responded that they have no post-graduate programmes, while the remaining 23.9 per cent responded that there were specific courses or modules on the subject of administrative or leadership ethics in their post-graduate diploma programmes. Excluding the participants who have no postgraduate diploma programmes, the percentage of who indicated that there were specific courses or modules on the subject of administrative or leadership ethics in their pose-graduate diploma programmes was 55 per cent.

The participants maintained (about -7%) that there were specific courses or modules on the subject of administrative or leadership ethics in their masters' programmes; 17.9 per cent held the opposite view, while the remaining 5.4% marked "not applicable." Excluding the non-applicable participants, the percentage of those who responded that there were specific courses or modules an the subject of administrative or leadership ethics in their master's programmes came to 81.1 per cent.

In the Doctor of Education (Ed. D.) programmes, 14.6 per cent responded that there were no specific courses or modules on the subject of administrative or leadership ethics in their programme, 33.3 per cent responded "non-applicable," while the remaining 52.1 per cent responded that there were specific courses or modules on the subject of administrative or leadership ethics in their Ed. D. programmes. Excluding the "Non-applicable" participants, the percentage of those who have specific courses or modules on the subject of administrative or leadership ethics in their Ed. D. programmes to those who do not have was 78.1 % to 21.9 per cent.

Table 3 also shows that 18.4 per cent of the participants reported that there were no specific courses or modules on the subject of administrative or leadership ethics in their Ph.D. programmes. About 53 per cent responded "Non-applicable," while the remaining 28.6 per cent responded that there were specific courses or modules on the subject of administrative or leadership ethics in their Ph.D. programmes. Excluding the participants who reported that the question was not applicable to them, the percentage of those who claimed that their departments have specific courses or modules on the subject of administrative or leadership ethics in their Ph.D. programmes to those who claimed opposite was 60.9% to 39.1 per cent.

*Table 3*

*Availability of Specific Courses or Modules on Ethics*

| | *Certificate* | | *Post-Graduate Diploma* | | *Masters* | | *Ed.D* | | *Ph.D.* | |
|---|---|---|---|---|---|---|---|---|---|---|
| | N | % | N | % | N | % | N | % | N | % |
| No | 9 | 17.0 | 9 | 19.6 | 10 | 17.9 | 7 | 14.6 | 9 | 18.4 |
| Non-applicable | 17 | 32.1 | 26 | 56.5 | 3 | 5.4 | 16 | 33.3 | 26 | 53.1 |
| Yes | 27 | 50.9 | 11 | 23.9 | 43 | 76.8 | 25 | 52.1 | 14 | 28.6 |
| Total Respondents | 53 | | 46 | | 56 | | 48 | | 49 | |

*Manner of inclusion of ethics in curriculum:* Table 4 shows how participants described the inclusion of administrative or leadership ethics in their programmes. There were repetitions in the responses, as participants ticked more than one response. About 3.0 per cent reported "distinctive or specific half course." An ever smaller percentage (2.5%) reported "distinctive half course," while 1.0 per cent reported "distinctive or specific full course." About 3.5% of the responses indicated that in ethics was offered as a distinctive or specific but elective course, while 7.4 per cent of the responses illustrated that ethics is offered as a distinctive or specific but mandatory course. The remaining 71.8 per cent of the responses claimed that ethics is integrated into other courses. The percentages of the responses in terms of course integration are as follows: policy courses (11..39%), law courses (14.9%), leadership courses (18.8%), politics courses (5.5%), organisational behaviour courses (10.9%), and educational philosophy courses (7.9%).

The responses suggest that ethics was more integrated into leadership courses than other courses, followed by law, policy, and organisational behaviour courses.

*Table 4*

*Method of Including Ethics in Educational Administration Programmes*

| | | |
|---|---|---|
| Not Applicable | 4 | 2.0% |
| Distinctive or specific learning module | 6 | 3.0% |
| Distinctive or specific half course | 5 | 2.5% |
| Distinctive or specific full course | 20 | 9.9% |
| Distinctive or specific but elective course | 7 | 3.5% |
| Distinctive or specific but mandatory course | 15 | 7.4% |
| Integrated into policy courses | 23 | 11.4% |
| Integrated into law courses | 30 | 14.9% |
| Integrated into leadership courses | 38 | 18.8% |
| Integrated into politics courses | 11 | 5.5% |
| Integrated into organisational behaviour courses | 22 | 10.9% |
| Integrated into educational philosophy courses | 16 | 7.9% |
| Others | 5 | 2.5% |
| Total Responses (more than one permitted) | 202 | |

*Estimates of number of students (by programme) enrolled in courses providing ethics education:* Table 5 shows the percentage of graduate students from the last twelve months who had been enrolled in courses containing specific teaching and learning on the subject of ethics. From Table 5, it may be observed that the highest percentage of the participants reported that 100 per cent of their certificate graduate students have been enrolled in courses containing specific teaching and learning on the subject of ethics. Excluding the "non-applicable" responses in certificate programmes, 73.1 per cent of the responses confirmed that about

75 per cent and more of their certificate graduate students has been enrolled in courses containing specific teaching and learning on the subject of ethics.

The responses on postgraduate diploma graduates shows about 50 per cent or less of the students who had been enrolled in courses containing specific teaching anti learning on the subject of ethics. Excluding the "Non-applicable" responses which form about 73.8 per cent of the responses, 54.5 per cent of the responses indicate that 50 per cent or less of the students have been enrolled in courses containing specific teaching and learning on the subject of ethics, while the remaining 45.5 per cent shows that about 75 per cent and above have been enrolled. Excluding the "Non-applicable" responses, about 75 per cent and more of the graduate students, at the master level, have been enrolled in such courses.

The responses on Doctor of Education programmes indicate that about 75 per cent and more of the Ed.D. graduate students have been enrolled in courses containing specific teaching and learning on the subject of ethics.

*Table 5*

*Percentage of Enrolment in Courses Containing Specific Instruction on Ethics*

| | *Certificate* | | *Post-Graduate Diploma* | | *Masters* | | *Ed.D* | | *Ph.D.* | |
|---|---|---|---|---|---|---|---|---|---|---|
| | N | % | N | % | N | % | N | % | N | % |
| Non-applicable | 21 | 44.7% | 31 | 73.8% | 6 | 10.9% | 20 | 41.7% | 29 | 64.4% |
| 25% or less | 3 | 6.4% | 3 | 7.1 % | 10 | 18.2% | 5 | 10.4% | 5 | 11.1 % |
| About 50% | 4 | 8.5% | 3 | 7.1 % | 2 | 3.6% | 4 | 8.3% | 3 | 6.7% |
| About 75% | 4 | 8.5% | 2 | 4.8% | 16 | 29.1% | 5 | 10.4% | 1 | 2.2% |
| About 100% | 15 | 31.9% | 3 | 7.1 % | 21 | 38.2% | 14 | 29.2% | 7 | 15.6% |
| Total Respondents | 47 | | 42 | | 56 | | 48 | | 45 | |

The responses on Ph.D. graduates show that for two-thirds of the participants, such courses were non-applicable, about 10 per cent suggested 25 per cent or fewer Ph.D. students were taught ethics and about 16 per cent said 100 per cent of students had been enrolled in such courses.

Participants were asked to indicate the title of the specific courses) or modules they offer in ethics, participants gave different course titles which include "Values and Ethics for School Leaders," "An Exploration of Ethics as Relates to the Modern School Administrator," "Law and Ethics," "Ethics in Educational Leadership", "Legal and Ethical Issues in Educational Administration" "Ethical leadership Politics of Education" "Philosophy and Ethics of Education" and "Ethics, law, and Finance". Most of the course titles given by the participants showed that Ethics as a subject is often integrated with other courses such as law, policy, politics, philosophy, and finance.

*Table 6*

*Reasons for Excluding Ethics as a Subject in Education Administration Programmes*

| | | |
|---|---|---|
| Subject is inappropriate | 0 | 0 |
| Ethics can not be taught | 2 | 2.4 % |
| Curriculum is too full | 10 | 12.1 % |
| Lack of professional interest | 5 | 6.0 % |
| Insufficient student interest | 4 | 4.8 % |
| Lack of qualified professor in the subject | 6 | 7.2 % |
| Inadequate teaching and learning material | 1 | 1.2 % |
| Insufficient demand from the field | 4 | 4.8 % |
| Financial limitations | 2 | 2.4 % |
| Already integrated with courses | 13 | 15.7 % |
| Provided as an elective to another department on campus | 1 | 1.2 % |
| Other | 1 | 1.2 % |
| Not applicable | 34 | 41.0 % |
| Total Responses (more than one permitted) | 83 | |

*Reasons for excluding ethics education:* Table 6 shows the reasons given by participants for excluding administrative or leadership ethics as a specific subject offered in graduate programmes. None of the participants indicated that the "subject is inappropriate."

About 15.7 per cent of the participants indicated that the course has already been integrated with other courses, and 12.1 per cent of the responses showed that the curriculum was too full.

*Connections with other university departments:* As indicated in Table 7, 79.3 per cent of the participants indicated that their students were not encouraged to take ethics courses from other university departments.

*Table 7*

*Graduate Advisors Who Encourage Students to Enroll in Ethics Courses) from Other University Departments*

| | | |
|---|---|---|
| Yes | 12 | 20.7 % |
| No | 46 | 79.3% |
| Total Respondents | 58 | |

*Requirement of ethics education by an external authority:* Table 8 shows the responses on whether participants' departments are required by an authority (i.e., state and/or professional group) to offer ethics courses) or module(s). As this table indicates, 34.5 per cent of the participants stated that they were not required by an authority to offer ethics courses or modules, while 65.5 per cent responded that they were not required by an authority to offer ethics courses or modules. Most of the participants indicated that their departments were required to offer ethics courses) or modules) by the Department of Education and National Council of Accreditation of Teachers' Education.

*Table 8*

*Departments are Required to Offer Ethics Course(s) or Module(s)*

| | | |
|---|---|---|
| Yes | 20 | 34.5% |
| No | 38 | 65.5% |
| Total Respondents | 58 | - |

*Level of importance ascribed to providing ethics education for students:* Table 9 shows the extent to which administrative or leadership ethics was considered as an important subject for students. About

3.5 per cent of the participants indicated that ethics is not a very important subject for the students, while approximately 62 per cent signified that ethics is a very important subject for the students. About 91.4 per cent of the participants rated ethics in the two top-most scales of importance.

*Table 9*

*Extent that Ethics is Considered an Important Subject for Students*

| | | | |
|---|---|---|---|
| (Not very important) | 1 | 2 | 3.5% |
| | 2 | 0 | 0.0% |
| | 3 | 3 | 5.2% |
| | 4 | 17 | 29.3% |
| (Very Important) | 5 | 36 | 62.1 % |
| Total Respondents | | 58 | |

*Graduate student scholarship in ethics:* In Table 10 we see that 53.5 per cent of the participants claimed that they knew of students who had undertaken major papers, projects, theses, or dissertations related to ethics in the last three years.

*Table 10*

*Participants Who Knew Students Who Had Undertaken Major Papers, Theses, or Dissertations Related to Ethics in the Last Three Years*

| | | |
|---|---|---|
| Yes | 31 | 53.5% |
| No | 27 | 46.5 % |
| Total | 58 | |

*Faculty scholarship in ethics:* As indicated in Table I1, 74.1 per cent of the participants claimed that they or their faculty colleagues have been directly engaged in scholarly activity related to ethics and educational leadership in the last three years.

*Nature of faculty scholarship in ethics:* From Table 12 it is observed that 25.6 per cent of participants indicated that their engagements were in articles, 34.4 per cent in conference papers, 13.33 per cent in books, 22.2 per cent in form of workshops, and 4.4 per cent were categorised as "other." Those who categorised their engagement as "others" identified their participation in

Human Research Ethics Committee, organisation of study-day on ethics, and doing book reviews or dissertation studies in the area.

*Table 11*

*Participants or Colleagues Who Had Engaged in Scholarly Activity Related to Ethics and Educational Leadership in the Last Three Years*

| | | |
|---|---|---|
| Yes | 43 | 74.1 % |
| No | 15 | 25.9% |
| Total Respondents | 58 | |

*Table 12*

*Type of Scholarly Activity Related to Ethics and Educational Leadership that Participants and/or Colleagues Had Directly Engaged in the Past Three Years*

| | | |
|---|---|---|
| Articles | 23 | 25.6% |
| Conference papers | 31 | 34.4% |
| Books | 12 | 13.3% |
| Workshops | 20 | 22.2% |
| Other | 4 | 4.4% |
| Total Responses | 90 | |

*Relative importance of qualifications needed to teach ethics:* Table 13 shows the relative importance of qualifications for teaching ethics, according to Heads or Chairs of in a typical educational administration and leadership programmes. Table 13 displays that about 24.1 per cent of the participants rated formal study of ethics as very important, while 20.7 per cent of the participants placed it on the two least important levels. Table 13 also depicts that a greater percentage of the participants (53.5 per cent) indicated that professional administrative experience was a very important qualification, whereas only 10.4 per cent placed professional experience in the bottom two categories of importance. About 29.3 per cent of the participants indicated that professional development for teachers of ethics education was very important, while 12.1 per cent reported that it was not very important. In summary, participants reported valuing professional experience slightly more than professional development, and substantially more than formal study.

*Table 13*

*The Importance of Qualifications for Teaching Ethics in Educational Administration and Leadership Programmes*

| | Formal study of Ethics | | Professional Administrative Experience | | Professional development in Ethics Education | |
|---|---|---|---|---|---|---|
| | N | % | N | % | N | % |
| 1 (Not Very Important) | 2 | 3.5% | 2 | 3.5% | 3 | 5.2% |
| 2 | 10 | 17.2% | 4 | 6.9% | 4 | 6.9% |
| 3 | 19 | 32.8% | 5 | 8.6% | 14 | 24.1 |
| 4 | 13 | 22.4% | 16 | 27.6% | 20 | 34.5% |
| 5 (Very Important) | 14 | 24.1% | 31 | 53.5% | 17 | 29.3% |
| Total Respondents | 58 | | 58 | | 58 | |

*Connections with other faculty:* Table 14 shows that 36.2 per cent of the participants claimed that they or their faculty colleagues work with faculty from other disciplines to provide students with learning or research opportunities in the area of administrative or leadership ethics. Tie type of work in which participants and their colleagues have engaged with faculty from other disciplines were on dissertation advisory committees and projects relating to health and criminal issues. Participants also pointed out their interdisciplinary engagements with faculties from other departments such as religion, business, psychology, counselling, and law.

*Table 14*

*Responses to Whether Participants' Faculties Work with Faculty from Other Disciplines to Provide Students with Learning or Research Opportunities in the Area of Administrative or Leadership Ethics*

| | | |
|---|---|---|
| Yes | 21 | 36.2% |
| No | 37 | 63.8% |
| Total Respondents | 58 | |

**Summary of Preliminary Findings from Survey of Programme Administrators**

Less than a decade ago Beck and Murphy (1997) reported that slightly over half the programmes for preparing educational administrators gave "somewhat" or "a great deal" of attention to the study of ethics. In these preliminary findings from our survey of programme administrators that we conducted during the fall and winter, 2005-2006, we have learned that the ethical dimension of leadership is considered much more important than a decade ago. With 58 participants responding, our survey indicated that 87 per cent now give ethics "somewhat" or "a great deal" of attention. Moreover, 91 per cent of the programme administrators in our survey reported that they consider formal study of ethics important. However, most programmes (69.4%) preferred to integrate the study of ethics into existing courses rather than offering a separate and distinctive course in ethics (7.4%). Another notable observation regarding the prominence that ethics is gaining centers on scholarship. Programme administrators reported that over half of their students (53.5%) had investigated topics in ethics in major research papers, theses; or dissertations. In addition, a very notable -4.1 per cent of the participants reported that they had engaged in some form of scholarship involving the study of ethics (e.g., articles, conference papers, workshops, etc.).

In those instances where ethics was not included in administrator preparation programmes, reasons varied widely, although, the leading reasons given were that the existing curriculum was too full (12.1%) with mandated content or that appropriate expertise in ethics was not available among faculties (7.2%). Upon looking further into the extent of faculty expertise, we learned that most programme administrators consider professional experience the most important qualification for teaching ethics (81.1 % considered experience important or very important), followed by formal study in ethics (66.5% considered experience important or very important).

In summary, the study of ethics in administrator preparation programmes is gaining more prominence in comparison to a decade ago. More programmes include instruction specific to the study of ethics in educational administration, and more students and faculty are engaged in scholarship that focuses on ethics. In the next section we report findings from our survey of faculty who teach courses that contain the formal study of ethics, and in particular we direct our 4 attention to the design and delivery of instruction in ethics.

## PRESENTATION OF DATA: SURVEY OF FACULTY

This section reports the findings that stemmed from the Ethics Education Survey was provided to graduate instructors involved with ethics education. There were 61 participants to this survey. Because of the anonymity of survey and the natural potential for dual roles (i.e., department head or director as well as being an instructor of an ethics education course — there may have been individuals who completed both surveys. This second survey captained four major parts, with each section having sub-questions. The first section centered on the provision of curriculum and instruction in administrative ethics. The second section focused on personnel oriented question, while the third section asked participants to consider teaching and learning methods. Section four focused on research on administrative/ leadership ethics.

*Ethics learning opportunities:* Table 15 shows the extent to which responding graduate instructors believed their departments or units offered learning opportunities concerned with ethics. From Table 15, it is observed that 18.3 per cent of the participants indicated that "very little" was the extent to which their departments or units offered learning opportunities concerned with ethics, 50 per cent responded "somewhat", while the remaining 31.7 per cent reported that their departments offered a "great deal". None of the participants indicated that their departments do not offer learning opportunities concerned with ethics.

*Satisfaction level for ethics education*: Table 16 expresses the extent to which graduate instructors are satisfied with their departments' offerings of learning opportunities concerned with ethics. It is observed that 10 per cent of the participants were "very satisfied," 43.3 per cent responded "satisfied," while 16.7 per cent reported "neutral." On the other hand, 16.7 per cent indicated that they were dissatisfied with their departments' offerings of learning opportunities concerned with ethics, and the remaining 13.3 per cent were "very dissatisfied". In summary, a total of 53.3 per cent of the participants were "very satisfied" or "satisfied" with their departments' offerings.

*Table 15*

*Extent that Departments Offer Learning Opportunities Concerned with Ethics.*

| | *N* | % |
|---|---|---|
| Not at all | 0 | 0 |
| Very little | 11 | 18.3% |
| Somewhat | 30 | 50.0% |
| A great deal | 19 | 31.7% |
| Total Respondents | 60 | |

*Availability of ethics education by programmes:* Table 17 shows the availability of specific courses or modules on the subject of administrative or leadership ethics in the preparation programmes of participants. We observed that 51.0 per cent of the participants indicated that there were specific courses or modules on the subject of administrative or leadership ethics in their certificate preparation programmes. Excluding the non-applicable responses, 60.5 per cent of the participants reported that there were specific courses or modules on the subject of administrative or leadership ethics in their certificate preparation programmes.

*Table 16*

*Extent that Participants are Satisfied with Ethics Learning Opportunities*

| | *N* | % |
|---|---|---|
| Very satisfied | 6 | 10.0% |
| Satisfied | 26 | 43.3% |
| Neutral | 10 | 16.7% |
| Dissatisfied | 10 | 16.7% |
| Very dissatisfied | 8 | 13.3% |
| Total Respondents | 60 | |

With respect to diploma programmes, 24.4 per cent reported that there were specific courses or modules on the subject of administrative or leadership ethics in their diploma preparation programmes. Excluding the non-applicable responses, 52.4 per cent of the participants reported that their departments offered specific courses or modules on the subject of administrative or leadership ethics in the diploma preparation programmes.

The responses on the master's programmes show that 65.5 per cent had specific courses or modules on the subject of administrative or leadership ethics.

Also from Table 17, 65.4 per cent of the participants reported that there were specific courses or modules on the subject of administrative or leadership ethics in their Ed.D. preparation programmes. Excluding the non-applicable responses, the percentage of those who indicated that there were specific courses or modules on the subject of administrative or leadership ethics in their Ed.D programmes was 77.3 per cent. The responses on Ph.D. programmes show that 37.0 per cent indicated that there were specific courses or modules on the subject of administrative or leadership ethics in their Ph.D. preparation programmes.

Some of the participants indicated that they do offer specific ethics courses or modules in their departments, while others pointed out that ethics is integrated into some other courses. "We do not offer courses with specific title of 'ethics' but include ethics content in a range of educational administration and leadership courses." It was also pointed out that teaching ethics in its embedded courses, to an extent, depends on the professor. "Each professor covers ethics at his/her discretion. We do not have any specific requirements. I cover it a lot in my policy and law courses and to a lesser degree in my other classes."

*Table 17*

*Availability of Courses or Modules on Ethics in Administrator Preparation Programmes*

| | *Certificate* | | *Diploma* | | *Masters* | | *Ed.D.* | | *Ph.D.* | |
|---|---|---|---|---|---|---|---|---|---|---|
| Non Applicable | 8 | 15.7% | 24 | 53.3% | 1 | 1.7% | 8 | 15.4% | 16 | 34.8% |
| Yes | 26 | 51.0% | 11 | 24.4% | 38 | 65.5% | 34 | 65.4% | 17 | 37.0% |
| No | 17 | 33.3% | 10 | 22.2% | 19 | 32.8% | 10 | 19.2% | 13 | 28.3% |
| Total Respondents | 51 | | 45 | | 58 | | 52 | | 46 | |

Another respondent wrote, "The issue of ethic is implicit in many courses (e.g., moral leadership, critical theory.....), and in courses that deal with social gap. Yet it is not handled directly, as there is no specific course in that respect."

*Importance of types of qualifications for teaching ethics:* Table 18 shows how participants rated the importance of qualifications for teaching ethics in a typical educational administration and leadership programmes. It is observed that 53.3 per cent of the participants rated formal study of ethics on the two top-most levels of importance (4 and 5 levels), while about 18.3 per cent rated formal study of ethics on the two least levels of importance.

On professional administrative experience as a qualification for the teaching of ethics in a typical educational administration and leadership programmes, about 45 per cent of the participants reported that it was very important, while about 75 per cent of the participants rated it on the two topmost levels of importance (4 and 5 scales).

We noted that 61.7 per cent of the participants placed professional development in ethics education on the two topmost scales as a qualification for the for teaching ethics in a typical educational administration and leadership programmes.

*Table 18*

*Importance of Qualifications for Teaching Ethics in a Typical Educational Administration and Leadership Programmes*

| | | *Formal Study of Ethics* | | *Professional Administrative Experience* | | *Professional Development in Ethics Education* | |
|---|---|---|---|---|---|---|---|
| (Not Very Important) | 1 | 4 | 6.7% | 1 | 1.7% | 4 | 10.0% |
| | 2 | 7 | 11.7% | 5 | 8.3% | 4 | 6.7% |
| | 3 | 17 | 28.3% | 9 | 15.0% | 12 | 21.7% |
| | 4 | 23 | 38.3% | 18 | 30.0% | 20 | 33.3% |
| (Very Important) | 5 | 9 | 15.0% | 27 | 45.0% | 17 | 28.3% |
| Total Respondents | | 60 | | 60 | | 57 | |

We see that 53.3 per cent of the participants rated formal study of ethics in the two topmost levels as a qualification for the teaching of ethics, 75 per cent for professional administrative experience, while professional development in ethics education was 61.6 per cent. On the other hand, 18.3 per cent rated formal study of ethics on two least scales (1 and 2 scales). 16.7 per cent placed professional development in ethics education on the same levels, while only 10 per cent rated professional administrative experience on the two least levels of importance.

*Involvement in ethics education by years of involvement:* Table 19 shows time periods that participants had been involved in teaching courses in the area of ethics education. We observe that the greatest percentage of participants, 37.9 per cent, indicated that they had been involved with teaching courses in the area of ethics for less than five years, 36.2 per cent reported that they have been involved for between 5-10 years, 10.3 per cent for between 11-15 years, and 8.6 per cent reported that their involvement had been for between 16 and 20 years.

In a follow-up question, we asked the participants about their major speciality in teaching, writing, and research besides ethics, most participants indicated that ethics was not their major speciality. Among the areas indicated by participants were leadership, law, policy, curriculum administration, administration, catholic education, planning, finance, organisational theory, principalship, research, social justice, organisational culture, politics of education, and superintendency to name a few.

*Enjoyment of ethics education:* We also asked participants about what they enjoyed most about teaching ethics to people in educational leadership programmes. As expected, participants offered different remarks. One participant wrote, "Teaching ethics from a theoretical perspective, and from that, having students determine the connections between their personal and professional ethics." Another stated, "I enjoy exploring where ethical ideas originate. How an individual ethics impact how they treat and relate to those around them."

Also in response to the question of what participants enjoy most about teaching ethics to people in educational leadership programmes, one noted, "The opportunity to make a major contribution to their (students) development as individuals, professionals, and citizens — introducing students to a whole new paradigm orientation that can significantly extend the utility of their existing meta-organisers." Another wrote, "Challenging our thinking! Uncovering the real ethical issues that get buried in the economic and efficiency issues." Additional comments included, "providing diverse perspectives," "reflection on present and past practices," and "the interest expressed by students in the topic."

*Table 19*

*How Long Participants have been Involved with Teaching Courses in Ethics*

| | N | % |
|---|---|---|
| Less than 5 years | 22 | 37.9% |
| 5-10 years | 21 | 36.2% |
| 11-15 years | 6 | 10.3% |
| 16-20 years | 5 | 8.6% |
| More than 20 years | 4 | 6.9% |
| Total Respondents | 58 | |

*Approaches used to facilitate ethics education:* Table 20 shows participants opinion on the most commonly used approaches to facilitate administrative or leadership ethics courses/modules. The greatest percentage of the responses, 70.5 per cent, indicated that participants adopted the mixture of case study and principle-based approaches.

*Table 20*

*Approaches to Facilitate Administrative or Leadership Ethics Courses/ Modules*

| | N | % |
|---|---|---|
| Case studies | 8 | 13.1 % |
| Consideration and application of principles to situations | 5 | 8.2% |
| Mixture of case study and principle-based approaches | 43 | 70.5% |
| Another approach | 2 | 3.3% |
| Non-applicable | 3 | 4.9% |
| Total Respondents | 61 | |

While 13.1 per cent marked case studies, 8.2 per cent reported 'consideration and application of principles to situations,' and 3.3 per cent indicated that they adopt another approach. Other approaches used to facilitate ethics courses/modules included discussion of major critical theories and personal narrative.

In a follow up question, participants provided a variety of approaches which included case studies, use of reflective activities, role playing, discussion of real-life situations, discussion of major theories, and use of guest speakers that can talk about real ethical issues.

*Methods of instruction in ethics education:* Table 21 shows the methods of teaching leadership ethics that had generally been used in participants' course(s). About 16.5 per cent of the responses indicated the use of lectures which had been followed by or interspersed with discussion. We observe that 19.8 per cent reported seminar or discussion groups, 17.30 per cent reported directed reading, and 14.8 per cent have adopted the use of group projects. In is interesting to note that 14.4 per cent of the participants reported students presentation, 9.7 per cent use research papers. Seminar or discussion groups seem to be the most commonly adopted method, followed by directed reading.

Research papers seem to be the least adopted method of teaching and learning in area of leadership ethics. Participants also identified other methods of teaching and learning such as aesthetic representation, case studies, ethics audit, games and simulations, ethical platforms, journals, personal thinking, site interview with administrators, personal reflection, and personal critical thinking.

In response to our question asking for an indication of themes and contents that have resonated well with students in their learning about ethics, participants offered many themes, such as: professionalism, dying places, ethical dilemma, equity and opportunity, diversity and ethical relationship. Also noted were "Doing what the public wants or doing what's right," foundationalism vs. relativism, human resources issues, use of paradigm, fairness and honesty in teachers' evaluation, justice, issues of ethics in finance, servant leadership, politics, and moral compromise.

Participants are most enthusiastic about some renowned authors and most participants pointed out that they had used a variety of source materials. A respondent wrote, "This one is hard. I have variously used just about every one of the main folks out there — Starratt, Fullan, Rebore, Maxcy, Kidder and others. None of these is really adequate for a variety of reason. I find the most useful things are not so much from the ethics of school Admin world." Nevertheless, names such as Starratt, Shappiro, Stefkovich, Kidder, Perrow, Sergiovanni, Begley, and Beck dominate participants' lists of major authors. On major writers and/or researchers in the field of applied and professional ethics (as pertains to educational leaders), a respondent noted, "While I've read some who write in the field, and there are many who address the subject (more in articles than in books). I prefer to rely on major writers in general as opposed to those in the discipline." Another respondent wrote, "I have used a range of individuals within and outside the field ... . As a result, I have not presented to students individuals as major writers. Rather, I have dealt with them as individuals providing different lenses and/or taking different stances towards ethical analysis and ethical and moral leadership." Participants however, identified both the classic and recent writers in the field. Among the major classic writers identified by participants were Immanuel Kant, Aristotle, Plato, Socrates, Jeremy Bentham, Stuart Mill, John Dewey, and David Hume.

*Graduate student scholarship in ethics:* Table 22 shows that a lesser percentage of the participants, 25.9 per cent, indicated that they had students who have undertaken theses or dissertations related to ethics in the last three years.

*Faculty scholarship in ethics education:* Table 23 shows that 42.4% of the participants claimed that they have been involved in scholarly activity related to ethics in educational leadership during the last three years. In a follow-up question that asks the type scholarly activities that participants have been engaged during the last three years, participants indicated articles, books, research in ethical issues, conference papers, presentations, teaching, and dissertation supervision as their areas of involvement.

*Table 21*

*The Methods of Teaching Ethics Used in Participants' Course(s)*

| | N | % |
|---|---|---|
| Lectures followed by or interspersed with discussion | 39 | 16.5% |
| Seminar or discussion groups | 47 | 19.8% |
| Directed reading | 41 | 17.3% |
| Group projects | 35 | 14.8% |
| Student presentations | 34 | 14.6% |
| Research paper | 23 | 9.7% |
| Others | 15 | 6.3% |
| Not applicable | 3 | 1.3% |
| Total Responses (more than one permitted) | 237 | |

*Table 22*

*Responses on Whether Participants have Students Who have Undertaken Major Research Papers, Theses, or Dissertations Related to Ethics in the Last Three Years*

| | N | % |
|---|---|---|
| Yes | 15 | 25.9% |
| No | 43 | 74.1 % |
| Total Respondents | 58 | |

*Table 23*

*Responses to Whether Participants Have Engaged in Scholarly Activity Related to Ethics in Educational Leadership in the Last Three Years*

| | N | % |
|---|---|---|
| Yes | 25 | 42.4% |
| No | 34 | 57.6% |
| Total Respondents | 59 | |

## Summary of Preliminary Findings from Survey of Faculty

In summary, observations by faculty agreed with the programme administrators regarding ethics education in educational administration programmes with two notable exceptions. Whereas programme administrators reported that approximately three-fourths of the faculty had engaged in some form of scholarship in ethics, less than half the faculty (42.4%) reported that they were active in research on ethics. Similarly, when programme administrators were asked if students had engaged in research on ethics (e.g., major research papers, theses, or dissertations), over half (53.3%) reported that students had. However, when asked the same question, faculty reported that only a quarter (25.9%) of their students had undertaken major research papers, theses, or dissertations. Our observation that programme administrators overestimate the extent of ethics scholarship in their programmes in comparison to their faculties merits further exploration.

The central purpose of the follow-up survey with faculty who were instructors of courses in ethics, or courses that had ethics modules contained in them, was to explore the design and delivery of ethics education within educational administration programmes. Case studies, or some other form involving the application of principles to specific situations, emerged as the overwhelming preference expressed by instructors. Over ninety per cent of the faculty responding indicated that they planned their courses in this fashion. However, when reporting their instructional methods (e.g., lectures, directed readings, discussions, student presentations, etc.) the responses were much more varied. The five leading methods — lecture interspersed with discussion, seminar and discussion, directed reading, and student preservations — ranged from 19.8 per cent to 14.6 per cent respectively. Similarly, no consensus emerged regarding preferred textbooks.

In summary, the survey of faculty who teach ethics in educational administration programmes confirmed observations by programme administrators that interest in ethics continues to grow. A slight majority (53%) were satisfied with the extent that ethics was being emphasized in their programmes, and participants' comments revealed a high level of interest by students. A strong majority of instructors expressed a preference for course designs and that stress applications, such as case studies.

### Content Analysis of Syllabi

We conducted content analysis of syllabi that respondents submitted in order to gain further understanding into the scope of ethics courses and instructional methodologies utilised by instructors for ethics education. While 19 syllabi were submitted by respondents, two of the syllabi were designed for courses in counsellor education. Therefore, a total of 17 syllabi in educational leadership were available for analysis. Eight of the syllabi described courses designed solely for ethics, while nine of the syllabi were designed for courses with other emphases. In general, the content analysis confirmed the observations made from both the survey of the department heads/programmes administrators and the survey of faculty.

The courses designed solely as ethics courses did not present a consensus for textbooks, as only two authors were identified for the primary texts in more than one course (Ciulla and Strike, Hailer, and Soltis). Analysis of topics, however, revealed some degree of consistency in the topics that are covered in the courses. Most of the courses include a strong background in ethical theory, with a variety of ethical theories represented. Six of the eight courses include readings excerpted from Plato, Aristotle, Mill, and Kant. Jesus of Nazareth, Aquinas, Noddings, and Rawls also were found among the required readings in more than one course. In addition to ethical theory, the courses emphasize ethical issues that educational leaders are likely to encounter. Surprisingly, only two of the eight course syllabi indicated that professional ethical codes receive close attention. The prevailing instructional methodologies, in order of frequency, were discussion of readings, case studies, and individual reports. The case study approach appeared to be oriented toward ethical decision-making, with strong emphasis upon the process of validating ethical claims for decisions.

The majority of the syllabi that were analysed came from courses that were not designed expressly as ethics courses; but rather, they included a module on ethics. Of the nine syllabi in this category, the primary content of the courses varied widely (e.g., introduction to leadership, human resources, decision-making, and policy studies). Close examination of the primary texts, supplementary readings, and course bibliographies for these courses did not reveal any titles that deal primarily with ethics, suggesting that the study of ethics in these courses is informal. Moreover, the proportion of the course allotted to the study of ethics, in comparison to other modules listed, was less than 10 percent. Of these nine courses, three made reference to "issues" and "decision-making;" however, none made specific mention of professional codes. In brief, the courses containing modules on ethics appear to be designed to heighten awareness of ethical issues and the importance of ethical behaviour; but they do not provide rigorous instruction in ethical theory or a process for making ethical decisions.

## Discussion

A notable limitation of our findings stems from a disappointing response to our international survey. The international sample size was too small to allow for a comparative analysis. However, the total number of respondents was sufficient to draw some comparisons between the status of programmes in the mid-1990's and today. In this relatively short span of time, ethics education has become more prevalent. As noted in our overview of historical perspectives, the moral dimension of leadership is now acknowledged by numerous authors (Willower, 1988; Shapiro & Smith-Rosenberg, 1989; Hodgkinson, 1991; Slater, 1991; and Sergiovanni, 1992) and the preparation of leaders for school communities encompasses more than managerial skills. Coincidentally, this theoretical shift in the conception of educational administration has been accompanied by widely reported breaches of public trust in business and government. These two influences together — increasing acceptance of leadership as a moral act and frequent examples of moral lapse among high-profile leaders — provide some explanation for greater attention to ethics education in programmes that prepare school leaders. Beyond mere confirmation of an increase in attention, however, our investigation sought to add more insight into how extensive was the ethics education that future school leaders are now receiving.

While we observed that more programmes include ethics education now than in comparison to the mid-1990's, the curriculum design remains haphazard. Most ethics education is infused into existing courses, thus instruction in ethical theories and models for ethical decision-making remains spotty. Moreover, we were not able to observe any trends for instructional methods or materials other than a strong preference for case studies.

Content analysis of syllabi revealed that the courses designed primarily as ethics courses provide a wide spectrum of ethical theory and decision-making process. However, the study of ethics was much more informal when it was infused into other courses, and it did not appear to be informed by readings in ethics or professional codes of ethics. Given that most of the ethics education in administrator preparation programmes is infused into courses that deal primarily with other subjects, this contrast — the study of the discipline of ethics on the one hand and the awareness of ethical issues on the other — merits further study.

Participants in both phases of our survey voiced agreement that professional experience was the most important qualification for teaching ethics in administrator preparation programmes, although a substantial proportion considered professional development important. This observation suggests a desire by those who are teaching ethics, whether as a separate course or as part of another course, to provide more than a cursory treatment of the subject. The fact that so many faculty who are teaching ethics have little or no formal preparation to do so should encourage professional organisations to facilitate resource centers and professional development opportunities.

Since our report is preliminary we are hesitant to elaborate on our findings in the form of conclusions. Rather, we are re-directing future data collection in those areas where our findings indicate a need for further exploration. Specifically, we will continue efforts to collect data for our international sample for comparative purposes. In addition, we will be collecting more course syllabi from instructors who teach courses that claim to include ethics but are not primarily about ethics.

## Conclusion

We began this investigation into the status of ethics education in educational administration with two objectives. First, we intended to update Beck and Murphy's study of 1997; and second, we hoped to add an international perspective to our description. The study utilised mixed methods, consisting of a survey conducted in two stages (first with programme administrators and second with faculty who teach ethics courses) and content analysis of syllabi of courses that participants in the study volunteered to submit.

While we found that the inclusion of ethics education is more prevalent in comparison to observations reported by Beck and Murphy (1997), in most programmes the delivery is integrated into other courses. Case studies and other practical applications were reported as the preferred methods for instruction. Moreover, faculty preparation to teach ethics remains undefined.

Therefore, the observation that most educational administration programmes include ethics education must be viewed in the context of widely ranging approaches.

Since ethics education in educational administration programmes occurs most often in courses where it is ancillary, the follow-up to this preliminary investigation necessarily must focus on content analysis of the syllabi for these courses as much as courses dedicated primarily to ethics. In addition, the next stage this investigation will focus more sharply on the formal preparation of faculty to teach ethics, as well as their continuing professional development in professional ethics.

Educational leadership is, essentially, a moral act. We hope our continued investigation into the ethical education of future leaders of school communities will assist faculty and other mentors in facilitating this aspect of their professional education.

## References

Beck, L.G., & Murphy, J. (1997). *Ethics in Educational Leadership Programmes: Emerging Models.* Columbia, MO: The University Council for Educational Administration.

Campbell, R.F., Fleming, T., Newell, L.J., & Bennion, J.W. (1987). *A History of Thought and Practice in Educational Administration.* New York: Teachers College Press.

Culbertson, J. (1988). A century's quest for a knowledge base. In N. Boyan (Ed.) *Handbook of Research in Educational Administration.* (pp. 2-26). New York: Longman.

Crowson, R.L., & McPherson, R.B. (1987). The legacy of the theory movement: Learning from the new tradition. In J. Murphy & P. Hallinger (Eds.) *Approach to Administrative Training in Education* (pp. 45-64). Albany: State University of New York Press.

Elias, J.L. (1989). *Moral Education: Secular and Religious.* Malabar, FL: Robert E. Krieger.

Farquhar, R. (1981). Preparing educational administrators for ethical practice. *The Alberta Journal of Education Research,* 27(2), 192-204.

Hodgkinson, C. (1991). *Educational leadership: The Moral Art.* Albany, NY: State University of New York Press.

Norton, M.S., & Levan, F.D. (1987). Doctoral studies of students in educational administration programmes in UCEA member institutions. *Educational Considerations, 14(1),* 21-24.

Sergiovanni, T. (1992). *Moral Leadership.* San Francisco: Jossey-Bass.

Shapiro, J.P., & Smith-Rosenberg, C. (1988). The "other voices" in contemporary ethical dilemmas: The value of the new scholarship on women in the teaching of ethics. *Women's Studies International Forum,* 72(2), 199-211.

Silver, P.F. (1978). Trends in programme development. In P.F. Silver & D.W. Spuck (Eds.) *Preparatory Programmes for Educational Administrators in the United States* (pp. 178201). Columbia, MO: The University Council for Educational Administration.

Slater, R.O. (1991). On some recent developments in educational administration. *Organisational Theory Dialogue,* 1, 18-21.

Tyack, D.B., & Hansot, E. (1982). *Managers of Virtue: Public School Leadership in America,* 1920-1980. New York: Basic Books.

Willower, D.J. (1988). Synthesis and projection. In N.J. Boyan (Ed.) *Handbook of Research on Educational Administration* (pp. 729-747). New York: Longman.

# 12

# Institutional Reforms in the Context of New Zealand Tertiary Education

—*Jo Howse* and *Stuart Middleton*

The authors completed extensive and independent research on New Zealand tertiary and higher education institutions in the 1990's. This decade was a period of rapid expansion and dramatic changes as successive New Zealand governments sought to reform the economy, the state sector, the administration of education and the shape of tertiary education. Colleges of education and polytechnics were manoeuvred into a competitive and contestable environment that imported into education the principles of the "free market" The two researchers confirmed that there was a significant gap in the literature available on leadership and change management in tertiary and higher education.

The two qualitative and quantitative studies reported, showed the impact of the reforms on pre-service teacher education colleges and polytechnics. These tertiary institutions were granted a mandate to offer graduate and postgraduate degrees and subsequently transformational changes in administration and management infrastructure were critical for the development of a research culture that would underpin such a capability. The paper concludes with a set of principles that will add to and develop the existing knowledge on institutional leadership and change management in such reform environments.

## Socio-Political Context

During the past two decades, New Zealand has been subjected to the most radical and comprehensive reforms in its educational history. The social policies established by the first Labour Government were fundamentally maintained for almost fifty years, until the fourth Labour Government saw its election in 1984 and re-election in 1987 as an overwhelming mandate to pursue change. As Hermansson and Webb (1993) stated:

> With even more vigour than their reforming forbears of the 1930's who created the welfare state, the Labour Government of the 1980's set about dismantling it. In a little over a decade they, along with the National (Conservative) Government that has succeeded them, implemented economic and social policies that have totally changed the fabric of New Zealand society (Hermansson & Webb, 1993, p.215).

In the mid-1980s, a fiscal crisis, reflected in an increasing overseas debt and rising inflation, led to demands for financial reforms and accountability in all sectors of New Zealand society. New Zealand had become "one of the more highly indebted countries in the OECD" (New Zealand Government Treasury, 1987, p. 229). The National Government, under the leadership of Sir Robert Muldoon (1975-1984) and faced with an escalating overseas debt, had "gradually lost credibility in its traditional power bases, the agricultural and corporate sectors, by being so interventionist and yet could not control the frightening growth of external debt" (Macpherson, 1993, p. 247). Its fiscal policy of subsidies and heavy state borrowing contrasted sharply with other OECD countries that were privatising state assets and businesses (Howse, 2005, p.1).

During the 1980s, the discourse of government documents began to show a shift to a more 'technocratic' ideology (Codd, 1990, p. 141) and, that is there was a shift towards more technical notions of efficiency and consumer choice (Peters et al., 1994, p. 260). According to Lauder (1990), the newly elected Labour Government "created a New Right revolution in New Zealand, which has sought to change the relationships between the state, the economy and civil society" (p. 1). The Labour Government elected in (1984) believed that the inequities and inefficiencies which existed in New Zealand society could be corrected by a series of changes in the public sector, and by changes to structural, organisational and management aspects of the public service (Boston, 1991).

The Treasury Report, Economic Management, released in 1984, was the New Zealand Government's mandate for the radical economic reforms "that were to transform the New Zealand economy: deregulation of finance, floating the dollar, abolition of exchange controls, corporatisation, GST, reduced income tax, family care and so on" (Jesson et al., 1988, p. 43). The afore mentioned Treasury Report (1984) foreshadowed the radical changes to follow in tertiary/higher education, by., commenting on the failure of education to deliver the skills required in the reformed New Zealand labour market, "The poor performance of the education sector has adverse effects on the adjustment of the labour market directly and indirectly on the performance of the overall economy" (New Zealand Treasury, 1984, p. 268). The report expressed deep concern for equity, "For instance, there is suggestive evidence, at least, that the education system is poorly adapted to Maori and Pacific Island students and devotes too few resources to special educational needs" (New Zealand Government Treasury, 1984, p. 249). The Treasury analysis strongly influenced the Labour Government who conducted reviews in every sector of education. Successive reviews of tertiary education from 1987 to 1994 led to the conclusion that given the Treasury's views of fiscal pressures, and current market demands, the tertiary sector required significant restructuring (Howse, 2005, pp.2-3).

## New Zealand Tertiary / Higher Education Reviews

The Labour Government released two extensive reviews of post-compulsory education in the report *The Management, Funding, and Organisation of Continuing Education and Training* (1987), known as the Probine-Fargher Report and the Report on *Submissions to the Tertiary Reviews* (1988). These two reports were consolidated by the *Report of the Working Group on Post-Compulsory Education and Training* (1988), known as the Hawke Report. The latter Report consulted widely with post-compulsory education interest groups and this consultative process was reflected in the revision of the original policy statements Learning for Life: One (1988) and *Learning for Life: Two* (1989) (refer to Figure 1).

***The Probine-Fargher Report***
***March, 1987***
*Issues:* equity, management autonomy, coordination in the delivery of education services, technological and scientific shortage.

***The Tertiary Review***
***February, 1988***
*Issues:* equity, management autonomy, funding, student grants & loans, community links, competitive tertiary environment, national qualifications framework, technological shortage, scientific shortage.

***The Hawke Report***
***July, 1988***
*Issues:* equity, management autonomy, funding, community links, accountability, governance role of non-technic councils.

**Learning for Life: One**
**February, 1988**
**Learning for Life: Two**
**August, 1989**
Government Policy Documents Issues: equity, management autonomy, funding, national qualifications framework.

**Todd Report**
**May, 1994**
*Issues:* funding, student giants & loans, community links, competitive tertiary environment.

*Figure 1 : Chronology of Reviews of Tertiary/Higher Education and Training (Commissioned by Various New Zealand Governments)*

A later Report of the Ministerial Consultative Group, *Funding Growth in Tertiary Education and Training* (1994), known as the Todd Report, examined the central policy dilemma, i.e, the challenge to fund the increased growth in tertiary education in a sustainable manner (refer to Figure 1). Difficult choices had to be made between either an increased government contribution or an increased private contribution (p. 15). The reforms of New Zealand polytechnics were underway when the Todd Report (1994) was completed and, with the publication of the report, the stage was now set for even more radical changes in the 25 polytechnics and six colleges of education. These four reviews of tertiary education and training were commissioned by various New Zealand Governments (1987–1994).

The above reports on tertiary/higher education from 1987 to 1994 clearly signalled that polytechnics and colleges of education were being positioned for radical changes with the concomitant granting of financial autonomy and academic freedom in the 1990s.

In the context of this framework for change the senior managers of New Zealand's polytechnics and colleges of education were required to plan strategically and to manage the continuing development of their respective institutions. This change in autonomous decision-making was a significant shift from the highly centralised policy and funding control traditionally exercised by the Department of Education.

The New Zealand Government's concern at this time was with the country's external economic position. The *OECD Economic Surveys*, New Zealand, 1992-1993, were considered to see whether New Zealand tertiary education was responding to labour, market and technological change in the 1990s. The Surveys recommended that young people should make the transition from secondary school to the labour market either by way of tertiary/higher education, or through further vocational education and training. Therefore the Government, through the Education Amendment Act (1990), attempted to ensure that tertiary institutions such as polytechnics and colleges of education, provided curriculum that matched labour market demands by ensuring improved access for minority groups and a broader academic curriculum extending to postgraduate qualifications. In requiring polytechnics and colleges of education to make these changes, a new managerial leadership was mandated to lead them through the reforms (Howse, 2005).

Just as *The Picot Report* had spawned *Tomorrow's Schools, The Hawke Report* gave birth to *Learning for Life* (Department of Education, 1988c), the Government's statement of policy intent for tertiary education. Its key features were:

- — decentralised decisionmaking for operational and management decisions;
- — a Ministry of Education to provide comprehensive policy advice on education and training;
- — a new mechanism for government funding based on a common formula across institutions, adjusted by weightings for different course costs, and an increase in the proportion of private funding;
- — changes in the funding of scholarship and research-based on accountability and effectiveness;
- — a National Education Qualifications Authority (NEQA) to provide an across-the-board approach to the validation of qualifications;
- — the encouragement of greater participation in PCET, and the removal of barriers to access for under-represented groups;
- — a Review and Audit Agency to monitor equity issues. (Patterson, 1991, pp.66-67)

This was followed a year later by *Learning for Life Two: Education and Training Beyond the Age of Fifteen* (Department of Education, 1989). This established the regulatory environment for the operation of tertiary education institutions through the 1990's. In summary this new setting had the following features:

- — institutions were recognised as being one of four types, a college of Education, a University, a Polytechnic or a Whare Wananga;
- — Institutions were bodies corporate, that is to say they were legal entities, that were the legal owners of their assets but establishment, disestablishment or amalgamation were to be public processes;

— councils were the governing bodies who appointed the Chief Executive Officer;
— each institution would have a charter and corporate plan which would be a public document;
— institutions were to be funded on an equivalent full-time student (EFTS) basis;
— each institution would be audited through a variety of processes involving the Auditor General, the Education Review Office (formerly the Review and Audit Agency), the NZQA (formerly the NEQA), and internal processes.

(Department of Education, 1989)

Specifically the *Learning for Life Two* report had a clear view of a role for colleges of education that reflected the general principles that informed the reforms:

— Colleges of education will be established as independent institutions, free to stand alone or to amalgamate with other tertiary institutions such as universities or polytechnics.
— Those colleges of education that remain independent and do not amalgamate with other institutions will negotiate charters and corporate plans with the Ministry of Education.
— Colleges of education will be able to offer a variety of courses in the manner of polytechnics and universities ... That is, they will not necessarily be restricted to teacher-training courses alone.
— Colleges of education will be able to contract with the Ministry of Education to provide in-service training for schools or for the post-school sector.
— The rolls of colleges of education will not be controlled by government projections of the future demand for teachers. As set out in *Tomorrow's Schools*, the Government will fund a minimum number of teacher trainees .....
— Qualifications for teaching may be offered by institutions other than colleges of education (Department of Education, 1989, pp.38-39).

As a consequence of the Act, the 25 New Zealand polytechnics and six colleges of education in the early 1990s were granted a high degree of autonomy for curriculum development and financial management. At the same time, these institutions were made highly accountable to the Ministry of Education, and competed and had to qualify for funding by a charter, statement of objectives and statement of service performance. It was clearly signalled in the Act (1990) that a balancing act between ostensible autonomy and strict accountability would provide the leaders of New Zealand polytechnics and colleges of education with a major challenge to manage and to lead the changes (Howse, 2005).

## Two Studies of the Impact of Reform

### The Polytechnic Sector

The study of 19 New Zealand polytechnics (Howse, 2005) in the 1990's adopted a multi-method approach using quantitative and qualitative research methods. The five modified case studies (fictitious names, Kowhai, Pohutukawa, Rimu, Kauri and Rata Polytechnics) employed an interpretative approach and councillors, senior managers and academic and administrative staff were interviewed to obtain their perceptions of the strategic changes, policy implementation and the emergent leadership. The national survey of 337 councillors, senior managers and academic and administrative staff of the 19 polytechnics provided a broad data set that allowed for quantitative analysis and comparison concerning the respondents' views on change management and the educational leadership evident.

For example, a Senior Manager of Kauri Polytechnic noted that since the Education Amendment Act (1990) there were "fantastic changes" which were at "the highest level of generalisation, a relative gain in autonomy, a trend towards self-management and the running of the polytechnic, not as a business, but in a very business-like way." Similar comments were made by senior management in Pohutakawa and Kowhai polytechnics. It appears that New Zealand polytechnic and the seven new Australian universities (Sharpham, 1990) were following a worldwide trend of tertiary/higher education reforms and restructuring. Nevertheless, the data from the national survey suggested that slightly less than half (46.8%) of the polytechnics experienced wholescale restructuring. A Kruskal-Wallis test confirmed that there was a highly significant difference between the responses of senior managers, and those of staff; with senior managers tending to identify whole-scale restructuring and staff identifying incremental restructuring occurring during the changes. The responses from two of the polytechnics (Rimu and Rata) suggested that they did not experience whole-scale restructuring. An Allied Manager, Rata Polytechnic, commented that an "incremental approach" was taken as the Institute "dealt with structural issues as they arose," and while there were redundancies, they did not "rock the whole ship" only "departments from time to time," conceding, however, that "there were a couple of severe ones."

The data may suggest staff focused on incremental change, particularly the cultural elements of the organisation and the process of change itself, whereas the senior management team appeared to focus on whole-scale changes, particularly the structural elements of the organisation and the strategic changes. That Rimu and Rata polytechnics reported managing the change incrementally, and were among the more 'successful' institutions in this process, suggests that the cultural elements may influence structure and that the influence of culture is paramount in the process of change. A manager of Rata Polytechnic stated that the institute had a "values driven philosophy" and the process entailed a "modification of structures" and "regrouping" rather than "whole-scale restructuring."

These findings support Cranston (1993) who identified four common elements of change including structural transformation and cultural renewal, and claimed that the successful transformation of organisations is heavily dependent upon cultural renewal and that it should be interfaced with management of change processes. Likewise, the findings also support Fullan (1991) who argued that meaning is central to making sense of change at both micro- and macro-levels. Fullan linked this assertion to the importance of an informed and consultative process with staff at all levels. An allied/ administrative staff member at Rimu Polytechnic reported that the management team "worked really hard" at informing staff through e-mails and the Polyfiller (an in-house newsletter) and that the CEO "updated staff on the big picture" at staff meetings during the restructuring process. In addition, under their second CEO, Kauri Polytechnic also made effective changes. In this instance, the restructuring was rapid and whole-scale but the CEO reported that he used e-mail as his main form of communication with the staff, and that everything was reported and prompt feedback was encouraged. In broad terms, therefore, Fullan's suggestions re the management of the change process are supported by these data.

The Polytechnic staff interviewed indicated that there had been little time to consolidate or reflect on the changes during the decade. Typical of these responses were the comments of a Programme Leader, Rimu Polytechnic, who stated that "we are so busy changing that there is this sort of momentum happening, that maybe we have lost the ability at any level to stop and say no, we don't actually agree with this change." On the other hand the Kauri Polytechnic Council Secretary referred to the "domino pattern of change" when most staff accepted change after change. All of these interviewees welcomed the polytechnic study as their first opportunity to reflect and to consider the impact of the mandated reforms in the Education Amendment Act (1990). This suggests that a process that does not allow staff time to reflect and adjust to the changes creates a sense of hurried and forced changes and ultimate resistance of staff (Howse, 2005).

Robbins (1983) claims that a planned and systematic approach is essential, and Kilmann, (1987) talks about the importance of the development of shared understanding through an inclusive model of management. However, Gronn, (1983) and Handy (1993) caution that "We should not wait until change is forced upon us, as individuals or as organisations because change then is hurried, unpleasant and often beyond our control" (p. 318). It is important to note that the changes were mandated and in this sense were forced upon polytechnics and colleges of education. Given the findings it seems reasonable to say that while leaders should be proactive in the change process they must not act with such speed as to preclude reasonable time for staff to assimilate the new requirements, i.e., for shared understanding to develop, and that they should plan and control the process allowing for inclusiveness and thus a sense of control. There is however, evidence that the emergence of new management systems, in the polytechnic changes, created difficulties both in developing shared understandings and in implementing an inclusive model (Howse, 2005).

The changes in Rimu and Rata institutions were perceived to be generally effective and their internal processes during this period support the argument that effective change requires an inclusive model of management and the development of shared understandings and values (Gronn, 1983; Robbins, 1983; Schein, 1992; Hargreaves, 1996). Gordon (1991) argued that there is an important relationship between the context and the culture of an organisation in terms of the assumptions made about customers, competitors and society and these form the basis for the organisational values, structure, and strategies. In this context, therefore, the manner in which managers interpreted the government policies to which they are responding was also an important factor. Fullan (1991) similarly argued the importance of meaning to making sense of change at micro- and macro-levels. Hargreaves (1991) more strongly asserted that "Neglect of the phenomenology phenomenology of change ...is at the heart of the spectacular lack of success of most social reforms" (p.4). What was apparent from the data in the polytechnic study was that staff and management interpreted the constraints of the policy differently which, in turn, led to sociopolitical and educational stresses within and between the institutions (Howse, 2005).

Cultural transformation was also shown to be important to the internal environment of the polytechnics, typical of staff comments were those by a Senior Lecturer from Rimu Polytechnic who recommended a different approach — that change could be managed "on collegial grounds with budgetary constraints, if you take staff into your confidence, explain the situation and work through these issues together, you will have everybody on side." This important point about collegiality in the context of adversity has been advocated by Cranston (1993) who broadened it to argue, first, that the successful transformation of an organisation was heavily dependent upon the transformation of the culture and, second, that change management processes must be interfaced with human resource strategies. Handy (1993) likewise argued that "organisations are not machines" but rather "communities of people" who "compete amongst themselves for power and resources" with "differences of opinion, and of values, conflicts of priorities and of goals" (p.291). However, in this policy environment, as Leader (2004) reminds us, tertiary institutions such as the polytechnics and colleges of education were caught in the "twin paradoxes of planning for commercial intent and competitive market position, on the one hand, and the notion of a values driven commitment based on educational principles to meet the needs of a local learning community, on the other" (p.71).

Finally, an important finding in the study of 19 New Zealand polytechnics (Howse, 2005) was the considerable gap in experience and views between senior management (including Council) and the ground-level staff (academic and administrative) in relation to the change process. On 29 out of 38 questions in the strategic management practices questionnaire, the level of disagreement between the two groups was of statistical significance. Owens (1991) identified three likely strategies in change management — the first (empirical-rational) suggests that the values and culture of the organisation may be central to managing change, whereas the second (power-coercive) focuses on external factors or influences, taking into account the impact of internal variables such as the organisational structure and core values/culture. The third (normative re-educative) looked to the organisation's structure and development in the process of change. The current data would seem to reinforce the first of the strategies referred to by Owens (1991) — (empirical-rational) which emphasises the importance of the values and culture of the organisation in the process of change. The importance of structural elements in the process of cultural renewal together with the finding of the significance of organisational culture suggests that the nature of the initial structure and culture of an organisation may in itself be a major factor in the likely success of any strategic changes that are initiated. Some of the polytechnics may well have been better placed in terms of their initial structure and culture, to move forward into the changes successfully, e.g. Rimu and Rata Polytechnics began with good structural bases and systems, and appear to have then handled the changes better than many of the others studied.

Formerly, the principal of a polytechnic or a college of education was an instrument of government policy with control and direction from the Department of Education. There was perhaps an assumption, by the New Zealand Labour Government, that the former principal would automatically qualify for the new position of CEO and possess the necessary attributes and skills. The studies of Pohutukawa and Kauri polytechnics showed that this was not the case. These two CEOs had functioned well as principals under the umbrella of the Department of Education but when this systemic infrastructure was removed, they struggled to preserve their roles as academic and educational leaders with the new bureaucratic demands of the new and significantly changed job.

The five polytechnics studied showed the urgent and sudden establishment of a new middle management infrastructure for financial management, quality assurance, marketing, and student services. The comments of a manager from Kauri Polytechnic were typical of those interviewed. The manager noted the "infrastructure explosion" when new divisions and departments were structured and non-academic middle managers were appointed to cope with the administrative responsibilities relinquished by the former Department of Education. This was confirmed in the national survey by almost one half of the respondents (51.4%). Staff generally recognised an improvement in middle management performance (44.1 %); however, this was less well recognised by senior managers (18.42%) and councillors (16.0%). These results suggest that the staff had more direct and regular involvement with middle managers while the council and senior managers had peripheral relationships with middle managers and, perhaps, were more distanced from the core business of the polytechnics. Staff, while being removed from direct relationships with senior management, were able to communicate more directly with the newly appointed middle managers (Howse, 2005).

It is significant that in response to the open-ended question on effective leadership in the polytechnic survey, many respondents noted that effective leadership also came from middle management leaders: the Deans, Heads of Schools and Programme Leaders. The suggestion here is that the appointment of Faculty Managers, to handle the more usual administration, freed the Deans and Heads of Schools to function as academic or educational leaders. Beachum and Dentith (2004) have suggested that teachers can take leadership roles where linear structures are broken down and mutually agreed values and goals developed and promoted. It does appear from these data that the changes afforded opportunity to various groups within the polytechnics to broaden and deepen their contributions.

Notwithstanding this positive outcome the five 'modified case studies' showed that the emergence of the new non-academic posts at middle management level often led to a concomitant blurring of managerial roles as was described by (Simkins & Lumby, 2002). These findings, in fact, would seem to challenge claims that distributive leadership is an essential and positive ingredient in successful change management (Beachum & Dentith, 2004). Instead, leaders and managers become too stretched over tasks to focus appropriately on the essential core business of education and learning. This was illustrated by a Senior Manager (Rata Polytechnic) who commented on the difficulty in gaining consensus, saying that there was a "scramble for degree development and all sorts of people were trying to do their own thing and it was like trying to herd cats." There were other more personal challenges also; for example, a head of school opted for lecturer status citing as the reason the demands of the head of school position and saying, "I pulled the plug on my managerial career. I decided that having a life was much more important." The data suggest that inclusiveness is not dependent on a 'flat' organisational structure, nor necessarily a distributive approach to leadership (Howse, 2005).

Finally, it is significant that the two CEOs of Rimu and Rata Polytechnics remained in post during the restructuring years and successfully led their respective polytechnics through substantial academic development and the establishment of a new managerial infrastructure. These examples illustrate the strength that can come from utilising existing structures, people and strategies to create new approaches and structures (Mintzberg, 2000.)

Parry and Proctor-Thomson (2003) noted in their New Zealand study of public sector organisations that transactional and transformational cultures are not mutually exclusive and they argued that public sector organisations such as polytechnics and colleges of education require a different leadership style and culture than those found to be appropriate in private sector organisations to manage the change. The experience described in relation to Kauri Polytechnic suggests that an organisation can experience different leadership styles consecutively but given the very different outcomes under each style it seems unlikely that they would occur concurrently in the one organisation.

One somewhat unexpected factor was identified in looking at those managers (CEOs) who were most effective in leading the changes. In the case of two polytechnics, Rimu and Pohutukawa, the original CEOs were removed early in the process and replaced by the deputy principal of the polytechnic. These two deputy principals went on to demonstrate highly effective leadership and this was not necessarily expected by all observers. This finding may further illustrate the importance of organisational structure and systems to successful strategic change. In both of these situations in their role as deputy principal the people involved had a significant responsibility for establishing and maintaining appropriate systems and structures while, at the same time, being seen as an integral part of the existing organisational culture — possibly even an exemplar of that organisational culture. At Rimu a director commented on the stability of the Senior Management Team as many were long serving employees.

The data here tend to suggest that when the deputies took on the leadership role they were not only able to lead by example but with experience in establishing structure and systems; they were able to achieve an appropriate structure for the necessary cultural renewal to take place while at the same time being free to focus on the more innovative transformational change. From Pohutukawa Polytechnic the CEO who had previously been a deputy was spoken of highly, a manager commented that, "he was kind of an injection, of maybe a different philosophy." And that, "whether some of the staff liked it or not, we had to have that change." These comments were supported by a middle manager who commented that, "things have changed here, especially because of [the current CEOs] appointment. The difference was that he has very high integrity. He's trustworthy. But he is also financially accountable."

A recurring theme in the present study has been the importance of communication throughout the change process. Fullan (1991) argued that meaning is central to making sense of change at the micro- and macro-levels. Meaning is created through communication — that there was such a significant gap in the views between management and the academic staff suggests that shared meaning was not effectively established in most instances. Those managers who were seen as most effective in managing the changes were seen also as effective communicators. What has not been recognised perhaps is the extent to which communication is effected by the size and structure of the organisation. These two factors impact on communication and thus the emergent culture, especially during strategic change. As a comment (typical of many interviewees responses) by a Director of Rata Polytechnic illustrates, "as the institute got bigger ... everything was getting too complicated... you could not consult everybody on everything... it was harder for the institute to get all the symbols, motifs, messages, anecdotes and stories that added meaning to what was going on conveyed to staff across the institute."

## A College of Education

While all the above was unfolding in the polytechnic sector, the recommendations of the various reports, subsequently confirmed in legislation, set out an agenda for colleges that on the one hand included new freedoms which had not been available to them under the control of the Department of Education, while on the other it removed protection through introducing contestability for the provision of teacher education courses. The price of autonomy had been the requirement that colleges enter into the pressured world of market ideology (Keen, 2001, pp.50-51).

Colleges had been subject to significant control by the Department of Education. (This is dealt with more fully below in "The Institutional Context".) The prospect of being released from the control of the Department of Education was significant.

> Linkages between the colleges of education and the universities were developed; but against the grain of the formulae by which the Department of Education controlled the disposition of college resources. The formulae which determined the behaviour of both college students and college authorities depressed professional standards and ensured that subject teaching was replicated on college and university campuses. Apparently innocent of any

> acquaintance with systems theory, the Department of Education exercised financial control by regulation in depth. The extent of regulatory control over teachers colleges could, in fact be surmounted by careful juggling of academic regulations between the colleges and the universities on a case by case basis. (Butterworth & Tarling, 1994, pp.40-41)

An earlier report had also made explicit the degree of control exercised by the Department over the colleges when, around 1977, the Department had sponsored a series of workshops to address the issue of college-university relationships. The reforms then were to have particular significance for the Auckland College of Education because a "degree" was now able to be taught by institutions other than a university. To qualify to do this, an institution was required to show that the degree was taught by people engaged in research and that the programme emphasised general principles and basic knowledge as the basis for self-directed work and learning.

The *Picot Report* had proposed "that each teachers college move towards becoming a semi-autonomous school within the local university" (Department of Education, 1988a, p.ix) and this became something of a national concern during the period of this study. Mergers between colleges and universities were a characteristic of the United States in the 1950's, were promoted by the Government in the United Kingdom in the 1960's and were common during the period of the move of the Australian Government towards a binary system in the 1980's. In New Zealand, in 1990, there was one imminent formal amalgamation between a college and a university (i.e., Hamilton Teachers College and the University of Waikato) and another under discussion (Palmerston North College of Education and Massey University). All colleges had some arrangement or accommodation with their local university to provide for the teaching programmes that, through an arrangement of cross-crediting, led to the award of both a degree and a professional teacher education qualification.

The *Learning for Life* reports set up an environment in which amalgamations with universities seemed both realistic and even possibly financially advantageous (Peters & Roberts, 1999, p.17). The possibility of colleges offering a degree, and the requirement that such a degree be taught by those predominantly engaged in research, was an additional impetus for many of the developments within colleges.

Clearly with those changes/reforms, the framework that shaped the environment in which tertiary education was to operate over the decade of the 1990's had been put in place. In analysing the reforms undertaken in New Zealand, Jane Kelsey (1995a) noted that they were in large measure based on purist economic theory with little regard for the impact on real life, were implemented by a Labour Government from a social democratic background and continued by a traditionally interventionist conservative government. Finally the 'fundamentals' — market liberalisation and free trade, limited government, narrow monetarist policy, deregulated labour market and fiscal restraint—were taken for granted and were assumed to illustrate good common sense (pp. 1-2).

In summary, the implication for the colleges of this period of reform clustered around changes to the governance structure, the role of the Principal (now Chief Executive Officer), concomitant industrial issues, a new funding and financial management regime, an increased contracts approach and widespread contestability (Fletcher, 2001, p.322).

It has been suggested that despite the fact that the reforms were being applied to three different sectors — the pre-school sector through Before Five (Department of Education, 1988b), the compulsory sector through Tomorrow's Schools (Department of Education, 1988e), and the post-compulsory sector through the Learning for Life reports (Department of Education, 1988c; 1989)—there were similarities which characterised all of the reforms (Peters, Marshall, & Massey, 1994). These are listed as:

> Control of education was transferred from the central state to elected boards and councils; employment of staff was transferred to the newly elected authorities; management of property and assets was placed in the hands of the institutions; there was an increased emphasis on consumer choice and the notion of user pays; a new management incentive was initiated in all sectors; and educational institutions were encouraged to adopt efficient business practices. (Peters et al., 1994, p.259)

Jesson (2000) provides a tidy summary of the impact of the changes overall on teacher education. (See on next page)

An interesting feature of the education reforms was that they were not initiated from within education or perhaps even from a concern for education but derived their force from a wider restructuring of the state and administration. At the same time a series of legislative reforms was changing the state context within which tertiary education operated. The Treaty of Waitangi Act was amended in 1985, 1986, and 1988 and together with the State Owned Enterprises Act (1986), the State Sector Act (1988), the Public Finance Act (1989) and the Employment Contracts Act (1990) helped change the state environment within which the education reforms were planned and implemented.

This study set out to identify the key changes that took place within teacher education programmes at the Auckland College of Education during the period 1985 to 2000. Five change narratives emerged in the study (see Middleton, 2002, Chapters 5-9). Each of these was a cluster of changes that centred respectively on the effects of mergers, an administrative and professional restructuring, the promotion of a research culture, the experience of jointly teaching a degree with the university and the development of a college provider degree.

Patrickson, Bamber and Bamber (1995) have provided a set of descriptions that for them typify transformational changes. They claimed that such changes:

I. are triggered by environmental and internal disruption;
II. involve shifts in most organisational components;
III. result in the adoption of a new organisational paradigm;
IV. are driven by senior executives and line management;
V. involve considerable innovation and learning. (p.3)

Taking each of Patrickson, Bamber and Bamber's (1995) criteria in turn and applying it to the college leads to the conclusion that the changes experienced in that setting were transformational in both scale and nature.

| *Status/Task* | *Old Bureaucratic System* | *Marketised Model* |
|---|---|---|
| Operational entity | Department of Education controlled organisation | Autonomous institution set up as a Crown enterprise |
| Funding decisions | Department of Education | EFTS price + student 'user pays' fees |
| Number of students | Department of Education set by quotas for subject and level | No quota, but nationally set number of teacher education EFTS |
| Purpose of teacher education | Training of teachers | Production of qualifications |
| Selection of students | Department of Education panels, national minimum qualification 6FC | Individual enterprise decisions, usually university bursary |
| Status of students | Teacher trainees with allowances | Fee-paying students / clients seeking qualifications |
| Pre-service curriculum | Nationally set in hours | Individual enterprise decisions in line with academic freedom under TRB influence |
| Approval of courses for teaching | N/A | TRB |
| Quality of courses | N/A | NZQA accredited via various sectorial bodies |
| Employment of lecturing staff | Under Department of Education | Individual enterprise |
| Culture of the institution | A professional (i.e., school) culture | Individual enterprise |
| N/A | | |

(Jesson, 2000, p.63)

*Changes in ACE Teacher Education Paradigms*

| *Pre-Reform (c1985) Paradigm The "T.Coll." Model"* | *Post Reform (Late 1990's) Paradigm "The College of Education Model"* |
|---|---|
| *The Socio-Political Context* | |
| Government funds college. College by attrition becomes the only site for teacher education in Auckland. Teacher education at the college post-secondary school but not tertiary. College operates within a protected market. | - Teacher education becomes full member of the tertiary education institutional class.<br>- College funded on the same basis as all other tertiary institutions based on student numbers.<br>- Teacher education part of a highly competitive and contestable market in Auckland |
| *Place and Time* | |
| College is one of six institutions that were originally the "Teachers Training Colleges". | - Universities, polytechnics, Wananga and private providers able to offer teacher education programmes. |
| Steady increase over 100 years in course length from 1, to 2 to three years. From 1970's all early childhood education courses undertaken at the college. | - Three year degree replaces the four year conjoint programmes as the norm. |
| From 1990 joint four year degree programme in association with the university. | |
| *Students* | |
| Traditionally those who were not going to university and had clearly lower academic qualifications. | - Students required to meet university entrance standard on entry.<br>- Students represent wide range of ages and a wide mix of ethnic groups. |
| Typically young pakeha school leavers. Students receive remuneration to attend College. | - Students pay fees and enter into government loans to finance years at College. |

*Staff*

| | |
|---|---|
| Staff expected to be top school teachers who exemplify best practice in their activities (teaching and school partnership). | - Staff required to demonstrate the academic qualities of a tertiary education in terms of qualifications and activities (teaching, school partnership and research). |
| Staff work in silos identified by sector and subject. | - Staff work in academic groups (centres) based on teacher education curriculum focus. |

*Governance*

| | |
|---|---|
| College controlled by the teaching by the Department of Education and influenced by the Education Board. | - Autonomous institution, which has a purchase agreement with the Government through EFTS funding. |
| Students recruited and selected for teaching by the Department of Education Autonomous Council in the latter part of the period but with limited control. | - College recruits and selects its own students. |

*Curriculum Content and Process*

| | |
|---|---|
| Certificate and diploma qualification | - Degree qualifications |
| College organisation and structure reflects that of the senior secondary school. | College reflects typical tertiary model of organisation. |
| Heavy emphasis on the craft of teaching — the tricks of the trade. | |
| Programme focuses on curriculum studies, teaching practice, personal development, and teaching studies. | - Focus on teaching as a learned profession — the reflective practitioner. |
| A smorgasbord approach to compilation of the programme. | - Programme focuses on the needs of teaching the curriculum in a social and political context by reflective teachers. |
| | - High levels of integration and coherence. |

*Figure 2: Changes in Tertiary Teacher Education Paradigms (Middleton, 2002)*

A transformation such as that outlined in this study is arguably in the order of a paradigm shift. Using the philosophic construct of a paradigm (see Kuhn, 1962) provides a useful way of describing sets of beliefs, values and techniques that are shared by a given community — the "distillation of what we think about the world" (Lincoln & Gruba, 1985, p.15).

> A paradigm is a world view, a general perspective, a way of breaking down the complexity of the real world. As such, paradigms are deeply-embedded in the socialisation of adherents and practitioners: paradigms tell them what is important, legitimate, and reasonable. Paradigms are also normative, telling the practitioner what to do without the necessity of long existential or epistemological consideration. But it is this aspect of paradigms that constitutes both their strength and weakness — their strength in that it makes action possible, their weakness in that the very reason for action is hidden in the unquestioned assumptions of the paradigm. (Patton, 1978, p.203)

The aggregated shift from one paradigm to the other, produced by the changes, is summarised in the figure below. It shows that the context within which pre-service teacher education operates, underwent a significant change over the period being studied; a transformation from the old "T.Coll"[1] that operated in a benign and protected environment to a modern "College of Education" that had to survive in a competitive and tough environment.

**Shared Conclusions**

The studies showed many areas of communality. These can be expressed as a set of principles for the management of transformational changes such as those which occurred in tertiary education in New Zealand during the last two decades of the century. These principles are transferable to the international context of further and higher education.

1. *The Principle of Mutual Growth/Advantage:* The collaborative relationship to effect change between institutions and/or between groups within an institution must be premised on a belief that mutual growth/advantage is both an intended and likely result of that relationship. Change occurs at both

a micro and macro level and this principle is able to be applied to different degrees at each level.

2. *The Principle of Agreed Direction:* Both parties in a collaborative relationship must share a set of goals and objectives that is based on principles and philosophy, made explicit, understood and agreed on. The use of educational consultants, relatively unknown previously, became rampant during the time of change as groups within institutions and wider sector groups sought to establish shared understandings and commitments.
3. *The Principle of Complementary Activity:* The activities undertaken by both parties in a collaborative relationship must address points of difference but at the same time focus on areas of complementarity. Rather than throw out the baby with the bath water, or worse the bath itself, institutions sought to establish their strengths and to identify weaknesses in an effort to find points of difference.
4. *The Principle of Effective Expression:* The collaborative relationship must have a vehicle for expressing the relationship in operational terms and in ways that can be understood by a wider public. Rather than engage in discussions and conversations largely within education circles, institutions had to develop a discourse that reached the wider community.
5. *The Principle of Recalled Lessons:* Parties in a collaborative relationship must look to their past experiences at working with another institution or with other groups and be forthright in using lessons from those connections in developing a new collaborative relationship and develop more formal links through such mechanisms as advisory structures. Institutions took some time to recall the highly cooperative *modus operandi* of the tertiary sector prior to the reforms and it was only later in the 1990's that this strength returned to some degree.
6. *The Principle of Professional Growth:* Staff involved in change need to know clearly the nature of the professional growth that will be required and in order for a change to be effective, this professional growth must be supported. Staff were required to upgrade their skills to a degree and

postgraduate level in both kinds of institutions. Funding and time were issues and resources were sought to enable this to happen.

7. *The Principle of Status/Esteem:* Professionals have clear views of their status and change projects must acknowledge this status and where such projects involve working with other institutions there must be a demonstrated parity of esteem. The highly competitive atmosphere masked the traditions of academic respect that institution once held for each other. The different contribution and roles of the different kinds of institution were placed into a hierarchy from which both colleges of education and polytechnics were to take many years to correct.

Both studies concluded that the changes brought about in the tertiary education sector during the 1980's and into the 1990's were indeed transformational.

## References


Beachum, F. & Dentith, A.M. (2004). Teacher Leaders Creating Cultures of School Renewal and Transformation. *The Educational Forum 68,* 3, pp.276-286.

Boston, J. (1991). The Theoretical Underpinnings of Public Sector Restructuring in New Zealand. In J. Boston, J. Martin, J. Pallot, & P. Walsh. (Eds.). *Reshaping the State New Zealand's Bureaucratic Revolution.* Auckland: Oxford University Press.

Butterworth, R., & Tarling, N. (1994). *A Shakeup Anyway: Government and the Universities in New Zealand in a decade of reform.* Auckland: Auckland University Press.

Codd, J. A. Harker, R. & Nash, R. (1990). *Political Issues In New Zealand.* (2nd ed.). Palmerston North: The Dunmore Press.

Cranston, N. (1993). *Interfacing the Management of Change, Organised Culture and Human Resource Management: A System-Level Examination.* Unicorn, 19,1, pp. 36-44.

__________, (1988a). *Administering for Excellence: Effective Administration in Education* (The Picot Report). Wellington: Government Printer.

__________, (1988b). *Before Five: Early Childhood Care and Education Working Group (The Meade Report).* Wellington: Government Printer.

__________, (1988c). *Learning for Life.* Wellington: Government Printer.

__________, (1988d). *Report of the Working Group on Post-compulsory Education and Training* (The Hawke Report). Wellington: Government Printer.

__________, New Zealand. (1988). *Report On Submissions To The Tertiary Reviews.* Wellington: Government Printer.

__________, (1988e). *Tomorrow's schools: The Reform of Educational Administration in New Zealand.* Wellington: Government Printer.

__________, (1989). *Learning for Life Two.* Wellington: Government Printer.

Fletcher, W. J. (2001). *A Sense of Community: The Christchurch College of Education 1877-2000.* Christchurch: Christchurch College of Education.

Fullan, M.G. (1991). *The New Meaning of Educational Change.* (2nd ed.). New York: Teachers College Press.

Gordon, G.G. (1991). Industry Determinants of Organisational Culture. *Academy of Management Review,* 16, 2, pp.396-415.

Gronn, P. (1983). Accomplishing the Doing of Administration: Talk as the Work, *Administrative Science Quarterly,* 28.

Handy, C. (1993). *Understanding Organisations.* (4th ed.). Auckland: Penguin Books Ltd.

Hargreaves, A. (1996). *Changing Teachers, Changing Times: Teacher's Work and Culture in the Post-Modern Age.* London: Cassell.

Hawke, G. (1988). *Report of the Working Group on Post-Compulsory Education and Training.* Wellington: Government Printer.

Hermansson, G.L., & Webb, S.B. (1993). *Guidance and Counselling in New Zealand: Weathering a Decade of Transformation.* The International Journal for the Advancement of Counselling, 6(3), 231-227.

Howse, J. (2005). *Strategic Management Changes in New Zealand Polytechnics (1990-1999).* Unpublished PhD thesis. University of Tasmania, Tasmania, Australia.

Jesson, B., Ryan, A. & Spoonley, P. (1988). *Revival of the Right. New Zealand Politics in the 1980s.* Auckland: Heinemann Reed.

Jesson, J. (2000). *Caught in the Contradictions: New Zealand Teacher Education.* In A. Scott & J. Freeman-Moir (Eds.), Tomorrow's teachers: International and critical perspectives on teacher education (pp. 56-73). Christchurch: Canterbury University Press/Christchurch College of Education.

Keen, D. (2001). *In a Class of its Own: A Dunedin College of Education Anniversary History.* Dunedin: Dunedin College of Education.

Kelsey, J. (1995 a). *The New Zealand Experiment.* Auckland: Auckland University Press/Bridget Williams Books.

Kilmann, R.H. (1987). *Beyond the Quick Fix: Managing Five Tracks to Organisational Success.* San Francisco: Jossey-Bass.

Kuhn, T. S. (1962). *The Structure of Scientific Revolutions.* Chicago: The University of Chicago Press.

Lauder, H. (1990). *The New Right Revolution and Education in New Zealand.* In S. Middleton, J. Codd, & A. Jones. New Zealand Education Policy Today. Sydney: Allen Unwin.

Leader, G. (2004). *Further Education Middle Managers. Their Contribution to the Strategic Decision-Making Process.* In Educational Management Administration & Leadership, BELMAS 32, 1, pp.67-79.

Lincoln, Y. S., & Gruba, E. G. (1985). *Naturalistic Inquiry.* Newbury Park: Sage Publications.

Macpherson, R. J. S. (1993). Challenging 'Provider - Capture' with Radical Changes to Educational Administration in New Zealand. In Y. M. Martin, & R.J.S. Macpherson. *Restructuring Administrative Policy in Public Schooling: Canadian and International Studies.* Calgary, Alberta: Detselig.

Middleton, S.; Codd, J. & Jones, A. (1990). *New Zealand Education Policy Today.* Sydney: Allen Unwin.

Middleton, S.A. (2002). The Dynamics of Transformation: A Study of the Impact of Change on Pre Service Teacher Education at the Auckland College of Education 1980-1995. Unpublished PhD Thesis. Massey University, Palmerston North, New Zealand.

Mintzberg, H. (2000). *Rise and Fall of Strategic Planning.* London: Pearson Education.

New Zealand Government. (1990). *Education Amendment Act, 60.* Wellington:, Government Printer.

__________, (1989). *Learning for Life: Two. Education and Training Beyond The Age of fifteen. Polite Decisions.* Wellington: Government Printer.

__________, (1988). *Learning For Life: One. Education and Training Beyond The Age Of Fifteen. Policy Decisions.* Wellington: Government Printer.

__________, Treasury. (1987). *Government Management.* Wellington: Government Printer.

__________, (1984). *Economic Management.* Wellington: Government Printer.

OECD. (1993). *OECD Economic Surveys 1992-1993. New Zealand.* Paris: OECD.

Owens, R.G. (1991). *Organisational Behaviour in Education.* Boston: Prentice-Hall.

Parry, K.W. & Proctor-Thomson, S.B. (2003). Leadership, Culture and Performance: The Case of the New Zealand Public Sector. *Journal of Change Management*, 3, 4, pp.376-399.

Patrickson, M., Bamber, V., & Bamber, G. J. (1995). *Organisational Change Studies.* Melbourne: Longman Australia Pvt. Ltd.

Patterson, G. (1991). *New Zealand universities under the Fourth Labour Government.* Palmerston North: Department of Management Systems, Massey University.

Patton, M. Q. (1978). *Utilisation Focused Evaluation.* Beverly Hills: Sage Publications.

Peters, M.; Marshall, J. & Massey, L. (1994). Recent Educational Reforms in New Zealand. In E. Coxon, K. Jenkins, J. Marshall, & L. Massey, (Eds.). *The Politics of Learning and Teaching in Aotearoa-New Zealand.* Palmerston North: The Dunmore Press.

__________, Roberts, P. (1999). *University Futures and the Politics of reform in New Zealand.* Palmerston North: The Dunmore Press.

Probine, M. & Fargher, R. (1987). *The Management, Funding, and Organisation of Continuing Education and Training.* Wellington: Government Printer.

Robbins, S.P. (1983). *Organisation Theory: The Structure and Design of Organisations.* Englewood Cliffs: Prentice Hall.

Schein, E.H. (1992). *Organisational Culture and Leadership.* (2nd ed.) San Francisco: Jossey-Bass.

Sharpham, J. (1990). *Institutional Planning and Staff Vitality.* AAIR Forum Proceedings. Rockhampton: University College of Central Queensland.

Treasury. (1984). *Economic Management.* Wellington: Government Printer.

__________, (1987). *Government Management: Brief to the Incoming government.* Wellington: Government Printer.

Todd, J. (Chair). (1994). *Funding Growth in Tertiary Education and Training Report of the Ministerial Consultative Group.* Wellington: Government Printer.

## Reference

1. In the New Zealand, vernacular, colleges of education were frequently referred to as "T Coll" (i.e. "tea coll" an abbreviation of Training College and later, Teachers College.)

# 13

# Educational Leadership in Pluralistic Society: Indian Perspective

*—Hemlata Talesra*

The design of Indian society is found in the Constitution of a comprehensive culture bound together by the normative and value structure of democracy, socialism, secularism and scientific ethics. The comprehensive culture presupposes sub-societies of the plurality of ethnic groups. The general characteristic of Indian society permits the existence of caste society and for that matter of Muslim society, a Christian society, a Parsi society and so forth. The caste society has maintained its continuity despite several historical upheavals.

The plurality of ethnic groups including the caste, linguistic and religious groups pursue to retain, and have succeeded to a great extent in holding their cultural identity. All over the country, they have enjoyed the status of target groups for massive social transformation. In the contemporary situation on one hand they are struggling hard to hold their traditional society together, to retain their ethnic character, and on the other hand incorporate themselves in the wider society to improve their style of living.

## Traditional Unifying Bonds

The individual caste group is a part of the large whole the caste system. The tribal group enjoys a distinct identity, its society has shared values, style of life, exclusive symbol of identity and a consciousness of kind. Sociologists working on the caste system argue that the system is kept united on two principles: Segregation and hierarchy. Segregation means that each caste has its own separate identity from the rest of the innumerable castes in terms of (1) Caste name, (2) Occupation, (3) Residence and (4) Diacritical customs.

The caste principal of hierarchy is non-existence with the tribal society. Each tribal group has its own life ethos, historical, individuality and ethnicity.

### Leadership in a Pluralistic Society

Leadership is vital to the very survival of organisations. The point of concern in this connection however is that we usually take a leader as the one who possesses certain traits of character. We regard that person as a good leader who is open-minded, approachable, patient in listening, fair in dealing, consistent, reasonable and has respect for and understanding with his subordinates and so on. There is nothing wrong with this approach but it lacks a very vital factor.

A good leader must be a person of vision "Where there is no vision, the people perish", so days a proverb in the Old Testament. It is from the vision that a leader gets energy and direction. An effective leader must work for a goal. "Arise, Awake and Stop Not till the Goal is reached", said Swami Vivekananda.

The Indian scriptures repeatedly emphasize this very noble thought. Most effective leaders are highly motivated persons. They are forward-looking. They have an aim to achieve. They believe in mothers saying, "An aimless life is always a miserable life." Every one of you should have an aim, but do not forget that on the quality of your aim will depend the quality of your life. Your aim should be high and wide, generous and disinterested. This will make your life precious to yourself and to others. But whatever your ideal, it cannot be perfectly realised unless you have realised perfection in yourself."

So a good leader strives willingly for high objectives and sets high standards of performance for himself. Effective leaders in a pluralistic society are curious, energetic and challenged by the unsolved problems surrounding them. They eagerly assemble all their energies to overcome any barrier blocking their successful achievements of the goal being sought.

The right type of leader acts and behaves with a difference. His action and the way his followers perform tasks significantly affect not only the material results achieved but also the satisfaction of the followers in performing the work. A leader of this kind triggers a person's will to do, shows the way, guides and inspires the group members towards group accomplishment. A non- or a poor leader drives the followers while a real leader is the one who inspires the followers. A non-leader accomplishes work at the expense of the followers while the desirable one accomplishes work and develops the followers. A leader assumes obligation whereas a non-leader believes in passing the buck. In a pluralistic society like India we need a leader who inspires the group and followers with the right direction.

## Educational Leader

In any type of society every organisation in the field of education, big or small, needs strong and able leaders not only at one level but at all levels of the education leaders. In the pluralistic society members of an organisation do not respond effectively to dull, lifeless and unimaginative leadership. Under such leadership their full power will not be tapped. Abilities will die idle, ideas will go untried and obviously, the ultimate sufferer will be education itself. Education in that case will fail to prove itself as an agent of social change, reconstruction, national progress and prosperity.

## Indian Perspective

When we see the educational leadership perspective in India after its freedom in 1947, we have been very much alive to the single role that education could play in national reconstruction and development. The University Education Commission headed by Dr. S. Radhakrishnan (1948-49), the Secondary Education Commission headed by Dr. L. Mudaliar, the Indian Education Commission headed by Dr. D.S. Kothari (1964-66), formulation of the National Policy on Education (NPE) 1968 and then in 1986 the Committee chaired by Rammurti (1990) to review the NEP (1986) and the programme of Action (1990) — all these national commissions and documents prove beyond doubt our abiding faith as a nation in the potential of education. All along our national leaders have been realising it fully well that only a sound educational system could put the country on a firm footing for continued progress and prosperity.

As a result of these and other efforts our performance on the quantitative side has been highly creditable. Just to quote a few examples, we had 5,279 secondary schools in the whole country when India became free. The number of such schools rose to 52,279 in 1982-83 and 761,000 in 1989-90. In the realm of higher education, expansion has been remarkable. There were only 636 pre-degree colleges in general education and 17 universities in all, at the time of partition.

There were 5,276 colleges and 184 universities in 1993. The follow-up action of New Education Policy (1986) in the form of Programme of Action (1990) is surely a landmark in the success story of our educational endeavours and achievements.

In no way does all this imply that there have been no lapses and shortcoming in the world of the New Education Policy (1986). Education in India stands at the crossroads today. The problem of rapid growth of our population (about 1,000 million) is that life in the coming decades is likely to bring new tensions together with unprecedented opportunities to enable the people to benefit in the new environment. We should require new designs of human resource development. The coming generation should have the ability to internalise new ideas constantly and creatively. They have a to be imbued with a strong commitment to human values and to social justice. All this implies better education.

For better education leadership occupies the most important place. It is the kind of leadership on which would depend the implementation and also the quality and quantity of the desired results. Leader of the desirable type is a rare commodity but there is no substitute for an efficient and effective leader. We cannot deny the fundamental principle that competent and inspiring leaders are the urgent need of today, tomorrow and for all time to come.

### LEADER WITH 'VISION'

Benjamin B. Tregoe in his publication *Vision in Action* mentioned that vision should be put into practice by a leader. For this a conscious approach and thinking process is required. The new direction in leadership demands a clear vision of the goal to be achieved. Short-term operational planning must not lose sight of the woods for the trees. To preserve the long-term strategic well being the leader must go beyond the quarter-by-quarter operational outlook.

Through vision the leader determines the direction of the organisation and complete the process of transaction, development, monitoring, evaluation, etc. To accomplish day-to-day operations the leader must keep in mind the following three broad points for guidelines:

1. Articulating vision and formulating a focused, strategic direction.
2. Linking vision to operational plans and resources.
3. Ensuring that the strategy is effectively implemented.

A leader of such vision and action never believes in his own supermacy. Rather, he aims at leaving behind not just one person but a cadre of competent people with the talent to run the organisation successfully. The best legacy of such a leader is to leave an organisation with people who are gifted enough to set a clear strategic direction, committed enough to bring it about and courageous enough to admit that the vision may have to be modified or changed with the passage of time.

Human resources in the field of Indian education are immense. All what is needed is truly motivated, dedicated, competent and inspiring leaders who could give the desired direction to the present system of education. Worth quoting in this connection are a few lofty thoughts of Jawaharlal Nehru. He, in his inimitable style, says, "A Nation cannot progress if it mearly imitation its ancestors. What builds a nation is creative and vital activity." He firmly believes that greatness comes from vision, the tolerance of the spirit, compassion and temper which is not ruffled, ill-fortune or good fortune.

# 14

# Theory to Practice of Developing High Quality Leadership and School Effectiveness

*—Clifford E. Tyler, Robert G. Scharf and Jeanne Yamamoto*

An exciting and innovative Field Experience Portfolio Program for school leadership graduate students to apply learned leadership theory and concepts is successfully underway at National University, California. This University has established partnerships with local school district employers, that provide prospective administrators (students) the opportunity to collaborate with their mentor, and university supervisor as a group on current practical administrative issues, and requires them to complete extended activities for each regular course that translates theory into practice. This happens with the student formulating a set of 22 leadership activities in eleven different administrative categories. During the implementation of these activities, the university supervisor meets with the intern's mentor at the school site as needed for six to 12 months for guiding, supervising, and evaluating the student's fieldwork activities and his/her working relationship with their mentor.

This study will examine the collaborative reflection on practical school leadership activities in relationship to administrative theory, and varied content domains from the knowledge and content of the activities in the student's completed portfolio. It will also analyse the partnership linkage between the university and the school district mentors. This study will gather and analyse important information regarding the support network for intern administrators, and how that translates into success for intern administrators once they complete the university programme and become full time school leaders. Since this revised school administrative Portfolio Programme is only in its fifth year of implementation, this study will analyse the strengths and weaknesses of the program.

## Description of the Field Experience Portfolio

Realising that the school administration internships are of major importance to any preservice program, National University has designed an effective program that meets the needs of both students and school districts. Prior to participating in the program, students must complete at least three of the eight required courses. The eight required courses are Legal & Financial Aspects of Education; Theories, Assessment & Application of Educational Leadership; School Community Relations in a Diverse Society; Management of Education Personnel: Social, Political, & Policy Issue; Schools as Organisations: Development and Resource Management; Supervision of Instruction: Curricula, Evaluation & Staff Development; Leadership, Technology & Its Application; and Preliminary Administrative Field Experience; this last class is the Field Experience Portfolio Program.. With faculty approval for field placement and assignment of a University supervisor, the student can now enrol in the program. At the first meeting, the university supervisor obtains a signed agreement from the site administrator (mentor) stating that they would provide students the opportunity for a Field Experience toward a Preliminary Administrative Services Certificate. During the implementation of the activities, the university supervisor continues to meet with the site administrator as needed.

In the Field Experience Portfolio Program, the students participate in real life field experiences that are designed to facilitate the application of theoretical concepts in practical settings. Each candidate addresses the major duties and responsibilities authorised by the administrative services certificate in a variety of realistic settings. Field experiences include intensive as well as extensive activities, both in the day-to-day functions of administrators and in longer term policy design and implementation. These activities provide the intern with a foundation that will help them in making important and sound decisions when they become an administrator.

The university supervisor, site administrator (mentor) and the student intern work collaboratively to determine field experience assignments to be completed at the student's current school site. During the six to 12 months the student is participating in the fieldwork, the university supervisor is in contact with the student on a regular basis to provide guidance, assistance, encouragement and to continuously evaluate the student's fieldwork activities and progress. If the student is currently assigned to a school site at a level other than middle school or junior high, he must conduct at least 20 per cent of the field experience at the other school level. Such duties and responsibilities shall be performed by the student in at least two school levels: i.e., elementary, junior high school, middle school or school. In most of these situations, the site administrator will contact the appropriate level school and assist the student intern in making arrangements with the neighbouring school to complete the assignments.

Two to three activities must be identified for each of the areas unless the activities are so comprehensive in nature that they may meet the requirements for more than one area. For example, if the students are writing an entire grade-level curriculum, this activity could fulfil the requirements for more than one category.

The categories and some suggested activities are as follows:

---

Category 1. Curriculum, Instruction and Assessment

- — Participate in the assessment of an education programme. Develop instructional guides, resource materials.
- — Participate in decision making process through involvement in the assessment of educational needs the definition of goals, planning of the educational program and evaluation of the school and its academic effectiveness.
- — Coordinate the testing program.
- — Develop, evaluate student awards recognition program. Develop experimental teaching units.
- — Conduct of demonstration lesson.

- Assess the characteristics and behaviour of exceptional pupils in terms of program and developmental needs.
- Conduct a demonstration lesson.
- Become involved in the process of textbook selection and plan to implement use of the selected text.
- Present a training session on current research on one of the following: learning theories, brain research, alternative methods for assessing student and/or teachers and the impact it has on student learning and improvement of instruction.
- Review schools' reading intervention plan and data and make recommendations for revision.

Category 2. Administrative Concepts and Management Strategies

- Create a new student master scheduling system.
- Develop a lunch-time sports program.
- Develop a plan to utilise community and parent groups to assess the climate of the school.
- Assess staff needs for next year.
- Plan the faculty in-service meeting program.
- Demonstrate two techniques for diagnosing staff problems at your school site; indicate several strategies for resolving or improving each problem you identify,
- Conduct a teacher-staff meeting on a key topic.
- Develop a schedule for campus supervisors to assure adequate and continuous supervision of students during the school day.
- Follow through on three difficult pupils (one attendance case, one counselling case and one discipline case) and review the process used in handling each one.

— Develop and conduct a parent volunteer in-service training program.

— Develop a plan to involve the staff, parents and community including representation from all socio-economic and ethnic groups in the school community — in the review of the school's current goals, evidences of attainment and a process for revising them.

— Demonstrate two techniques for diagnosing staff problems at your school site; indicate several strategies for resolving or improving each problem you identify.

Category 3. Role of Schooling in a Democratic Society

— Attend a school board meeting and outline procedures regarding meeting structure, and minutes and present an oral summary of an item discussed which affects your school site and the implications to the faculty.

— Serve on the School Site Council and participate in a school or consortium review and/or assist with development of the School Site Council Budget.

— Assist in developing the PTA school program budget, support activities, and fund raisers.

— Prepare and submit articles on education to the community newspaper and/or the school's PTA newsletter.

— Participate in a professional educational organisation.

— Represent the school/district in one of the community's service clubs. (i.e. Rotary, Exchange Club, etc.)

— Serve as teacher liaison to the school's PTA for the school year and solicit teacher input for sharing at the meeting, prepare a written or oral report on the meeting for dissemination to the staff.

— Serve as the Student Council sponsor for the year and develop and coordinate with the students assemblies, awards ceremonies, special events, such as Red Ribbon Week, and other student-centred activities.

Category 4 : Working with Diverse Populations

— Work with community youth organisations, law enforcement agencies, welfare agencies anti similar groups in developing programs/services for the school.

— Design a program to deal with drop- out problems in the school.

— Mediate several parents with complaints.

— Locate instruments which would help you measure students, staff and parents awareness of the cultural contributions of various ethnic groups. Use a selected instrument in your school setting.

— Make home visits regarding truancy, serious adjustment problems.

— Develop a student tutor program for students who are having difficulty with English using bilingual students as tutors.

— Organise and assist in an in-service meeting to share ideas and techniques for working with non-English- speaking students.

— Design a school-wide Multi-cultural Diversity Fair involving both students and parents.

— Work with specialised support personnel on a case (nurse, psychologist, resource teachers, etc.).

— Review procedures for referring abused students for assistance.

— Develop and conduct a series of meeting for parents whose primary language is other than English on how to help their children succeed in school and how they can participate in the school.

Category 5. Organisational Management

- Plan and conduct a community, parent and/or school meeting.
- Participate in school; closing activities.
- Conduct a problem-solving session with staff focusing on a problem such as diversity, truancy, budget priorities, graffiti, etc.
- Analyse the effectiveness of staff meetings and take steps to improve quality of the meeting.
- Plan new pupil groups for next year.
- Develop a handbook for substitute teachers containing a lesson plan model and all pertinent information necessary to insure continuity of a classroom program.
- Develop a student policy handbook.
- Design a plan for introducing a year-round school in your school or district.
- Construct a schedule of classes and teacher assignments for a new year.
- Review all support services at your school site and make recommendations for improvement.
- Evaluate the School Lunch Program — supervision, lunches students like, flow patterns, inclement weather.
- Assist teachers in developing a consistent grading program.

Category 6. Human Resource Administration

- Evaluate a probationary teacher. (actual or simulation)
- Arrange for teachers to visit and observe the work of master teachers at your site or within the district.
- Participate in or conduct a clinical supervision workshop. Screen confidential papers of candidates for a position.

— Identify how employees are assigned to particular schools or specific jobs. What preference, if any, is given district employees when supervisory or administrative openings occur?

— Discuss teacher evaluation procedure with your principal or assistant superintendent of personnel or human resources and participate in the process where possible.

— Become familiar with all aspects of the district's processes for selecting both certificated and classified personnel.

— Interview and evaluate a prospective teacher.

— Discuss classified employee evaluation procedure with principal or director of classified personnel and participate in the process where possible.

— Participate in the evaluation of the instructional aides at your site either in a supervisor role or a supportive role.

— Interview and evaluate a prospective teacher.

— Identify human relations problems in your school and develop approaches to the solution for one of these problems.

Category 7. Fiscal Resources & Business Service Administration

— Assist with the preparation and administration of the school level budget.

— Identify available resources in the community for external funding for educational programs.

— Examine the regular financial reports and become familiar with the methods used in preparing the reports.

— Assist with the management of student body funds.

— Review the process for ordering supplies for the school and assist with the ordering.

— Develop and assist with an application for a program funded by Federal or State agency.

— Conduct a school site survey with stiff and determine budge strategies.

— Conduct school community budget planning committee. Inspect and evaluate the maintenance of the building.

— Evaluate and list plant needs (maintenance long term and short) summer projects.

— Develop a plan for appropriate staff arid community involvement in the school's budget process.

— Work with key teachers and parents to raise funds for a special school or district need, such as computers, VCR's, science equipment, educational materials, music/ art experiences, or items that have been cut due to budget constraints.

Category 8. Legal and Regulatory Applications

— Prepare a written analysis of the policies, rules, and regulations officially adopted by the school board for the operation of the district.

— Review or revise the school faculty handbook.

— Observe or participate in the development of an Individualised Educational Program (IEP) for a student.

— Review district policies regarding site level responsibilities in contract management.

— Determine the district liability coverage for teachers; share the data with faculty.

— Conduct a staff in-service which addresses P.L.94.142 and its implication.

— Outline the steps a principal must take in dismissing an unsatisfactory teacher.

— Review the legal procedures far searching pupils and their lockers; read the district's/school's procedures to determine their compliance to the legal regulations.

- Complete a student and an employee accident report, prepare a written summary explaining the process and the school's legal obligations, and share the results with the staff.
- Develop a handbook of laws which directly affect teachers or students or both.
- Contrast and explain individual protections of special education legislation as it pertains to parents, teachers and students.
- Review district suspension and expulsion policies and evaluate in terms of state statutes and common law.

Category 9. Policy and Political Influences

- Attend a Board of Education meeting and prepare a report which analyses the group's dynamics.
- Identify and describe federal and state projects in the school.
- Serve as a member of a committee preparing a proposal to the District Office.
- Work with a community/parent or student group in changing or shaping school policy.
- Identify and describe federal and state projects in the school.
- Attend an advisory committee meeting to present and communicate teacher concerns.
- Determine how the superintendent of your region/district receives input from the administrative staff as well as line personnel. (principals)
- Review several legislative bills affecting education currently before the state assembly/senate; meet with the superintendent or assistant superintendent and identify which of the bills has a high priority for the district and write a letter or send an e-mail to your

local state representatives stating the district's position on one or more bills.

— Identify and describe federal and state projects in the school.

— Interview the head of the teacher's association/union to identify the organisation's top three to five action priorities for the district in the school year.

— Meet with either your state or federal legislator(s) and review what they see as the major educational issues for the state or the nation and what their positions are on them.

— Attend a meeting of the school board and record briefly how each of the following items are handled.

a. Use of an agenda

b. Recording of minutes

c. Provisions for hearing speakers

d. Provisions for securing superintendent's recommendations on items requiring action.

Category 10. School Community Collaboration

— Establish a partnership with a community business.

— Speak at community or business meetings on general educational matters.

— Organise and participate in an extracurricular activities program.

— Plan a parent visitation program, Open House, Back to School, etc.

— Plan a parent Education Night.

— Assist in developing a community survey to determine satisfaction with school and its programs.

— Establish an after school homework assistance club.

— Establish and coordinate a School Beautification Committee (staff, students, parents).

- Develop a brochure describing the school's various programs, mission statement, vision and goals, awards and honours for distribution to local estate offices and businesses.
- Speak on school concerns/needs before a community group/organisation.
- Welcome and schedule the use of the school plant as a centre of community activities.
- Participate in the study process and development of plans for either the opening of a previously closed school or the closing of an existing school due to either increasing or declining enrolments in the district.

Category 11. Use of Technology

- Complete scheduling of each student for the school year using computer.
- Analyse the auditorium's sound system and submit written recommendations for upgrading.
- Meet with teachers to evaluate their instructional program. Consider computer-assisted instruction and record keeping.
- Review the entire curriculum at your school looking for objectives that could be taught using presently available computer software.
- Input staff manual into a software package for future updates.
- Administer and score tests to diagnose class performance using a computer.
- Assist individual teachers with technology.
- Conduct a parent orientation on your school's technology plan and demonstrate the various hardware and software currently in use by the students and faculty.

— Participate in the writing of a technology grant for the district or school.
— Prepare a technology needs assessment for the school staff to determine possible areas for staff in-service.
— Plan a new computerised approach for your school in the areas of pupil record keeping, pupil testing and score reporting, special education services or individual teacher grade recording.
— Observe or participate in staff development activity. Consider computer utilities such as word processing.

---

For each activity, the students must write a summary describing each step of how they started the activity and how they completed the activity. They must also attach any pertinent documentation, record and other artifacts that will attest to the scope and quality of the students' performance. Students must place all documentation into a binder that includes a self-assessment of the field experience, describing what they have learned and how they will apply this learning in the role of an administrator; a student evaluation of the Field Experience Portfolio Program and an extensive evaluation of the student by the site administrator. The administrators' evaluation has two parts: Part I contains the 11 areas in which the student participates in the activities; Part II contains the skills and attributes of the student intern in 10 domains. The domains are Leadership Skills, Decision-Making Skills, Problem Solving Skills, Organisational Skills, Written Communication, Oral Communication, Personal/Relationship Skills, Group Relationship Skills, Sensitivity to Diversity and Attitude, Initiative and Cooperation. The portfolio provides the materials that the university supervisors use to assess the students' performance in each of the categories and to issue a grade. The primary purpose for the culminating portfolio is that it allows the student the opportunity to integrate course theory and field experiences in the real world.

## Background

Research has shown that effective school site administrators are a key ingredient to the success of schools or as stated by John

Stewart in his article in the journal *Updating School Board Policies,* "Without proper background, education, guidance, and on-the-job training, a principal can create havoc within the school community". As early as 1981, states, school districts and universities saw a need to implement pilot intern programs in hopes of better preparing administration students for principal positions. The Kentucky General Assembly was the first in the United States to mandate the establishment of the Kentucky Beginning Principal Internship Program to upgrade the quality of educational leadership in the schools. In this program, a three member principal intern committee supervisors, assists and assesses each intern. The committee consisted of a mentor principal of a similar school level, the superintendent or a designee, and an administrator educator representing a state approved educational administrator program (Prickett, R.L. et. al., 1990; Richardson, M.D. and Prickett, R.L.., 1991). North Carolina's legislature also mandated changes in principal preparation programs and funded two-year full-time intern program which allowed Principal Fellows to receive loans. At the same time, the university maintained its program for part-time students. These students completed the same basic course work as did the Principal Fellows, but their internships were more limited in terms of duration and intensity. The Principal Fellows were clearly better prepared for entry-level administrative positions than their part-time counterparts (Bradshaw, L.K., 1997). There is little doubt that full-time intern programs have been and are beneficial to both administrative interns and school districts; however, this program is extremely expensive.

Stacey Edmonson reported on the intern program at Sam Houston State University which is similar to the program at National University. Students are involved in activities that are based on the Texas standards for effective school leaders and recommendations of their supervising administrator. These series of activities were designed for building a working knowledge of and actually applying the standards. In addition to the activities and other written components, the student interns must attend four seminars per each semester. The seminars provide the interns the opportunity to discuss and share their learning, their frustrations, and their evolving views of becoming and administrator. Stacey Edmonson reports that "the networking and growth involved with these seminars is tremendous". The seminars are the one area which is not included in the National program but perhaps, one that should be added.

In her report, Martha Ovando examined the assessment of interns' performance in a university-based internship program. Administrators, mainly principals, who supervised interns at school sites, completed the Assessment of Interns' Performance form. The assessment was designed to gather information about interns' experiences, field-based areas in which interns were involved, their potential as future administrators, their strengths and areas for further development, and recommendations for program improvement. Findings indicated that the interns were engaged in a variety of activities. The areas of demonstrated strength and ability included effective planning, organisation, time management, human relations, oral communication, written communication, taking directions, using organisation policies and procedures, and applying theory in educational administration. The supervisors had high regard for the interns and believed they had the potential to perform a variety of roles at both central office and school site levels. The supervisors were willing to continue supporting other interns.

In their research paper, Wade Devlin-Scherer, Roberta Devlin-Scherer and John Couture focused on principal interns' participation in activities at two universities. The internship was designed for interns to work closely with other educators in fostering school improvement by completing specific instructional and managerial tasks. The researchers examined the intensity of involvement in the activity; the program evaluation; the program implementation; and managerial leadership; classroom observations and teacher conferencing; job shadowing/ professional development; and independent leadership. They found that there was a wide variance in the amount of hours committed to this learning experience. They also found that the activities that the interns were involved in were legitimate and actually led to student learning.

With increasing interest in public education by the federal, state and local governments, universities and colleges are being challenged to improve the educational requirements for certificated personnel, especially the school site administrators.

The challenge is to develop a program that would graduate effective entry level school administrators at little or no cost to the districts. In addition to lack of funds, the difficulty is that the administrative roles which were once clearly defined in an organisational hierarchy as having complete autonomy have recently changed to a model of principal as "facilitator" (Schargel, F. P., 1994) and collaborator.. Teacher associations/unions and parent groups have become more vocal and involved in the decision making process at school sites, adding another dimension that school administrators must address. Keeping in mind that coming to consensus and making decisions utilising the collaborative model always takes more time; additional time that the administrator does not have. School site administrators are spending more time at the school site in order to accomplish all the responsibilities that go with the job. The principal is no longer a recognised leader in only instruction; the principal is now the manger of the school facility that is also responsible for the instructional program. As the role of leadership changes, the function and structure of internship will need to change (Hoekstra, .B. 1995) and has changed.

In order to meet the demand for the changing role of the administrator, requiring different skills and abilities, universities have recognised the difficulty of attempting to teach complex issues exclusively by lectures and textbooks. Therefore, administrative intern programs have become more popular (Jean, E.W. and Evans, R.D., 1995). Full-time internships are extremely expensive and most school districts are unable to release their teachers from their teaching obligations during their internship. In addition, more recently university education programs have included internship portfolio which ensures that the interns have an opportunity to perform real administrative duties while they are full time employees of the district (Edmonson, S. 2002).

National University has developed the Field Portfolio Program which combines the two strategies — field experience and portfolio assessments — to address the changing role of the school site administrator. The program is relatively new, only in its fifth year of implementation; some questions need to be answered, as well as, perhaps some changes.

## FINDINGS

Does the Field Experience Portfolio Program translate theory into practice? Each of the eleven categories was carefully designed to incorporate activities which would include the theories taught in the eight required classes. In selecting the activities, student interns were able to reflect back on their course work to determine which activities were of utmost interest to them. Without exception, the student interns stated in their reflections, that their activities were a real learning experience. The portfolio activities successfully translated theory into practice. This balance between theories and practice helped student interns realise that the administrative positions required a number of skills, in addition to knowledge of curriculum and instruction.

The Texas A&M University and the University of Texas at Arlington experience concluded that the portfolio assessment not only ties theory to practice but provided the students with a framework to continue their own professional development and also provided a tool to build upon (Wilmore, E. L., 1995). This same sentiment was echoed in the North Carolina experience (Bradshaw, L.K.;Perreault, J.O.;McDowelle, & Bell, E. W. 1997). In his paper, David Stader states, "The portfolio concept lends itself well to the challenges of assessing students in principal preparation programs in ways that are authentic and job-embedded". The one area of concern that teachers' working in traditional calendar schools was the few opportunities they had to participate in teacher observations/evaluations. Unlike teachers working in year-round schools, there were very few opportunities to observe teachers when they were not working, since all teachers at the school site were off at the same time. In some cases, the principal (mentor) was able to arrange for the student intern to observe at a neighbouring year-round school. In the North Carolina intern program, it was the part-time interns who reported that they had few opportunities to be involved in teacher observations (Bradshaw, L. K.; Perrault, G; McDowelle, J.O.; Bell, E.W. 1997).

Does the partnership linkage between the university and the school district mentor translate into success for the intern administrators? There are numerous models for administrative internships and many models involve a school site administrator, a University supervisor and the student intern. In most cases, as in the National university model, the administrative intern is a full time employee on the campus where he is completing his internship. Realising that most school site administrators have little time to accomplish all their tasks, and have little or no time to train an intern, collaboratively the university supervisor, the administrator (mentor) and the student intern, select activities which would help the administrator and be beneficial to both the school and the student intern. Recognising that most of these activities are completed by the student intern before and after their working hours, administrators give their teachers considerable latitude to become involved in their field-based activity. In some cases the site administrator will allow classroom teachers, in traditional calendar schools, as well as in year-round schools, to participate in teacher observation/evaluation by providing classroom coverage by other certificated staff members. Student interns, who are required to complete their activities at two levels, have a more difficult time completing their assignment. However, without exception, upon completing their portfolios all student interns feel better prepared and grateful for their experience. Just as the student interns at Sam Houston University, National University student interns become fully aware of the tremendous responsibility and the commitment required of a school administrator (Edmonson, S., 2002).

What are the strengths and weakness of the program? In his paper, John Greer states "that cooperation between universities and school districts is difficult". Although in the Danforth Program, in addition to collaborating in the selection of activities, and guiding monitoring, assessing and evaluating the student interns, school districts and the university shared responsibilities for the admission or program participants, and also for full-time internships, and the placement of program graduates in administrative positions. He found that the school district personnel were "enthusiastic" while university personnel were skeptical toward shared responsibility. In almost every situation, in the National university model, the relationship between the school district personnel and the University supervisor has been positive.. A definite strength of the program is hiring retired administrators from the school district to serve as the University supervisor for the student interns. Oftentimes, a positive relationship between the school site administrator and the university supervisor already exists. The school site administrator view having student interns at the school site as a win win situation. Having an enthusiastic intern that wants to become an administrator is one additional person who is able to take on some of the duties/activities.

In most cases the School Administrative Field Experience Portfolio Program has been successful. Some student interns, especially those who were classroom teachers, had a more difficult time completing the assignment in the allotted time. In cases of emergencies, time limits have been extended. Teacher interns working in year-round schools had a definite advantage over the students working m a traditional calendar school. A few interns had a difficult time completing their activities, when the intern did not have a positive relationship with his school site administrator. In this situation, it was most helpful when the university supervisor had a good working relationship with the principal. Depending on the problem, the University supervisors must be able to communicate with the school site administrator, as well as the student intern, to find a solution to the problem. The positive partnership linkage between the university supervisor and the school district mentor is definitely beneficial for the intern administrator.

## Conclusion

Research strongly supports the internship field experience portfolio programs. There is little doubt that real change can and does occur when student interns are involved in school based activities. First year principals in the University of Montana Internship Program were significantly more confident that they were well prepared for the job than first year principals who had no internship experience. The principals with internship experience felt better prepared in tasks most critical to schools, e.g., supervision and evaluation of teachers, team building, communication, facilitating, etc. (Jean, E. W. and Evans, R. D., 1995). A student intern at National University summed it best when he said, "The field experience exposed me to a realistic and hands on approach to administration and provided me with insight of how an administrator must be knowledgeable and aware of all aspects of administration — legal, financial, instructional, and at the same time be ethical, and professional". As for the portfolio notebook, without exception, all student interns made two copies, one to turn into the university and one for themselves to use as a source of information.

The internship model which came from other professional fields, particularly medicine, has long been regarded as a highly beneficial experience (Hoekstra, R. B., 1975). Today we know that this model is also most helpful to future school administrators. As the need for quality school administrators continues to grow, universities and school districts need to continue working together to refine and improve the internship program, in order to graduate effective and knowledgeable administrators.

## Recommendation

Since the Field Experience Portfolio Program is relatively new, it would be of interest for National University-Los Angeles to conduct a survey of graduate students who are now administrators. Did the experience help you to be an effective first year school administrator? Did you feel confident in your ability to fulfil the expectations of the job? Did the program translate theory into practice? Were you able to utilise the portfolio notebook in your first administrative assignment?

In addition, district supervisors should also be surveyed. Did the Field Experience Portfolio Program prepare the new administrators for the job? Were they better prepared than those new administrators who had no internship experience? Is there a need to periodically assess the program? Should the time spent in the field experience be extended?

Research should also be conducted regarding The Field Experience Portfolio Program utilising the research model, "The Principal Internship Portfolio: Evidence of Instructional, Managerial and Interdependent Leadership" used by Wade Devlin-Scherer, Roberta Devlin-Scherer and John Couture. Are the activities accomplishing what they were designed to do? Did the activities lead to student learning? Did the amount of hours committed to the tasks by the interns make a difference?

As the role of the school administrator continues to change, it is essential that the universities provide the very best preparation for student interns to be successful in a job that is demanding, challenging and very important.

## REFERENCES

Bradshaw, Linda.K.; Perreault, George; McDowelle, James O. Bell, Edwin W. *Evaluating the Results of Innovative Practices in Educational Leadership Programs* Southern Regional Council on Educational Administration, November 9 - 11, 1997, Charleston, S.C.

Brown, Genevieve; Irby, Beverly J. (2201). *The Principal Portfolio.* 2nd ed. Thousand Oaks, Calif Corwin Press, Inc.

Devlin-Scherer, Wade; Devlin-Scherer, Roberta; Couture, John. "The Principal Internship Portfolio: Evidence of Instructional, Managerial, and Interdependent Leadership". Annual Meeting of the American Association of Colleges for Teacher Education, February 26-29, 2000, Chicago, Illinois.

Edmonson, Stacey. "Effective Internships for Effective New Administrators." National Council of Professors of Educational Administration Annual Conference, August 7, 2002, Burlington, Vermont.

Greer, John T., The Danforth Program for the Preparation of Principals: A Project Update. "Changing Roles and Power Relationship." April; 1988.

Hoekstra, Ronald B., "Internships as a Means of Training Educational Leaders: An Historical and Contextual Perspective." April, 1975.

Jean, Ernest W. and Evans, Roberta D. "Internships/Mentorships for First-Year Principals: Implications for Administrative Certification and Graduate Program Design". A CSPAC Research Study, September, 1995, Missoula, MT.

Ovando, Martha N., *Assessment of Intern's Performance: A Key to Enhance School Leader Preparation Programs.* 1998.

Prickett, R.L. et. al., Richardson, M.D. "Opportunities for Success; Kentucky's Principal Intern Program." Annual Meeting of the National Council of Professors of Educational Administration, Los Angeles, Calif., August 12-17, 1990.

Schargel, F.P., *Transforming Education through Total Quality Management: A Practitioner's Guide. Eye on Education,* Inc., 1994, Princeton, N.J.

Stewart, John A., *Priming the Principal Pump: Interns in Polk Country.* Updating School Board Policies, 1991.

Stader, David, I., Neely, Robert O., "Portfolios for Professional Growth and Documenting ISLLC Standards "Annual Meeting of the

University Council for Educational Administration, November 2-4, 2001. Cincinnati, Ohio.

Wilmore, Elaine L. and Erlandson, David A. "Portfolio assessment: In the Preparation of School Administrators". Annual Meeting of the Southwest Educational Research Association, January 26-28, 1995, Dallas, Texas.

Wilmore, Elaine L. *Principal Leadership: Appling the New Education Leadership Constituent Council (ELCC) Standards*, Corwin Press, Inc., 2002.

# Index